I0900954

IMAGES
of America

GREAT FALLS

On the Cover: Chief inspector J. J. O'Mahoney (center) and two others are standing in front of the offices of the Port of Great Falls and U.S. Customs House, located on Central Avenue. In the early 1900s, north-central Montana was booming. People were coming by the trainload to settle in this new area. (Courtesy of The History Museum, catalog number 89.137.139.)

IMAGES
of America

GREAT FALLS

Don Peterson and The History Museum

ARCADIA
PUBLISHING

ISBN 978-0-7385-8084-5

Published by Arcadia Publishing
Charleston, South Carolina

Printed in the United States of America

Library of Congress Control Number: 2010921996

For all general information, please contact Arcadia Publishing:
Telephone 843-853-2070
Fax 843-853-0044
E-mail sales@arcadiapublishing.com
For customer service and orders:
Toll-Free 1-888-313-2665

Visit us on the Internet at www.arcadiapublishing.com

CONTENTS

ACKNOWLEDGMENTS

My sincere thanks to Marcia Clary, Jim Meinert, and Judy Ellinghausen of The History Museum for agreeing to sign on with this project and for providing unending support. Their archives collection made this work possible through the use of their photographic records as well as their voluminous historical and newspaper resources. All photographs are provided courtesy of The History Museum. Special thanks to local photographer Ray Ozman, who has provided numerous photographs from his private collection to The History Museum for their use. All images display The History Museum's catalog number immediately following the caption. All quotes from Lewis and Clark are taken from the *Journals of the Lewis and Clark Expedition*, University of Nebraska Press, edited by Gary Moulton. I would especially like to thank Judy for the level of support she provided and for her unending confidence in this project. I'd also like to give special thanks to Persis Webster, Maggie Nybo, Mary Rapp, Joann Edwards, and Fran Duncan for their contributions to this project. Special thanks to Bill O'Keefe for sharing history about power production and smelter operations in many conversations that helped to reinforce information I had collected. A special thanks to Richard Sterling, whose love of history and inexhaustible energy in digging out obscure facts has always been an unending source of information. I'd also like to give special thanks to John Poultney and Arcadia Publishing for making this opportunity to share our local history with the world. Saving the very best till last, a heartfelt thank you to my wife, Cherie, who worked beside me day and night for weeks getting me to the finish line. I understate this when I say I could not have managed this without her.

INTRODUCTION

Great Falls . . . just the words evoke a sense of power—waterpower. As the Missouri River follows its course for 3,000 miles from its beginnings at Three Forks in southwestern Montana to its confluence with the Mississippi River at St. Louis, Missouri, there is only one Great Falls. It was called "roar of stream" by the Blackfoot Indians. Meriwether Lewis was the first white man to see it, hear it, and experience it. He arrived about noon on June 13, 1805, and by doing so confirmed he was on the main course of the Missouri. He "hurried down the hill" to take his position on top of some rocks about the center of the falls to "gaze upon this sublimely grand spectacle." He was expecting only one "great falls." The next day he would discover four more falls. The river here drops over 550 feet in just 21 miles between the Lewis and Clark campsites at White Bear Island and Lower Portage Camp, less than a mile below the mouth of Belt Creek. Lewis, Clark, and their Corps of Discovery would spend over a month here as they portaged their cottonwood dugouts, supplies, and equipment over 18 miles across the prairie. During this time, Lewis, Clark, and several of their men kept detailed daily journals. The birth of Great Falls' written history can be traced back to these journals. Lewis and his men again visited the area a year later on their return journey to St. Louis. There would be other visitors in the next 50 years, but they left little, if any, record.

In 1853, Isaac Ingalls Stevens, newly appointed governor of Washington Territory, would bring his railroad survey crew through the area on the way from St. Paul, Minnesota, to Puget Sound. He and his group would also keep journals. Most importantly, he brought with him two illustrators who would leave a pictorial history: John Mix Stanley and Gustavus Sohon. Sohon created the first artist's rendering of the Great Falls that was done on site. It provided a wonderful image of the Great Falls of the Missouri as it looked before man came to change the face of the West forever. It would be another 30 years before a bankrupt St. Paul industrialist turned sheep rancher, struggling to provide for his family, visited the falls for the first time. Paris Gibson recognized the falls' potential for providing industrial power. He knew of efforts to harness St. Anthony Falls on the Mississippi River in his hometown of St. Paul, Minnesota. He had a vision of what harnessing these falls could mean to the development and growth of a new city on the plains. He had the vision—but not the capital. However, in James J. Hill, he had a friend that did have the capital. Hill, a successful railroad developer, would come at Gibson's invitation, and the two of them would work out a plan to take advantage of this wonderful natural resource.

The city of Great Falls sprang from the very falls that gave the town its name. The Missouri River drops over 550 feet in elevation in just 21 miles as compared to the 400 feet the Mississippi River drops in 1,000 river miles between St. Louis, Missouri, and New Orleans, Louisiana. Five hydroelectric dams would be built here over the next 65 years. These five dams would be built within a 12-mile stretch of the river, underscoring just how dramatically the river drops here. It makes the area unique in the entire world when it comes to hydroelectric development. There were five natural waterfalls within those 12 miles, but they accounted for only a third of the drop.

There is a 90-foot drop in elevation between two of the dams, and those dams are separated by less than 2 miles.

The river simply runs downhill. Thus, the river provided the perfect source for reliable power. The electricity would light and power a new city, providing local industry, recreation, transportation, communication, and residents with a source of dependable power. It would also provide power to the bustling mining town of Butte, 150 miles to the southwest.

Significant floods occurred in 1908, 1953, 1964, 1975, and 1997. These events had a profound impact on large segments of the area's population as they adversely affected transportation, communication, property, recreation, and health. The river influences everyone's daily lives.

The evolution and development of the city has been directly influenced by the Sun and Missouri Rivers. They have forced residents to adapt to their presence and work around them. In the early days, before the first bridge was constructed, the rivers forced people to find a suitable place to cross. The earliest wagon ford (called "rock bottom crossing" by the Blackfeet) still exists immediately downstream from the railroad bridge near the Mitchell Swimming Pool and Great Falls Water Park. Bridge building commenced early on; first was a railroad bridge and next a wagon bridge that connected early Johnstown (later known as the "West Side") with Great Falls. Then came a trolley bridge connecting Great Falls with Little Chicago and the smelter works on the north side of the Missouri. After that came three more bridges: ones on Tenth Street, First Avenue North, and much later, Tenth Avenue South. The Great Northern Railroad and the Chicago, Milwaukee, and St. Paul Railroad also had to span the river. After the Milwaukee Railroad's demise, its bridge was converted to a footbridge that is now part of the town's extensive River's Edge Trail system. The River's Edge Trail is an excellent example of how successful a rails-to-trails program can be. The river also provides residents with many forms of enjoyable recreation, such as boating, waterskiing, canoeing, kayaking, jet skiing, fishing, floating, and bird-watching.

Since the last ice age ended, the confluence of the Sun and Missouri Rivers has made available an enormous amount of water converging at a point just above a series of significant shelves of rock. By happenstance, Paris Gibson found himself uniquely positioned to exploit the available hydro energy produced by this rapid drop in river elevation. Hard rock mining in southwestern Montana, the development of railroads, the harnessing of electricity for industrial use, vast deposits of copper, and the emergence of people with the foresight and wherewithal to make dreams come true all came together at the right time and place, and what resulted was the city of Great Falls.

One

A River Runs through It

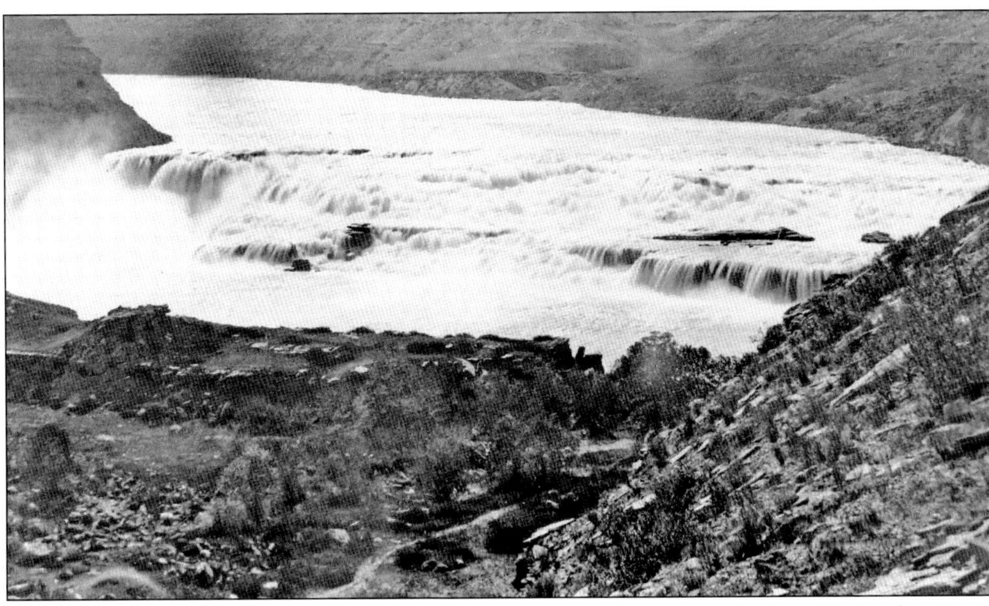

This is a view of the Great Falls of the Missouri as it could have looked to Meriwether Lewis on June 13, 1805, when he ascertained that he was on the right river—the one that Thomas Jefferson had directed him to explore. Lewis writes that he heard the noise and saw the spray while miles away. (98.2.1)

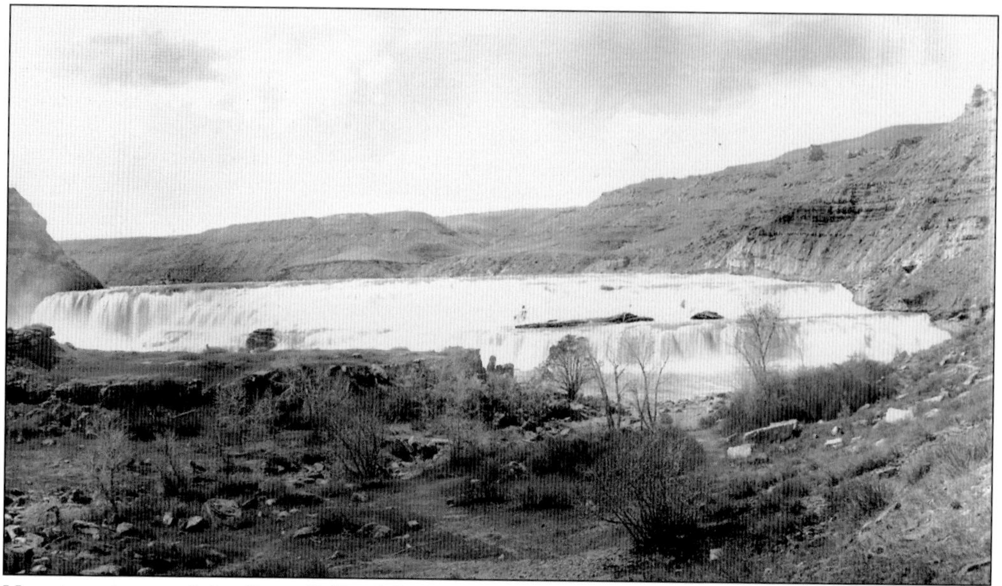

Here is a picture of the Great Falls of the Missouri taken from a point about 200 yards below the main falls. Meriwether Lewis noted the shallow or low area between the rocky eminence and the hillside. The dry channel that Lewis had to cross to gain a seat on the rocks near the center of the falls is now underwater after a deep channel was dug to accommodate the output from the turbines inside the powerhouse. (2007.17.717)

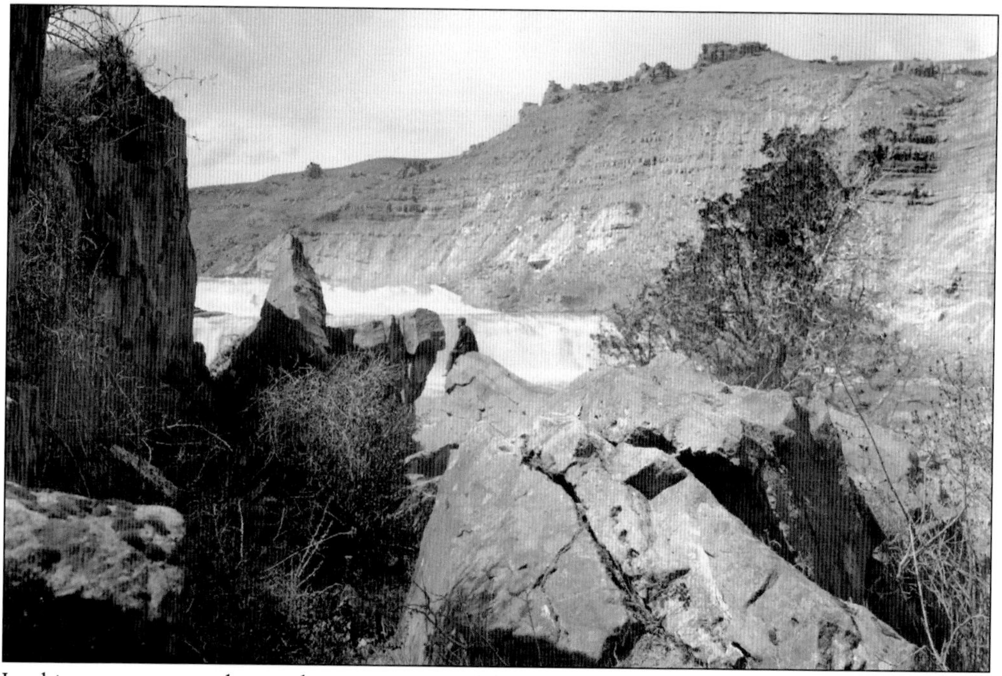

Looking upstream to the northern extremity of the Great Falls of the Missouri, one gets a distinct sense of the primitive nature of this area. Meriwether Lewis slid down the steep slope somewhere to the right on June 13, 1805. Lewis hurried down the hill to gaze on this sublimely grand spectacle. The gentleman sitting on the rock viewing the falls makes one reflect on Lewis and his first view of the falls almost 100 years before this picture was taken. (2007.17.0726)

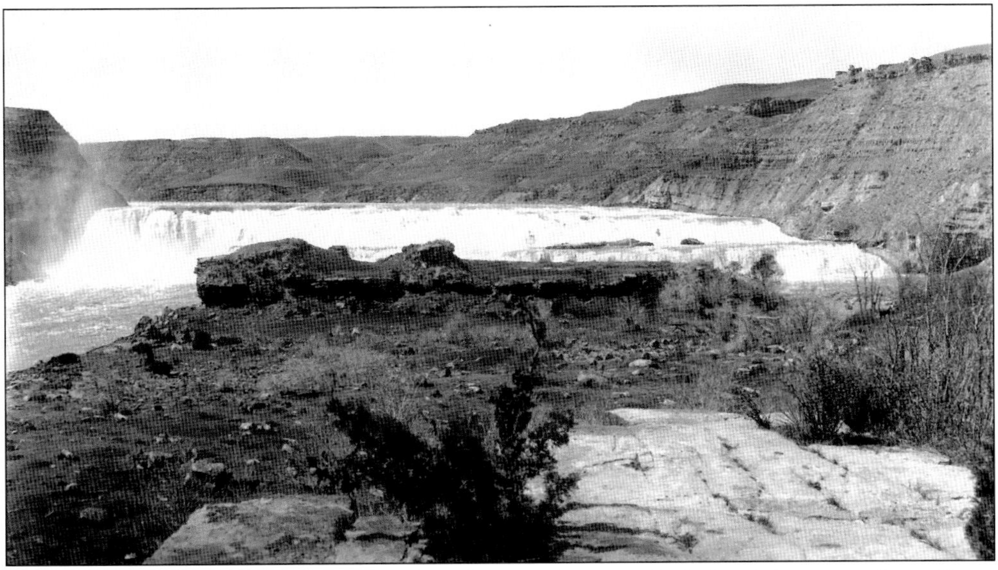

The Great Falls of the Missouri is seen here from the lower end of what is known today as Ryan Island. This boulder-strewn area below the falls became Lewis's camping site while he waited for Clark to arrive from downriver. The morning of June 15, 1805, Lewis awoke to find a rattlesnake coiled up not too far from his bed. (2007.17.029)

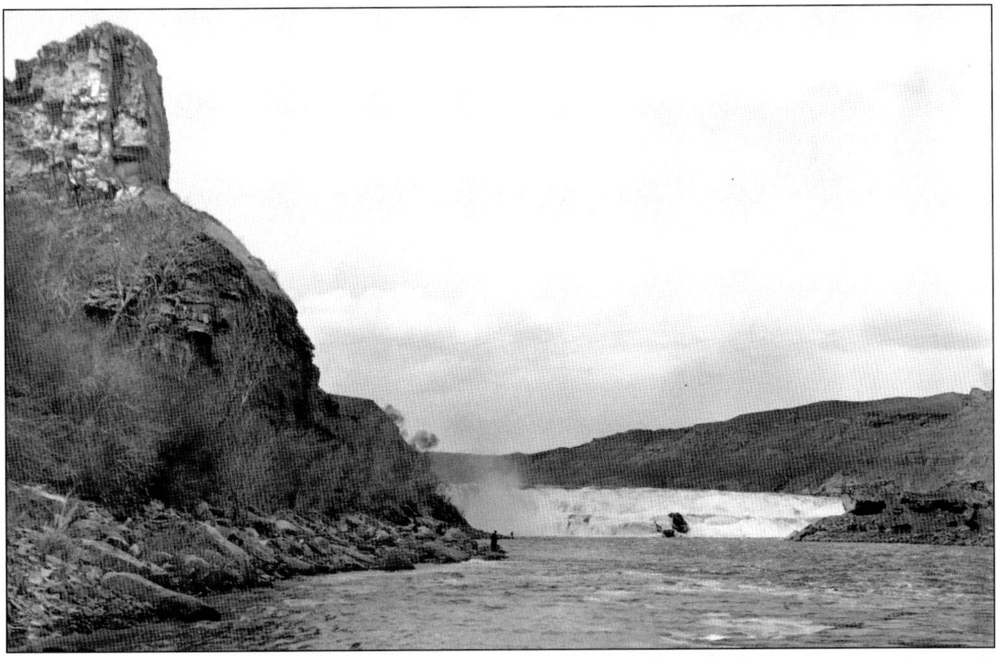

The Great Falls of the Missouri is shown here from a quarter of a mile downstream on the south bank. Note the fisherman standing on a rock near the falls. The river was full of cutthroat trout in 1805. Lewis and one of his party, a private named Silas Goodrich, spent a day relaxing here after their days of arduous hiking—first the 50-plus miles from the mouth of the Marias River on June 11–13, 1805, and then Lewis's 30-mile reconnoiter of the Missouri between these falls and the Sun or Medicine River the very next day. The next day, Lewis and Goodrich, whom Lewis notes as being "remarkably fond of fishing," spent the day fishing. (2007.17.725)

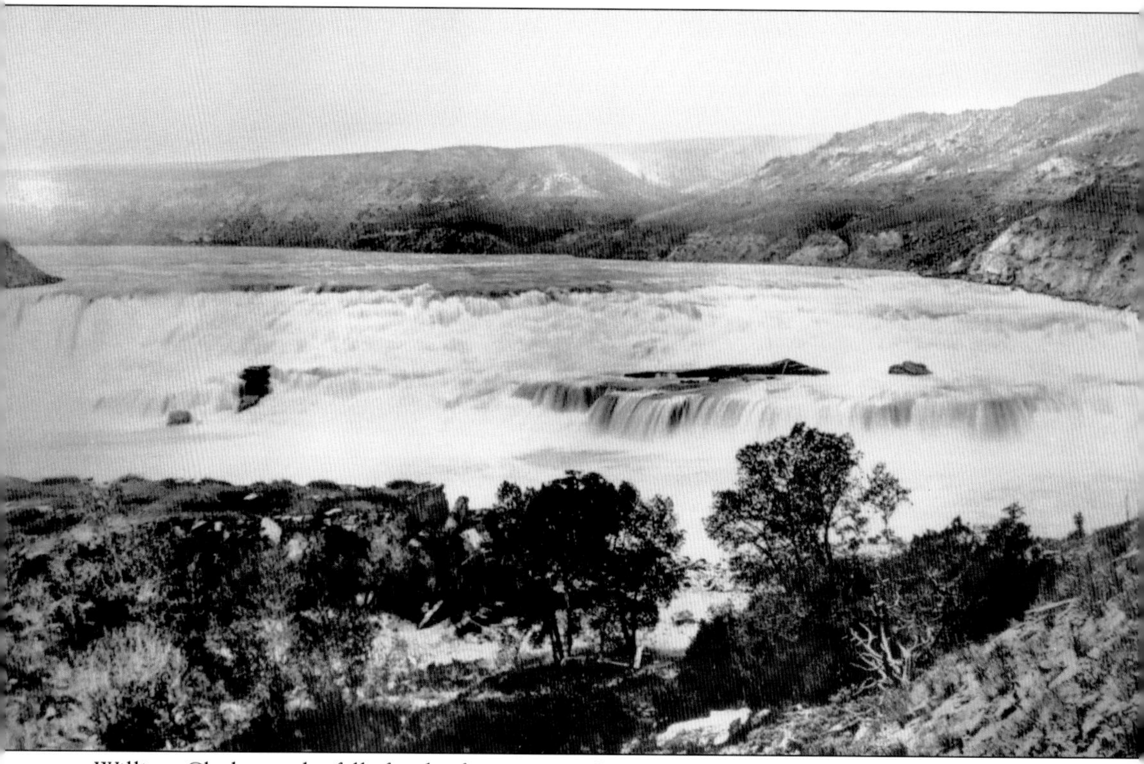

William Clark saw the falls for the first time on June 17, 1805. He was on his way to ascertain a course around the series of falls and rapids that would allow the Corps of Discovery to find an acceptable route to portage tons of boats, supplies, and equipment and enable the group of 33 people and a Newfoundland dog to continue its route of discovery to the Pacific Ocean. (98.2.8)

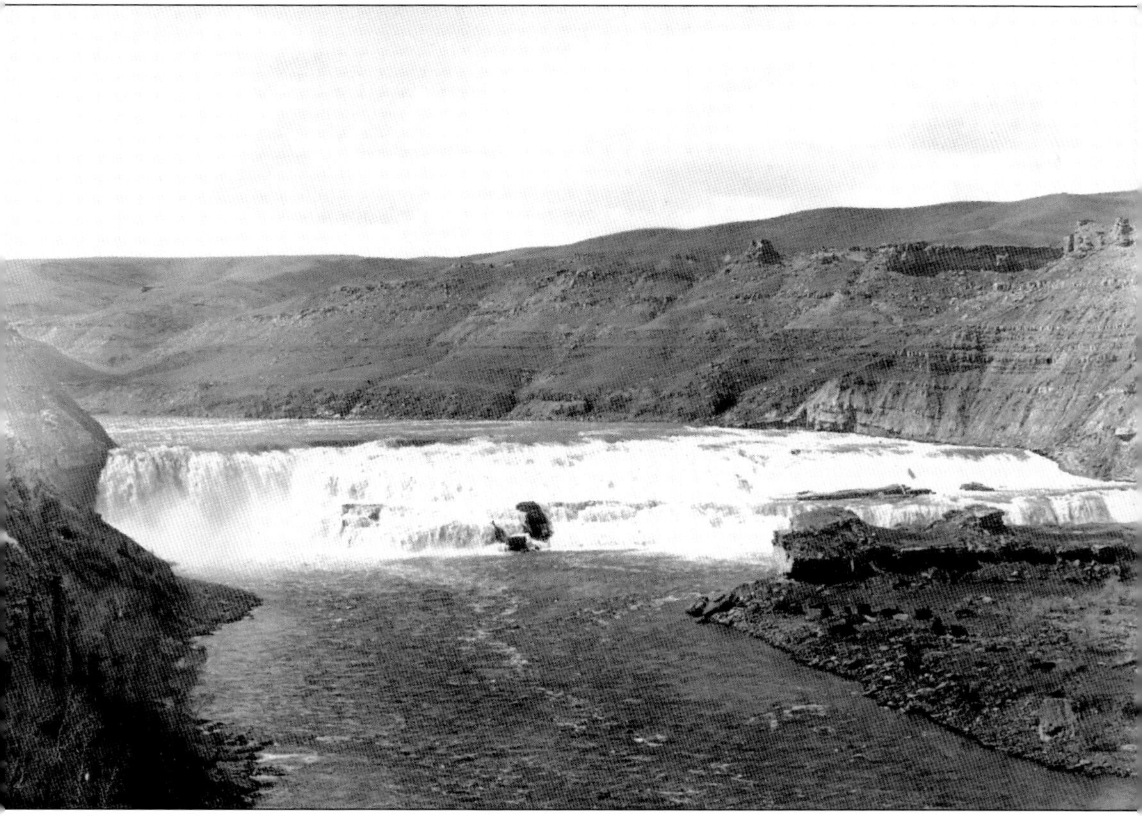

William Clark actually measured the falls themselves on June 17, 1805, as he ascended the Missouri with a small party of men. He was conducting a survey of the river channel, taking various measurements along the way. Here he first measured the height of the Great Falls at 87 feet, three-quarters of an inch. A second measurement read 97 feet, three-quarters of an inch. The first entry stands; the second entry may have been a simple mistake. Clark took his lunch that day immediately below where the photographer recorded this photograph. (2007.17.0731)

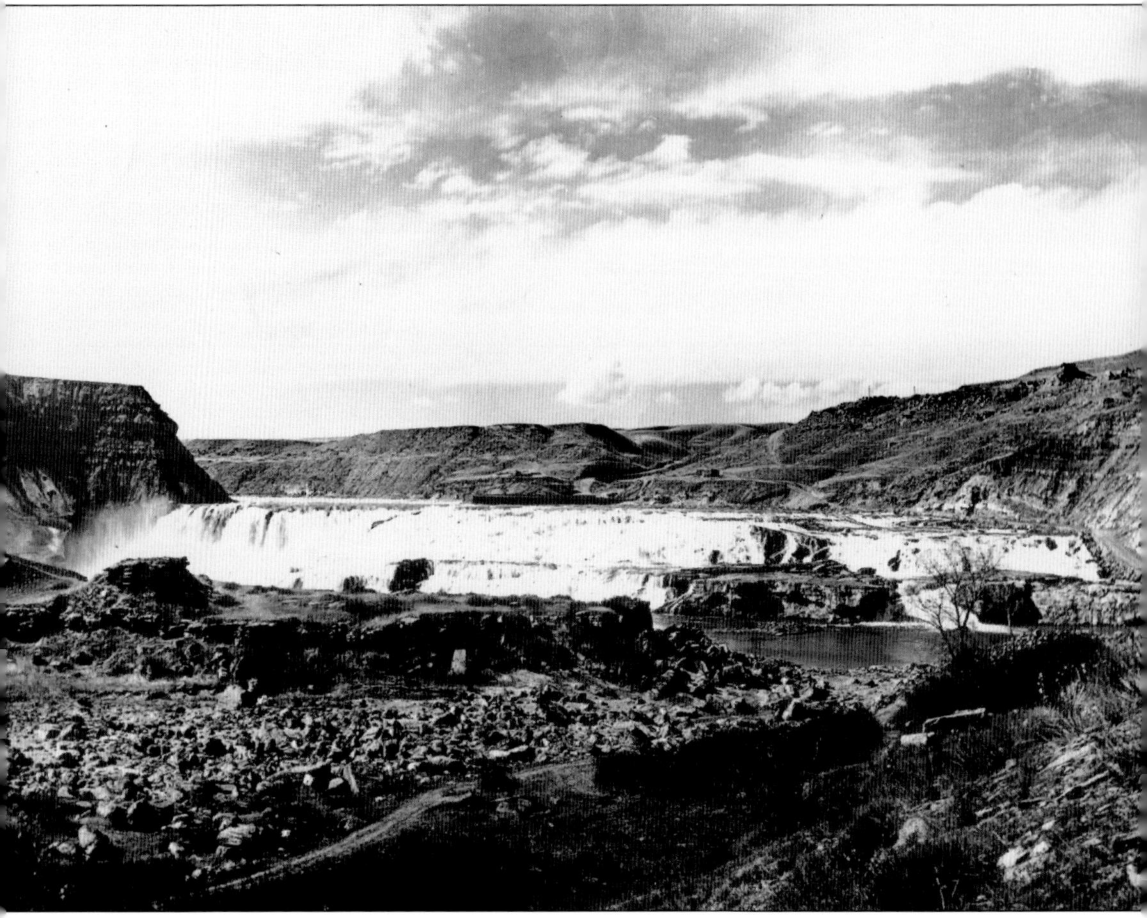

The Great Falls of the Missouri are seen here. The rubble that remains in the channel, separating the right shore from what would later become Ryan Island, must have witnessed eons of raging floods and extreme runoff. Both Lewis and Clark made several observations while in this area that lead researchers to believe that the river had a much greater flow in 1805 than anyone had imagined before. (2007.17.784A)

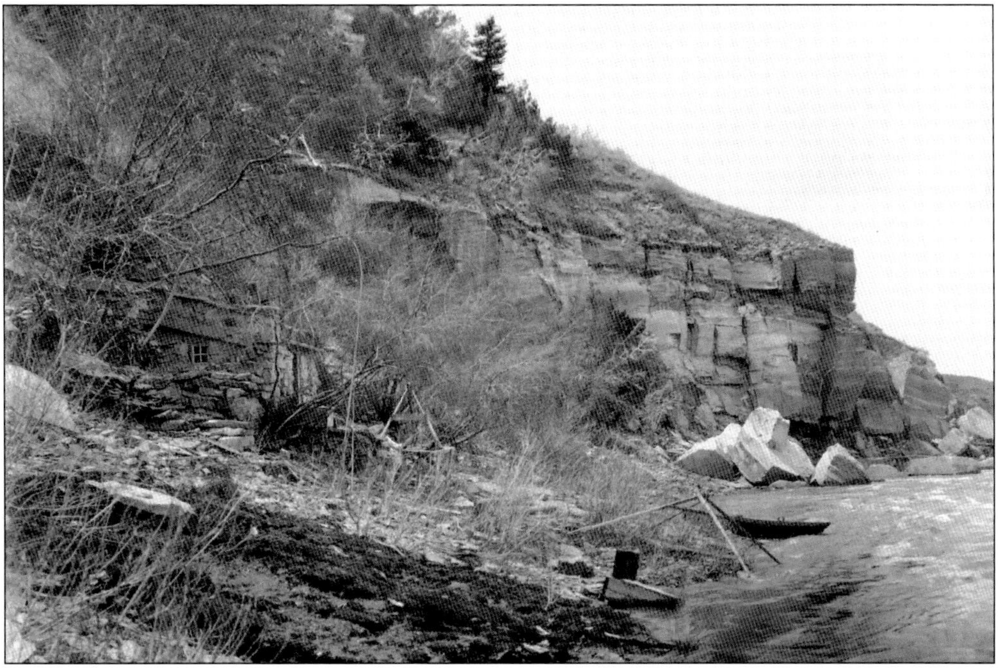

Just downstream from the Great Falls, someone constructed a very crude stone dwelling in the early 1900s. This dwelling provided only the most primitive accommodations for caretakers of a natural spring that had an output of about 1,100 gallons of sparkling pure water every hour. Note the little rowboat that was used to transport the caretaker to and from his little hut. (2007.17.0733)

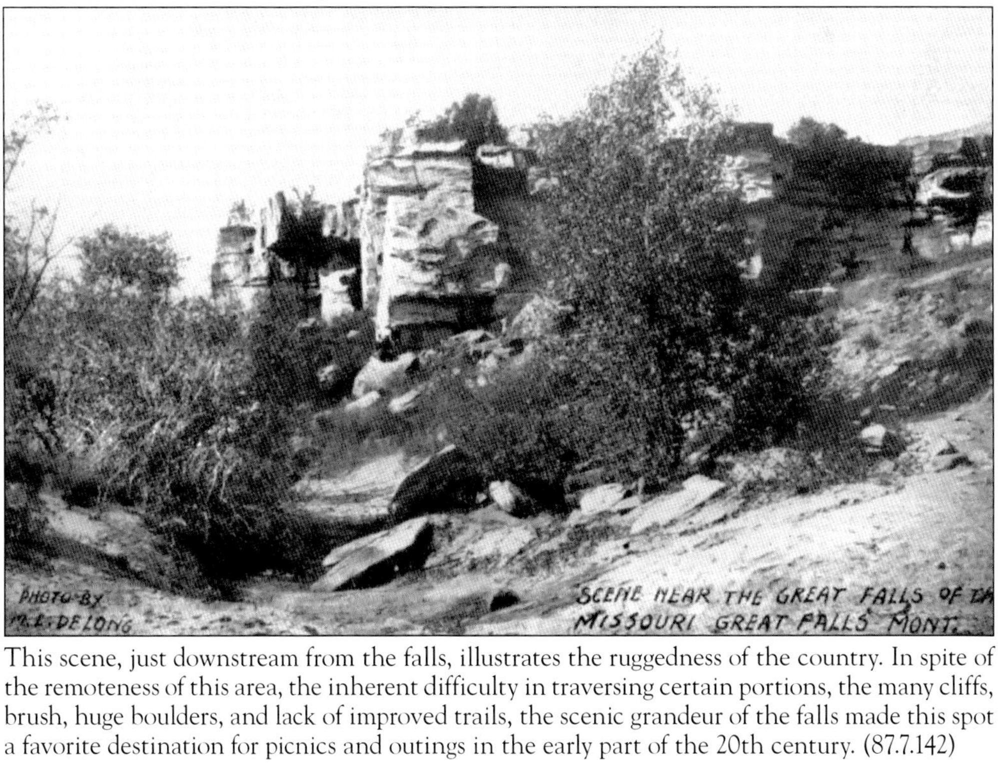

This scene, just downstream from the falls, illustrates the ruggedness of the country. In spite of the remoteness of this area, the inherent difficulty in traversing certain portions, the many cliffs, brush, huge boulders, and lack of improved trails, the scenic grandeur of the falls made this spot a favorite destination for picnics and outings in the early part of the 20th century. (87.7.142)

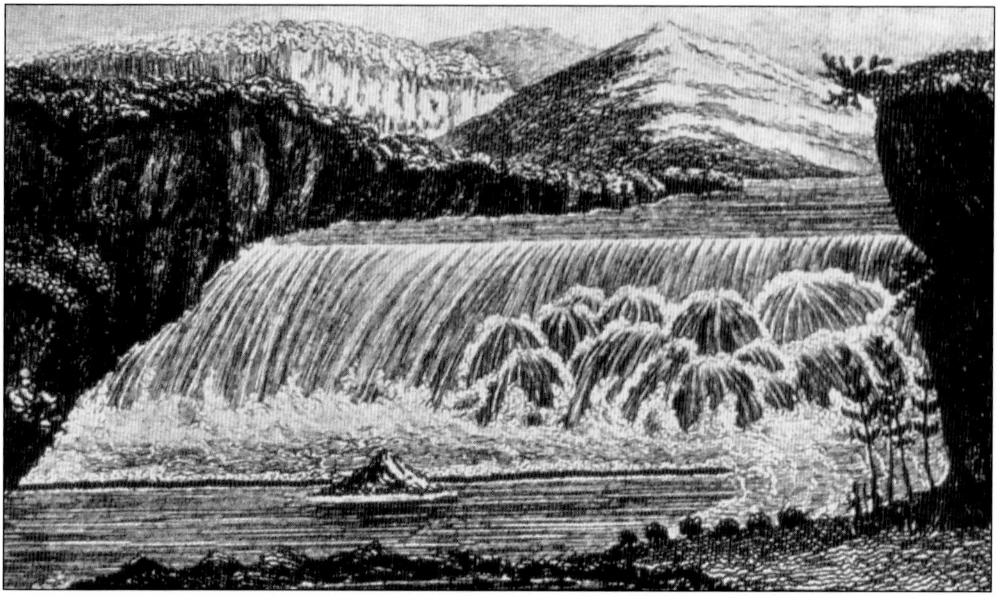

In 1807, when Meriwether Lewis began preparations to publish his journal, he wanted it to have professional illustrations. Since he had no artist with him in 1805, Lewis had Philadelphia engraver John Barralat create this image based on his description. Considering that it had been a year since Lewis had seen the falls, this image bears a remarkable resemblance to the real thing. (2010.1.010)

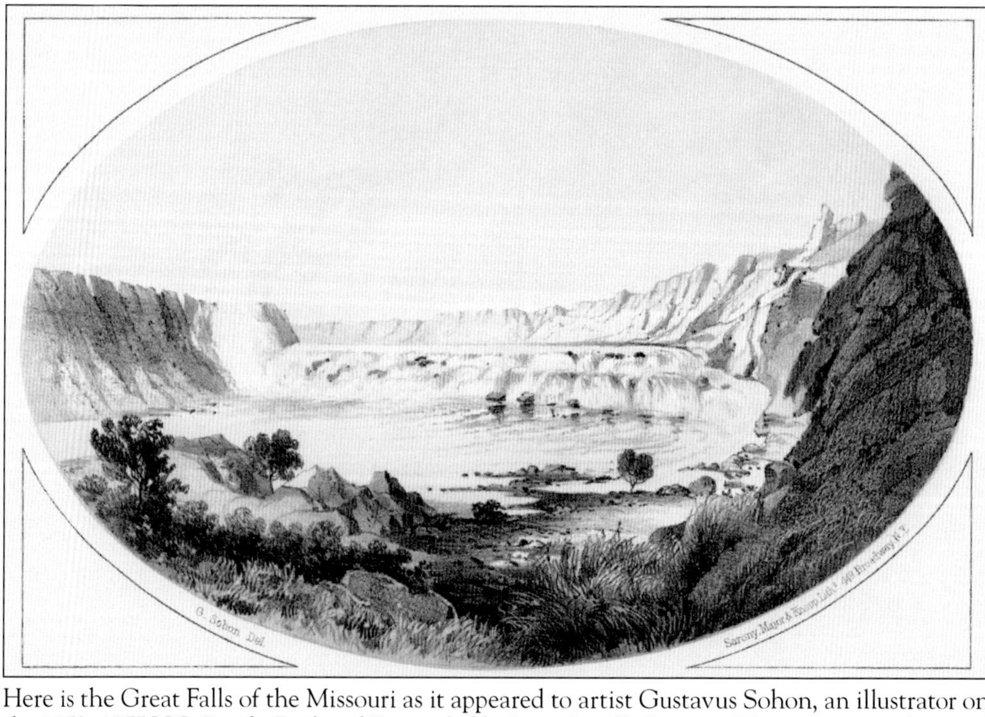

Here is the Great Falls of the Missouri as it appeared to artist Gustavus Sohon, an illustrator on the 1853–1855 U.S. Pacific Railroad Survey led by Isaac Ingalls Stevens. This survey was designed to provide information about topography and establish a route for development of a rail system between St. Paul, Minnesota, and Puget Sound. (2010.1.011)

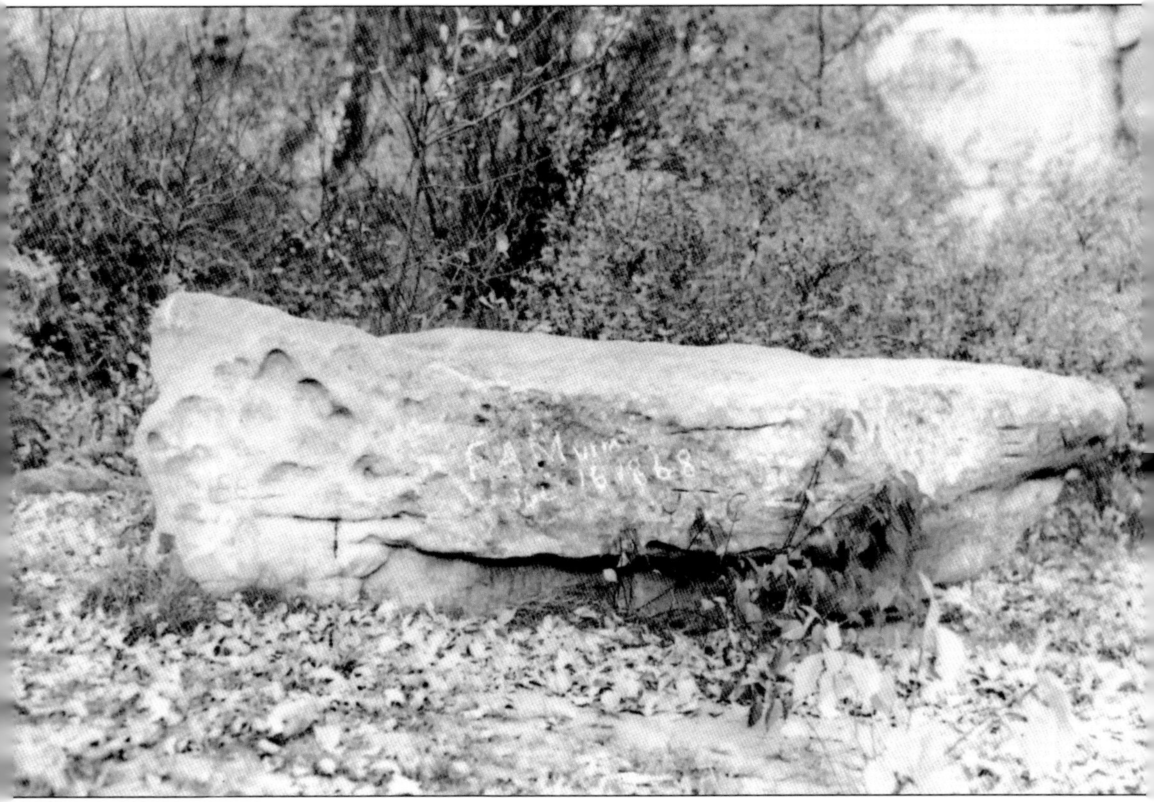

Murray's Rock, named for Frank A. Murray, is located on the island just below the Great Falls of the Missouri. Frank Murray was the pilot of a small packet steamer called the *Tom Stevens*. In a July 17, 1868, letter from Fort Benton, Montana Territory, to the editors of the *Missouri Democrat*, the author describes a trip from Fort Benton upriver to the Great Falls of the Missouri; he reports that the *Tom Stevens* was the only steamer ever to make it that far up the river. He also notes that Murray carved his name on the rock. (2007.17.339)

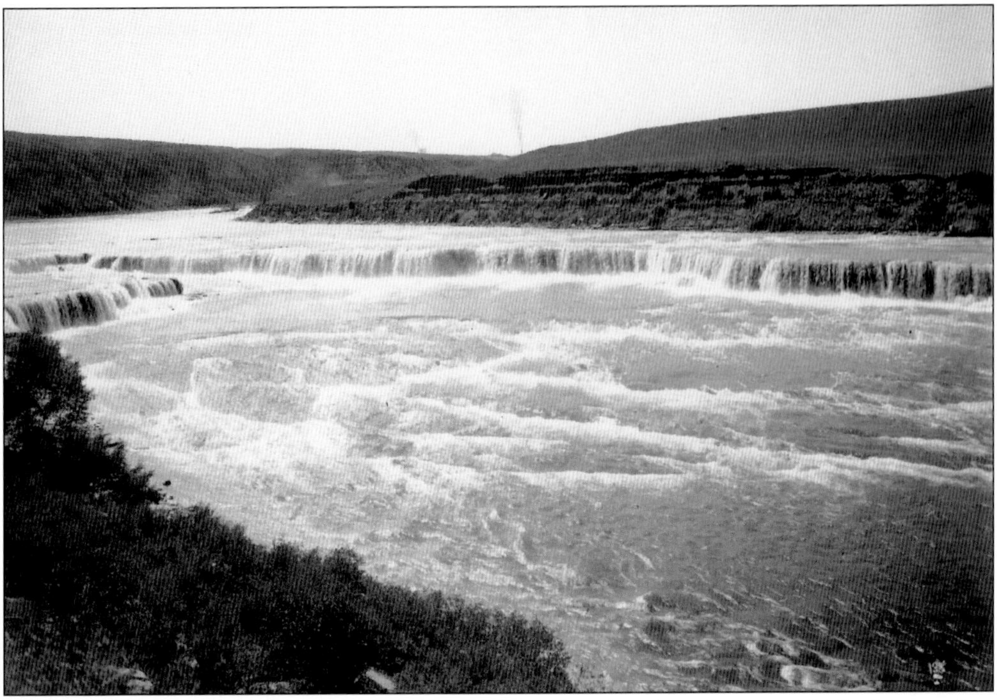

Crooked Falls is situated about a quarter of a mile below Rainbow Dam and Falls. Meriwether Lewis named these falls, and in truth they may be the only falls he actually named himself that retain the original name. (2007.17.785)

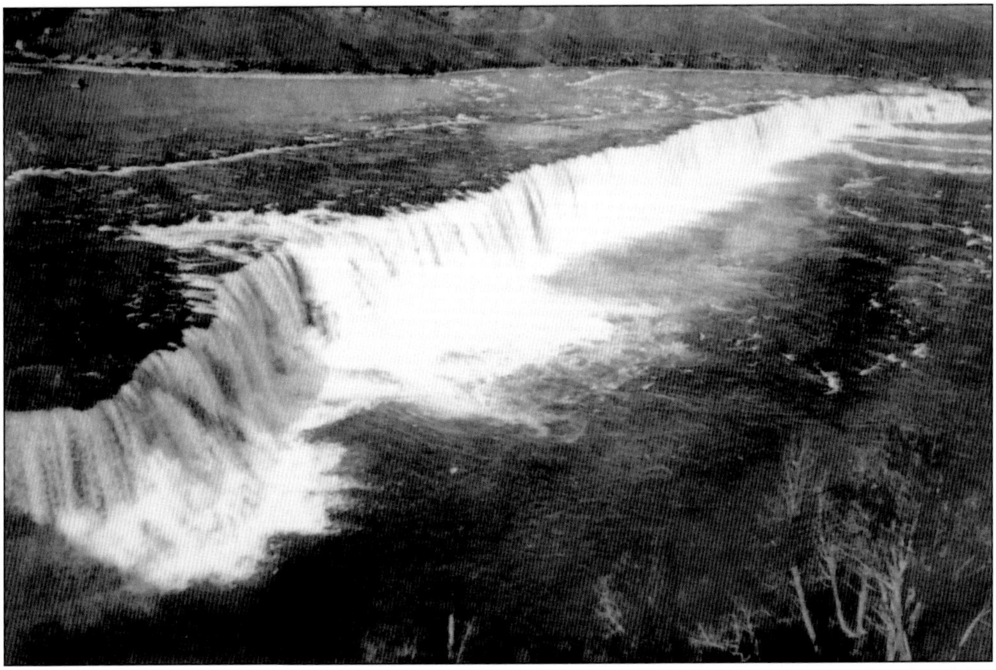

Rainbow Falls was first viewed by Meriwether Lewis as he made his way up the north side of the Missouri River on June 14, 1805. He had just discovered and named Crooked Falls when he heard the noise of these falls just above him. (2007.17.24)

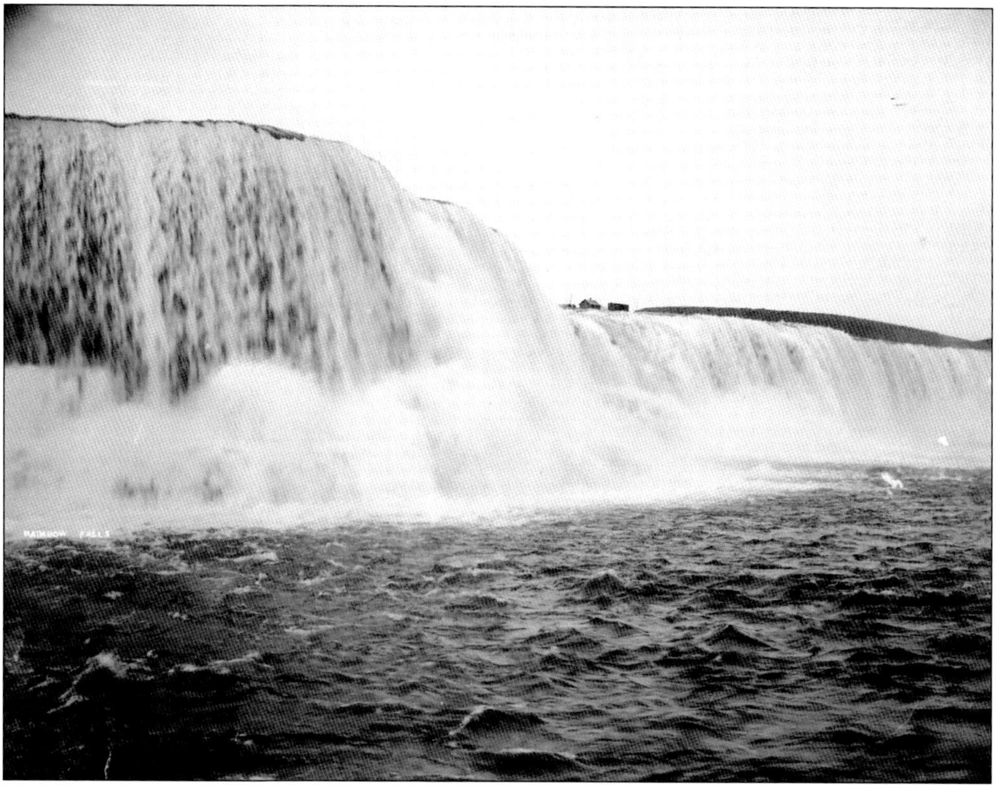

Here is a beautiful view of Rainbow Falls taken from the river's edge near the base of the falls. This photograph would be used later to develop an engraving that would become part of the bonds issued by the City of Great Falls for public works improvements. This particular engraving was taken for a street and sidewalk improvement bond issued in 1917. (Above: 227.1M; Below: 2010.1.012)

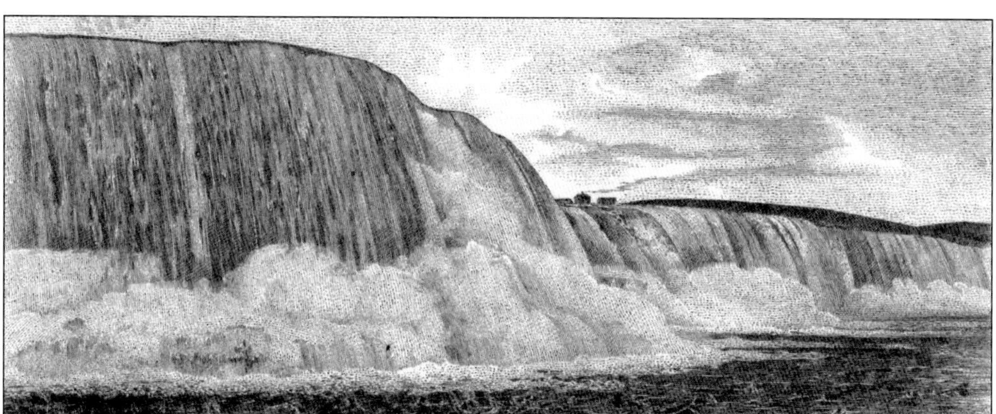

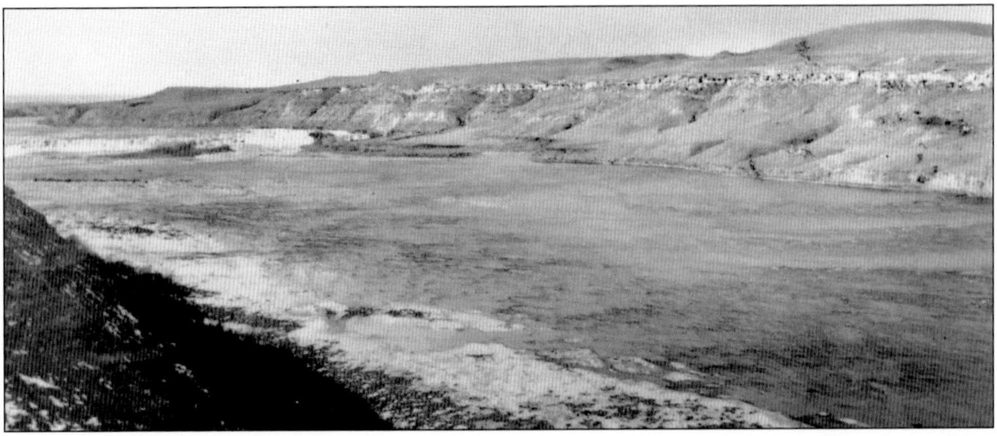

Black Eagle Falls and Indian Hill or Butte (where the smokestack stood) are seen here from about a quarter of a mile downstream. Lewis originally referred to these falls as "the upper pitch" or "head of the falls" and did not name them formally. The naming of the falls wouldn't happen for another 67 years. In 1872, a Northern Pacific survey engineer named Thomas P. Roberts formally named the cataract Black Eagle Falls after the eagle that Lewis had noted as nesting on a little island just below the falls in June 1805. (2007.17.431)

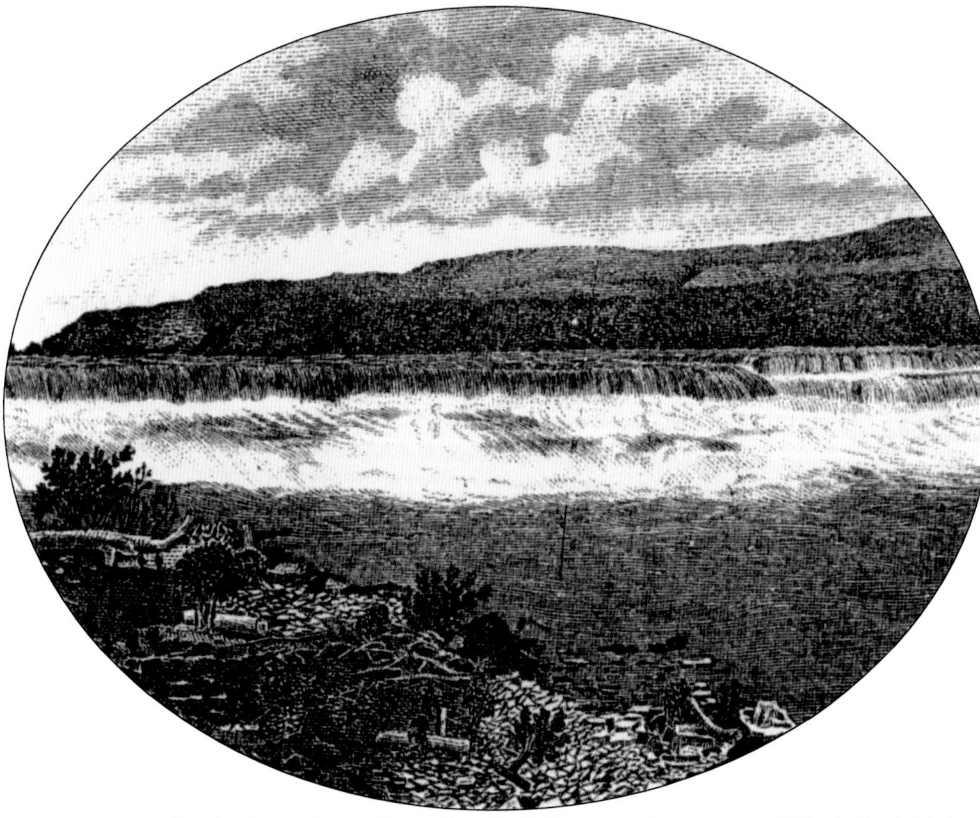

City of Great Falls checks in the 1890s and early 1900s carried an image of Black Eagle Falls as they appeared before development. It is quite accurate and shows the higher hills just north of the falls. The southwest slope of Indian Hill or Indian Butte is on the far right. It was on top of this butte that the 506-foot smokestack would rest after its construction in 1908. (2010.1.013)

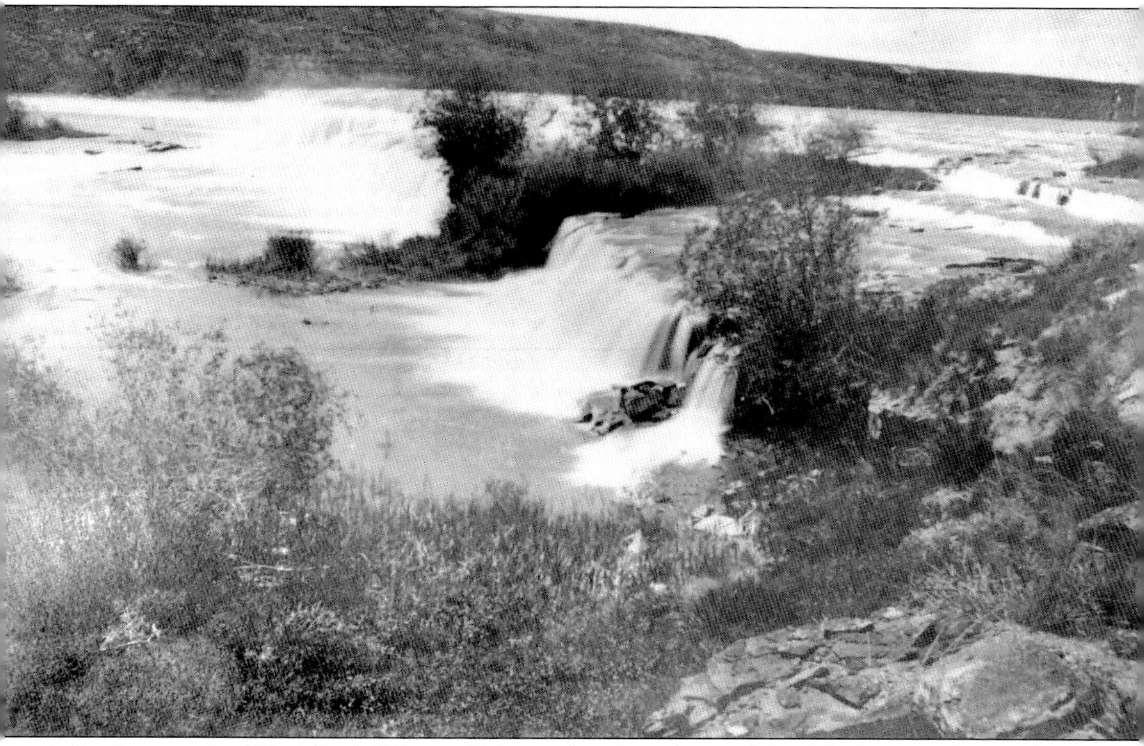

This photograph of Black Eagle Falls in 1883 was taken from the north bank looking south toward what would soon be the town site for the city of Great Falls. This view provides a wonderful perspective of the falls and a glimpse of a small part of an island that may have held the cottonwood tree and eagle's nest that earned the falls its name. (2007.17.034)

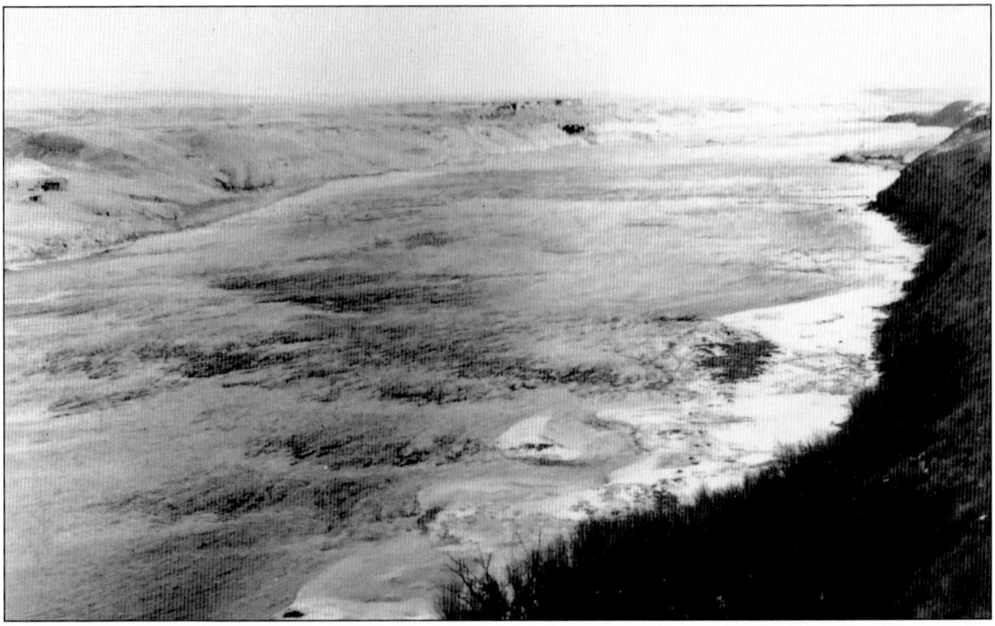

Between Black Eagle Falls and Giant Springs, the river ran very fast over a series of small cascades and rapids. Giant Springs can be seen as the last prominent point jutting out into the river on the right-hand side, far in the distance. There was a decided lack of vegetation at this time. (2007.17.504)

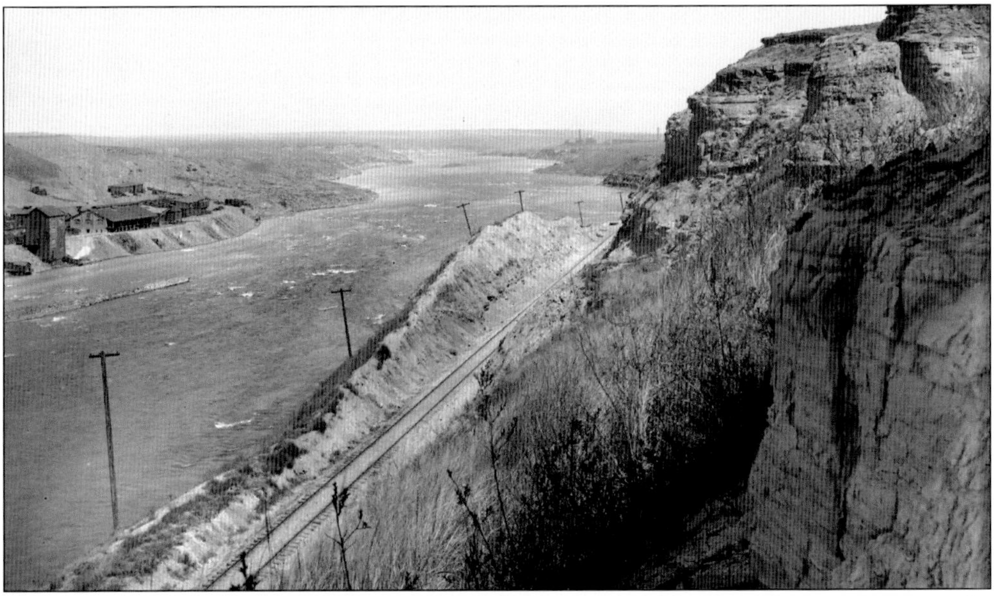

Looking downstream from about a quarter-mile below Black Eagle Dam, this view captures the primitive smelter works across the river, dating this image to about 1910. Far in the distance, on the right side of the river downstream, is Giant Springs, and to the right of Giant Springs, the smelter works from the old silver smelter can be seen. Two smokestacks are clearly visible. This smelter works was constructed in 1887 to smelt ore brought down from the rich mines in the Monarch-Neihart area of the Little Belt Mountains, about 70 miles southeast of Great Falls. (1998.72.82)

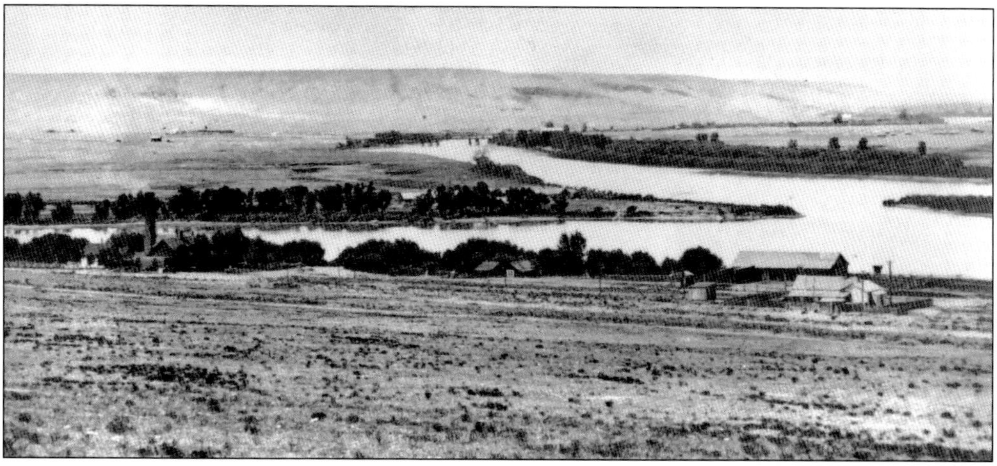

This view looks west up the mouth of the Sun River about 1889. At far left near the bank of the Missouri is the city's waterworks. It was opened in 1889 by T. E. Collins, Ira Meyers, and E. G. Maclay. The waterworks fed the city through a 12-inch main. (2007.17.433)

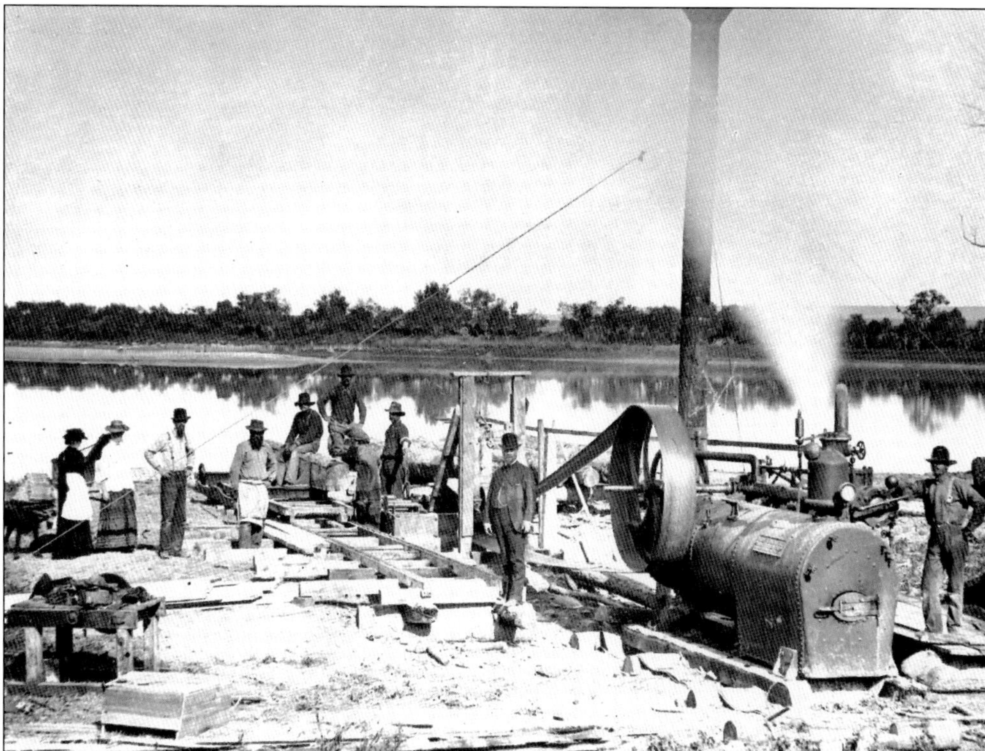

The quiet water of the Missouri River above the falls was a perfect setting for establishing a sawmill in the infant city of Great Falls. Lumber could easily be floated down the Missouri River in large rafts to this site not far from the mouth of the Sun River on the east bank of the Missouri. Ira Myers set up a sawmill near here in 1884. It provided a convenient processing point, turning logs into lumber that could be used for construction of homes and businesses as well as general construction. Ira, wearing a suit, is standing by the large flywheel to the left of the steam engine. (94.38.135)

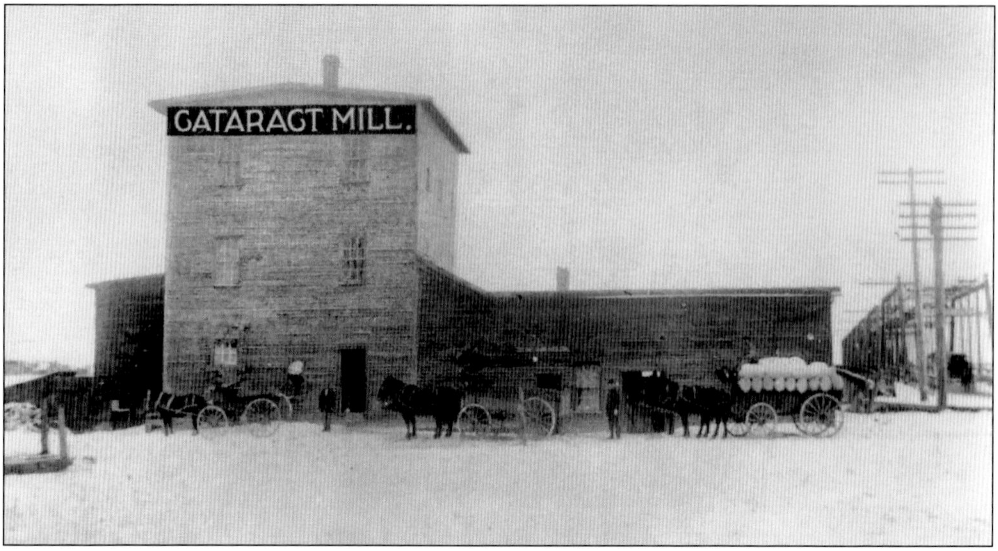

Cataract Mill was located on the east bank of the Missouri River and sat just south of the east end of the wagon bridge leading to Central Avenue West. It was first driven by harnessing the Missouri River and using waterpower to turn the stone used to grind wheat and other cereal grains. Cataract Mill was the first of three mills in Great Falls, the other two being the Royal Milling Company and Montana Flour Mills. It was built by a contractor named Vinegar Jones, a cousin of Paris Gibson, for H. O. Chowen and a man named Jamison over the winter of 1884–1885. (2007.17.187)

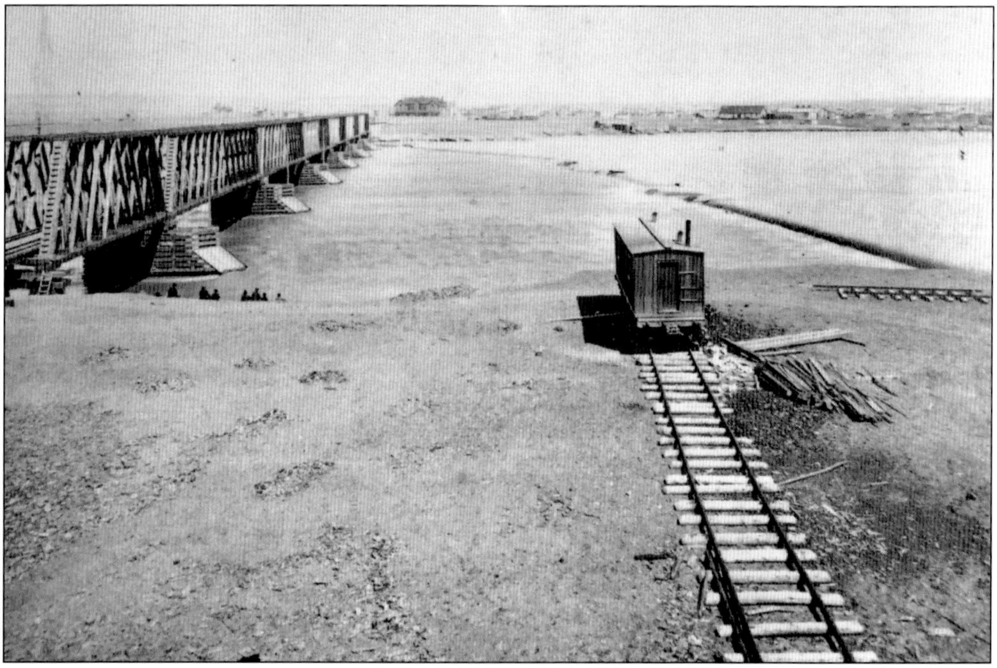

The Cataract Mill had a small dam built across the Missouri just upstream from the Great Northern Railroad Bridge. The purpose of the dam was to divert a small flow of water down the east side of the Missouri River from this point to the Cataract Mill site. This all took place before the advent of hydroelectric power in the area. (2007.17.250)

Two

GETTING DOWN TO BUSINESS

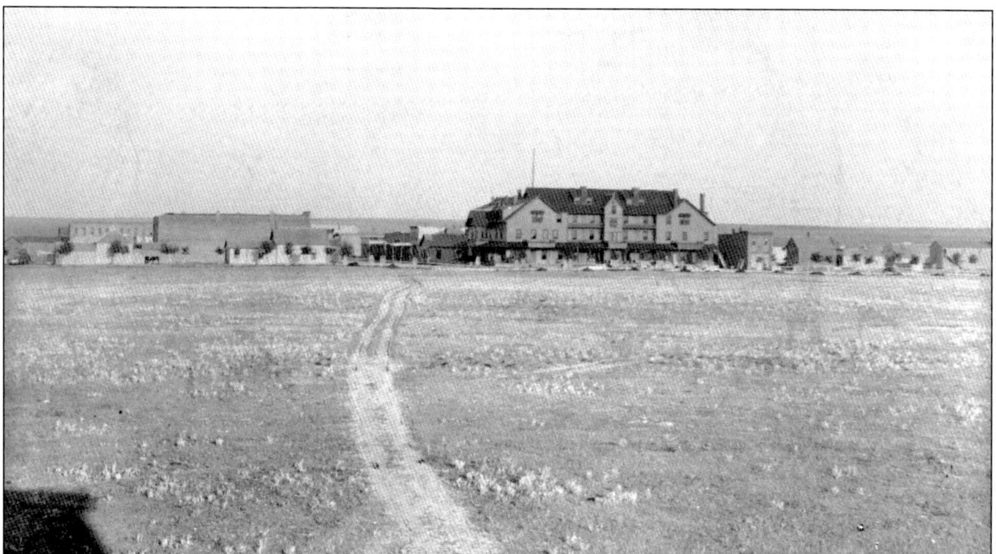

This very early view from 1887 shows the original Park Hotel sitting on First Street and Central Avenue. The photograph was taken from Cascade Park, named after numerous cascades in this area of the Missouri River. The cascades started at the Great Northern Railroad Bridge and continued on downstream for many, many miles. In 1903, a part of Cascade Park located north of First Avenue North would have its name changed to Gibson Park. The shadow in this image's lower left corner may be from the Cataract Mill's roof. (94.42.161)

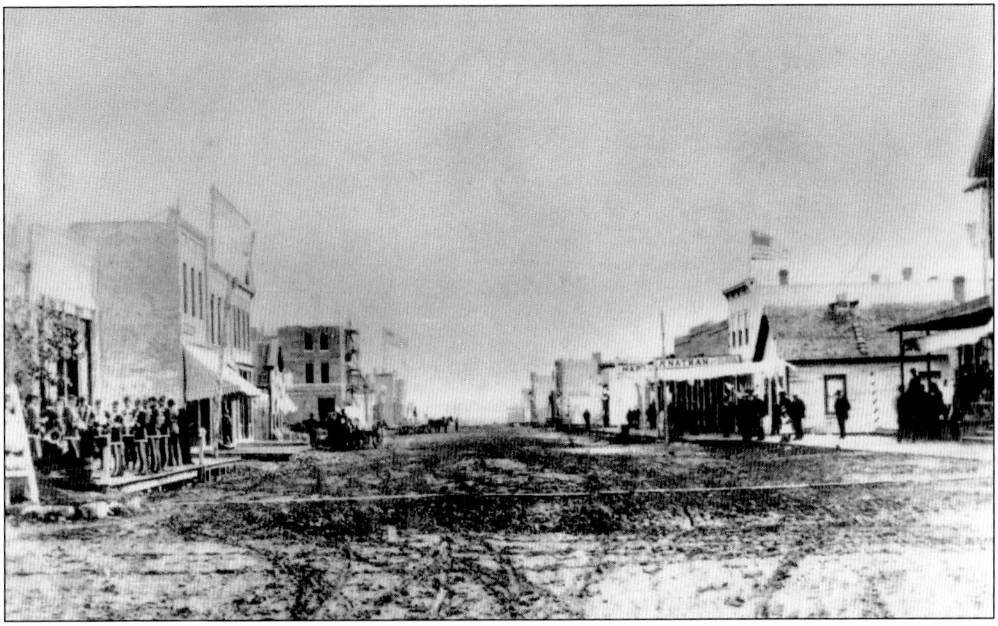

Mud and gumbo fill the streets in this July 4, 1887, scene looking east on Central Avenue across the street from the Park Hotel. The Fort Shaw Military Marching Band is gathered on the porch to the left. Everyone is in uniform, but the band was relegated to playing its marches on a dry porch that soggy July 4. A clothing store down the street to the right belonged to A. Nathan. He had left Fort Benton, along with Murphy Maclay, to make his footprint felt in the new city. (2007.17.500)

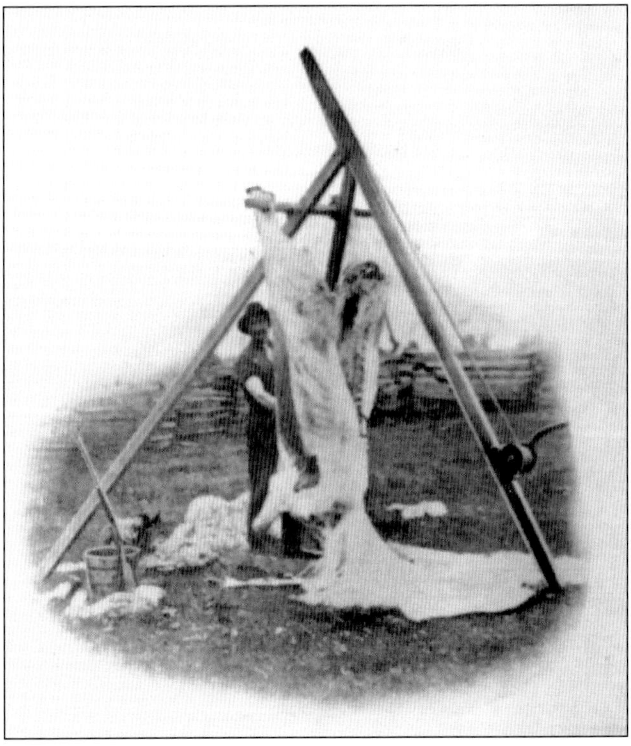

In 1885, the Great Falls Meat Company was located very near the downtown area. At left, one of the butchers has hoisted a beef up on a tripod and is carrying out the preliminary job of skinning and sawing it into halves. Note the rifle leaning up against the tripod to the left. It looks as though the whole operation—from leading the animal to slaughter, then skinning, then on to producing a workable carcass for the butcher—took place right here. (2007.17.177)

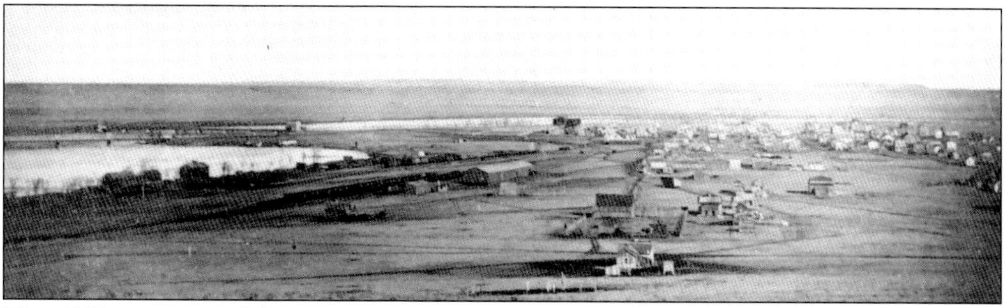

This 1888 panorama of the young city of Great Falls was taken from the hills south of the city, most likely in the Prospect Heights area. The only two bridges in this early photograph are the railroad bridge carrying the Great Northern trains into the city and the toll bridge linking the two parts of the city divided by the Missouri. The train station had not yet been built. (2007.17.873)

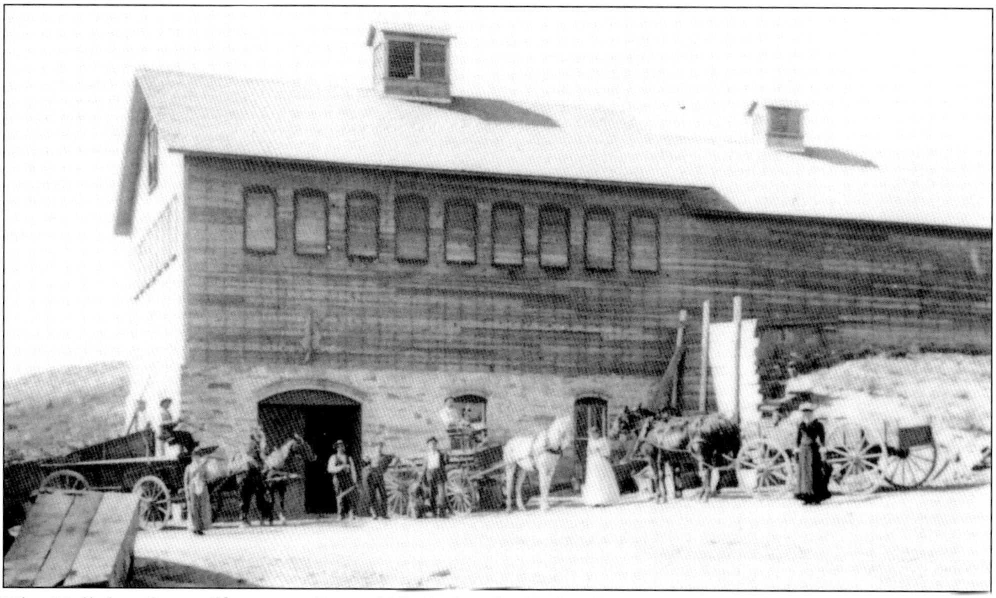

The Volk brothers, Christian Sr. and Nicholas, built the first commercial brewery in Great Falls in 1888. The Volk Brewery building was located south of the city on Upper River Road. It was constructed using native stone for the foundation and wood-frame construction for the upper portion of the building. This photograph was taken in 1891. Volk wagons delivered beer to the Great Falls area as well as to the Sun River Valley. The building burned in 1894, leaving only the stone foundation standing. (2007.17.160)

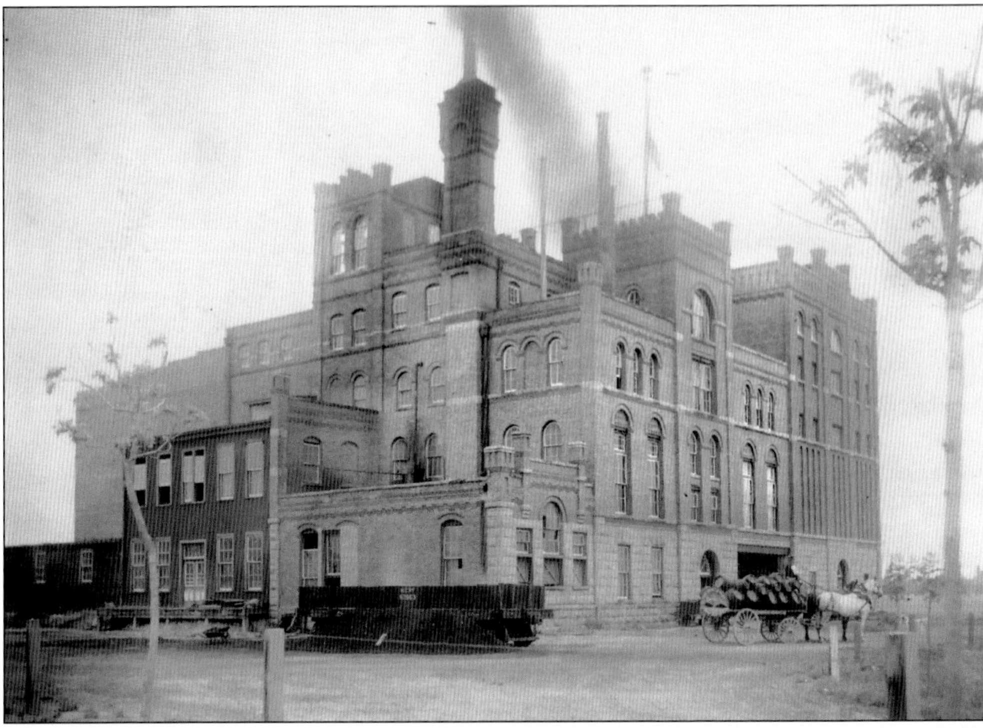

Built in 1892, the Montana Brewing Company was the second brewing company in Great Falls. The brewing complex was located on the west end of the First Avenue North wagon bridge, just north of Central Avenue West and right on the banks of the Missouri River. The last bottle of Great Falls Select was capped on August 31, 1968—economics had brought the brewery to its knees. However, the brand continued to be bottled by the Blitz-Weinhard Brewing Company in Portland, Oregon, for a number of years before it completely disappeared from store shelves in the late 1970s. (2007.17.885)

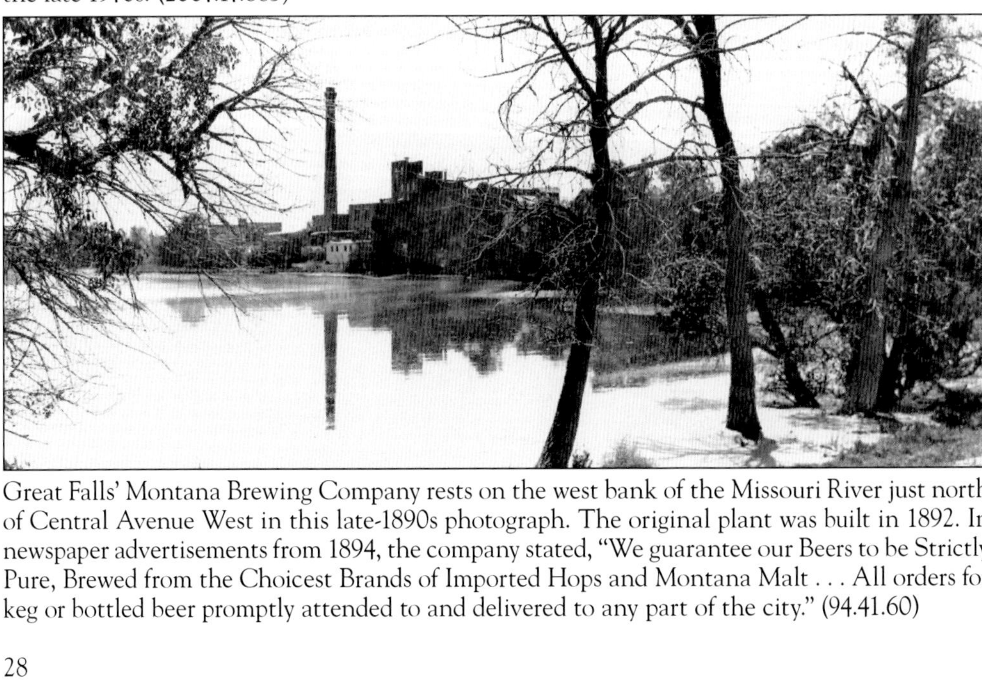

Great Falls' Montana Brewing Company rests on the west bank of the Missouri River just north of Central Avenue West in this late-1890s photograph. The original plant was built in 1892. In newspaper advertisements from 1894, the company stated, "We guarantee our Beers to be Strictly Pure, Brewed from the Choicest Brands of Imported Hops and Montana Malt . . . All orders for keg or bottled beer promptly attended to and delivered to any part of the city." (94.41.60)

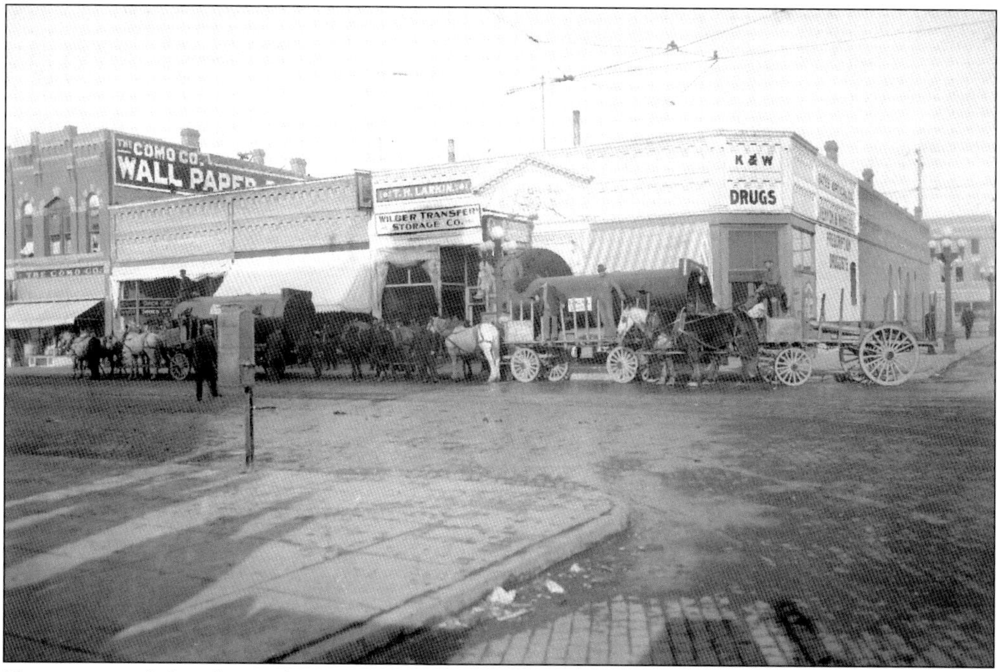

Teamsters and their horse-drawn wagons are getting ready to deliver some very heavy industrial iron pieces in this 1914 photograph. The Wilber Transfer and Storage Company was located on Central Avenue between Second and Third Streets. Wilber had earlier been a drayman for the city. The Como Company is seen here on the far left. Como specialized in art supplies and picture framing. Charles M. Russell had his paintings framed here. (94.40.4)

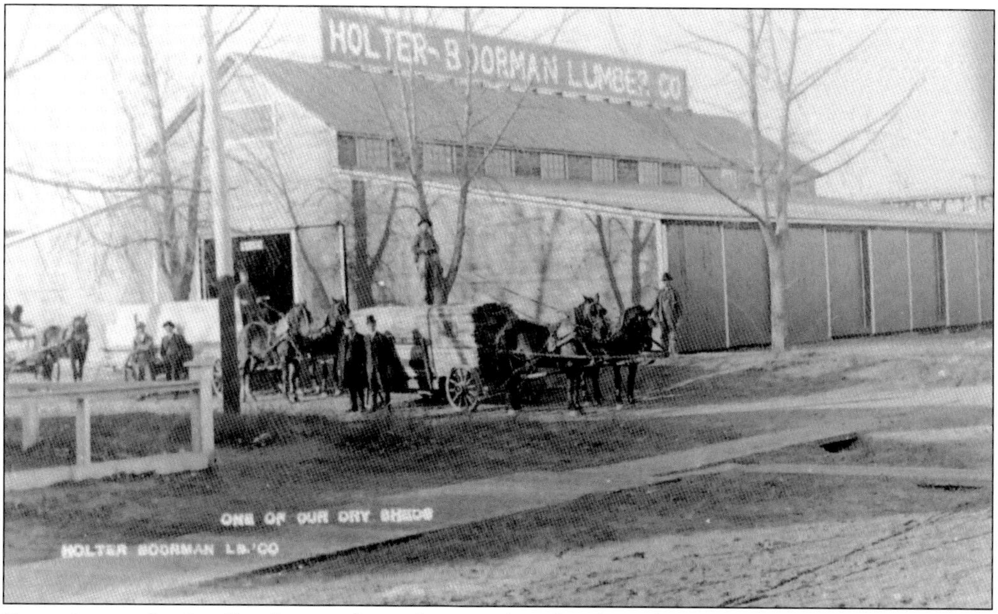

Several wagonloads of lumber are shown here ready to head out from the Holter-Boorman Lumber Company. The original Holter Lumber Company got its start with Anton M. Holter, one of the wealthiest men in 1800s Montana. It was the first business located within the current city limits of Great Falls, actually existing before the city was founded. (2007.17.185)

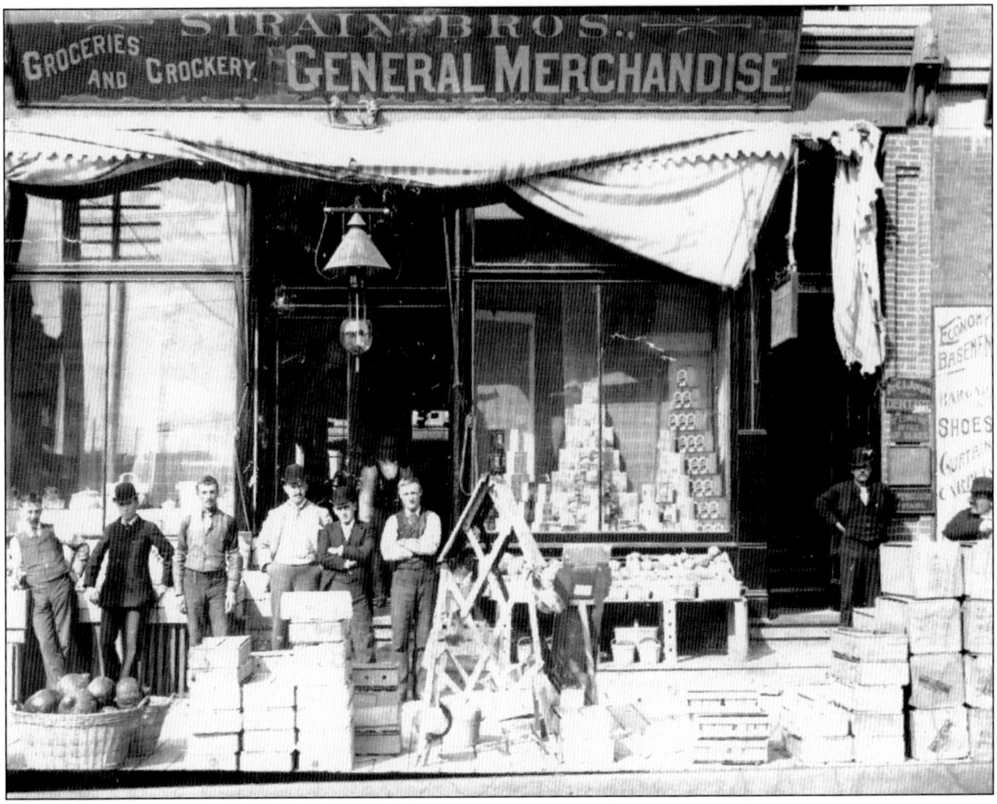

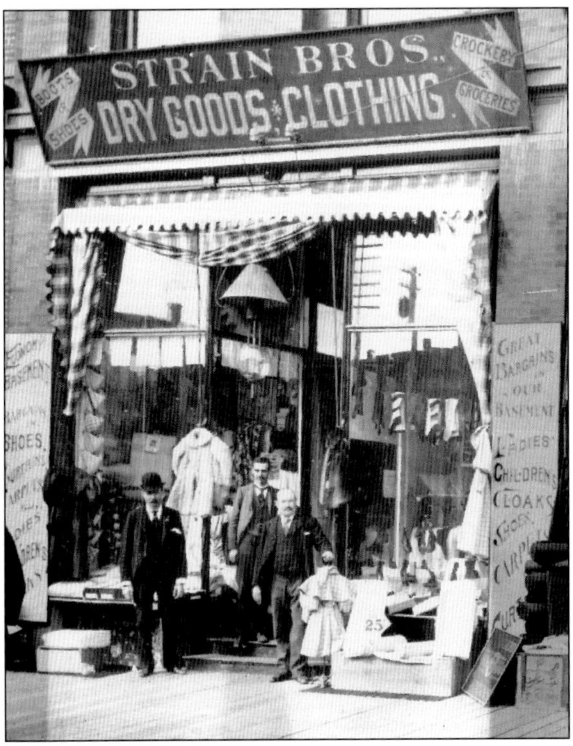

Crates of produce, including a large tub of squash, greet customers as they approach the Strain Brothers store on wooden sidewalks. The brothers started in 1887 when Herbert Strain rented a small warehouse at the rear of the Murphy Maclay Hardware Store. His brother W. J. Strain soon joined him from North Dakota. Together they formed a grocery business and a dry goods store. The grocery and hardware sections, seen above, continued in their Third Street location. (2005.16.44)

Three unidentified men stand in front of the Strain Brothers Dry Goods store in this early image. Adjacent to the grocery, the store offered ladies' attire, footwear, work clothes, carpets, furniture, and more. Situated on Central Avenue and Fourth Street, the business was an institution in Great Falls for many years. (2005.16.45)

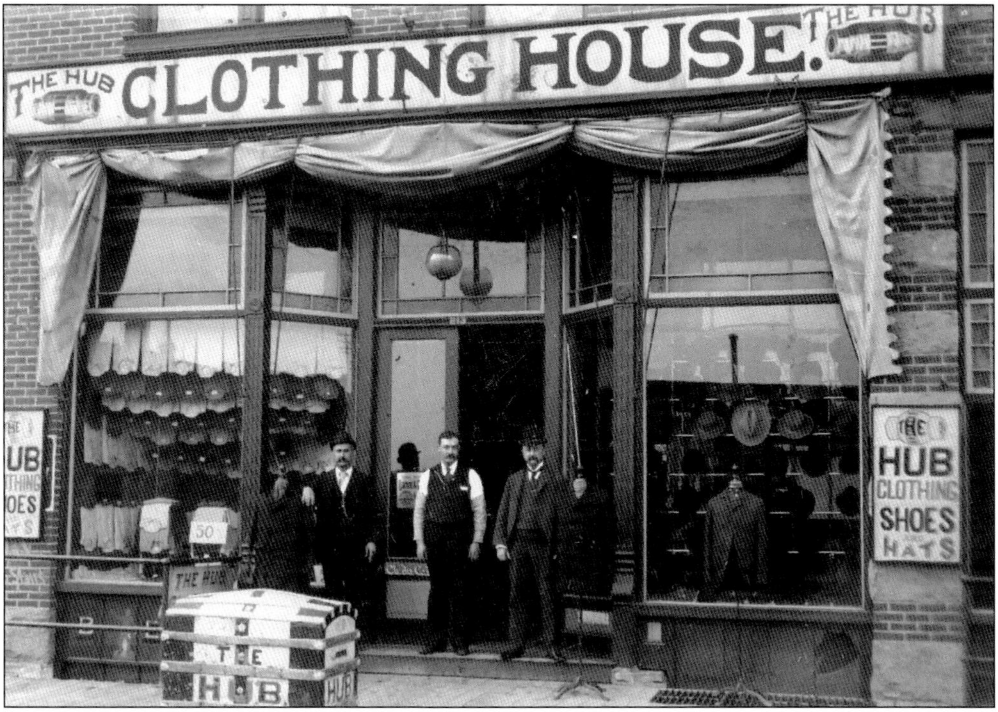

The Hub Clothing House was located on Central Avenue between Third and Fourth Streets. It was one of the earliest clothing stores in Great Falls, established in 1890 by T. W. Brosnan and Andrew Thisted. Brosnan went on to serve as a state senator. The store was a main source for all kinds of shoes and clothing and even offered delivery service. (2003.80.68)

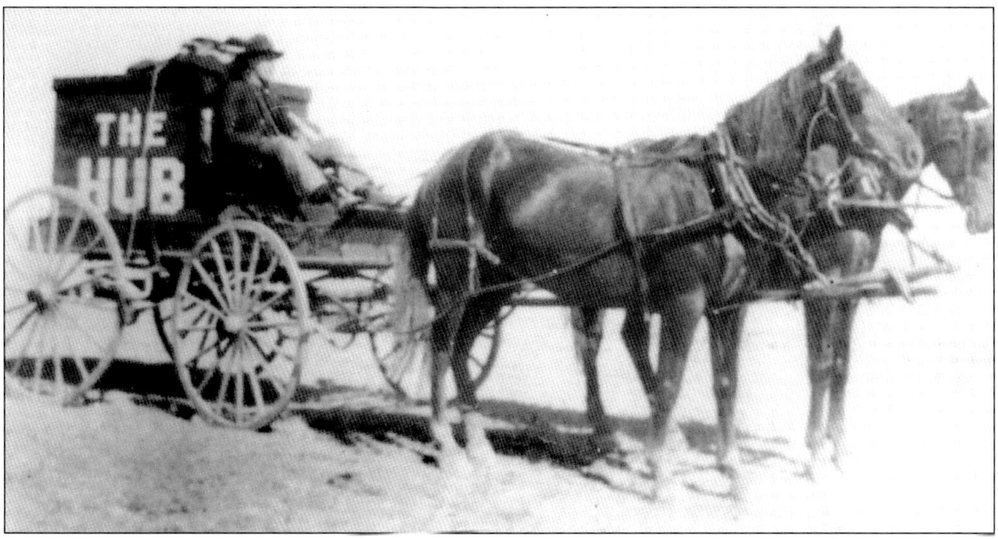

A wagon, horses, and their driver look ready to take on the world in this early photograph. The Hub Men's Store was one of the early haberdashers on Central Avenue. To provide its customers with the most up-to-date conveniences, a delivery system was put in place. Starting in late summer of 1890, the Hub grew to be one of the longest-standing and most prominent businesses on Central Avenue. Also known as Thisted, Brosnan, and Company, its slogan was "The Hub is the Center For Bargains In The Clothing Line." (2007.17.218)

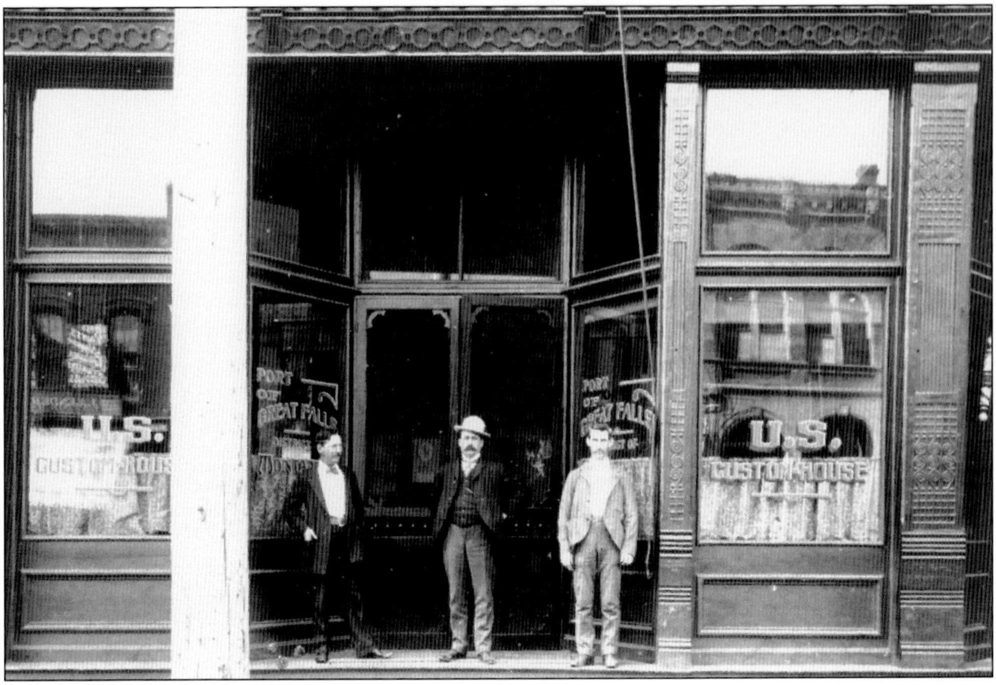

The U.S. Customs House and Port of Great Falls was located at 108 Central Avenue, not far from the Great Northern Railroad Station. Pictured at center is chief inspector J. J. O'Mahoney, standing with two companions. In the early development of the West, a lot of traffic flowed between Canada and the United States. Being only 140 miles from the Canadian border when business and populations were surging upward, the customs agent saw plenty of activity. (89.137.139)

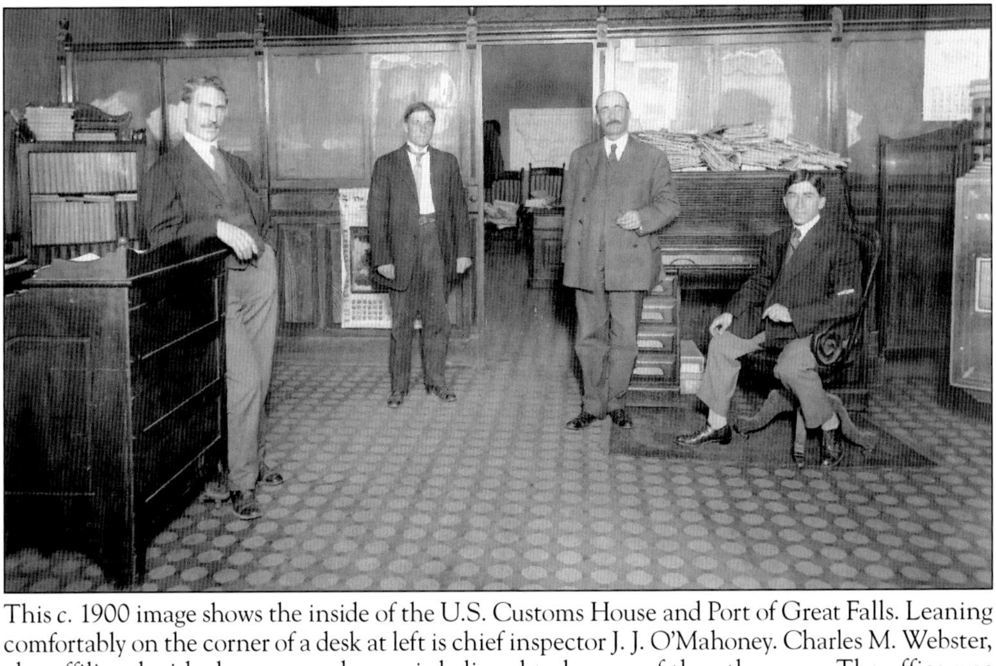

This c. 1900 image shows the inside of the U.S. Customs House and Port of Great Falls. Leaning comfortably on the corner of a desk at left is chief inspector J. J. O'Mahoney. Charles M. Webster, also affiliated with the customs house, is believed to be one of the other men. The office was located at 108 Central Avenue, beside the Park Hotel. (94.38.153)

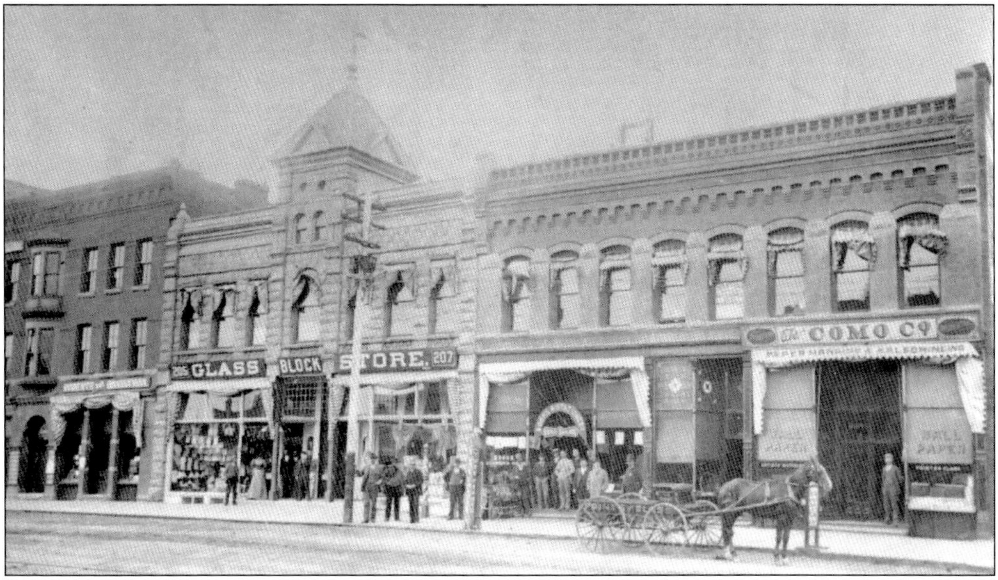

Central Avenue is seen here between Second and Third Streets looking north. The Como Company's earlier store at 211 Central Avenue is on the right. It sold various decorating and paint supplies, including watercolors, specialized glass, wallpaper, and calcimine. To the left of this is the Glass Block Store, which featured a variety of dry goods. In the store's second annual Clearing Up Sale in July 1894, it offered a variety of fabrics at 5¢ per yard. Ladies' corsets cost only 50¢ and were "guaranteed to be as good, if not better, than any 75¢ corset shown elsewhere." (2007.17.519)

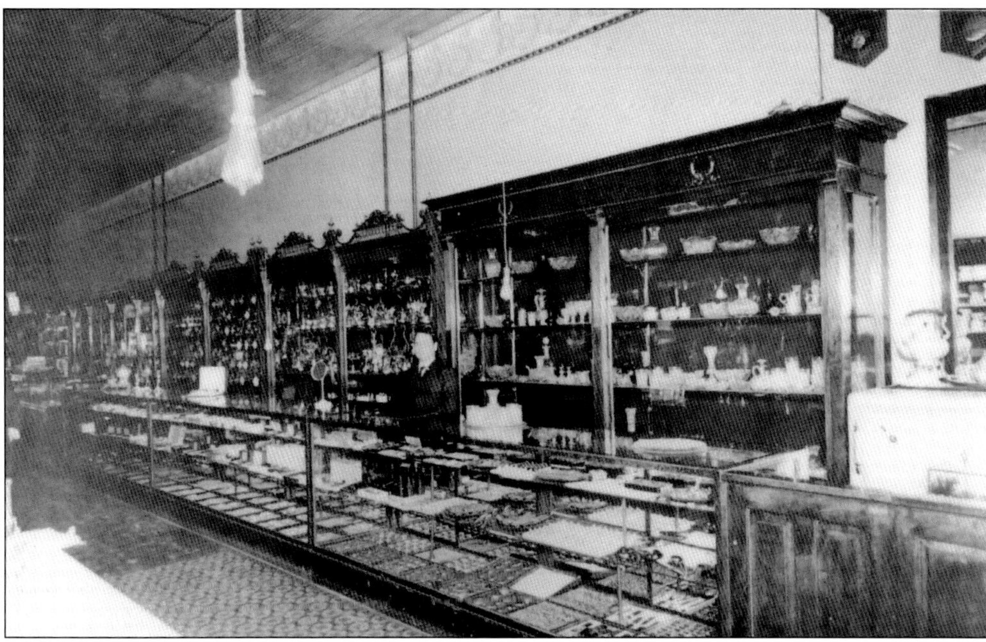

C. E. Davis Jewelry, at 317 Central Avenue, is seen here around 1900. Charles E. Davis advertised himself as an "Expert Watch Maker and Jeweler" and carried fine china, crystal, and a wide variety of the latest baubles. He also proclaimed, "We make a specialty of high-grade and complicated watch repair." (2007.17.186)

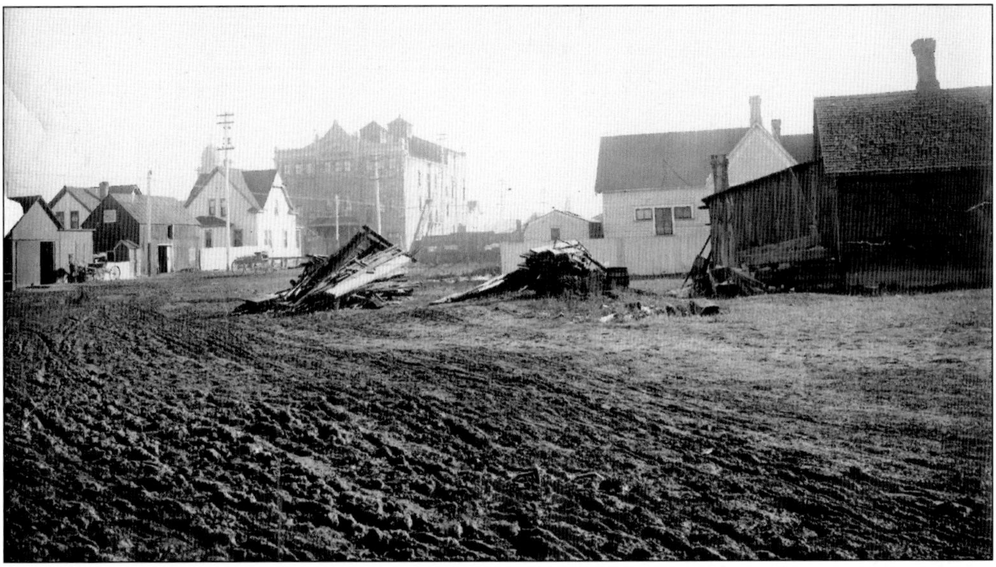

This October 26, 1908, photograph shows the spot where the U.S. Post Office would be built in a couple of years. Here it is nothing more than a mud track deeply rutted by wagon wheels. The sandstone Great Falls Opera House and the dome of the Cascade County Courthouse are visible in the background. (122.71)

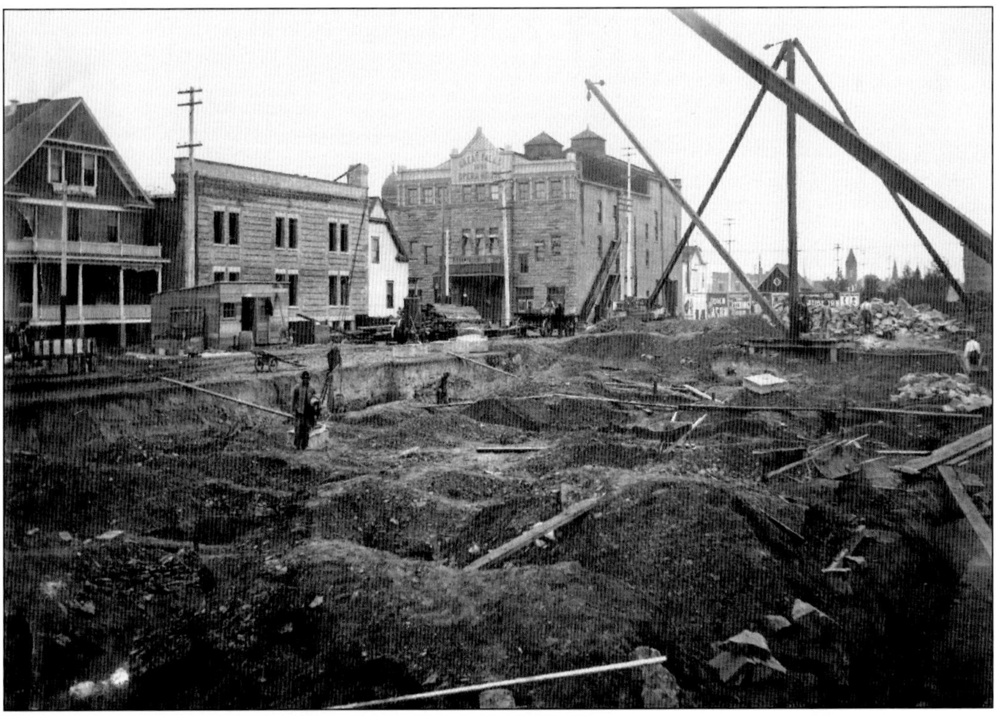

This September 1, 1910, picture shows that the groundwork is being prepared for the new post office on First Avenue North between Second and Third Streets. The contractor for the post office project was W. H. Maxwell. In the background is the original Great Falls (Grand) Opera House, built in 1891 and opened on January 4, 1892, when a crowd of 1,400 attended the play *Canuck*. (122.68)

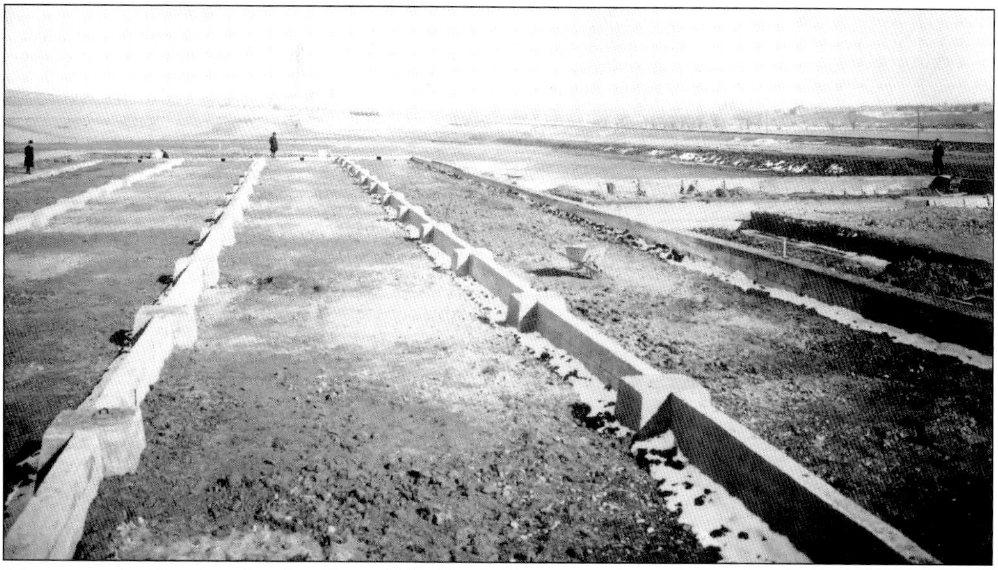

These are the footings for the Great Falls Brick Company factory, which was built just north of the Missouri River near an island named after Lewis and Clark's female traveling companion, Sacajawea. The brickworks would produce firebrick and building tile, hollow tile, fireproofing, drain tile, sewer pipe, and even flowerpots. The clay was taken from the Sand Coulee and Fields areas. As the city prospered, the demand for building brick increased. Consequently, the Anaconda Copper Company reopened its own brick plant in 1911. (2007.17.811)

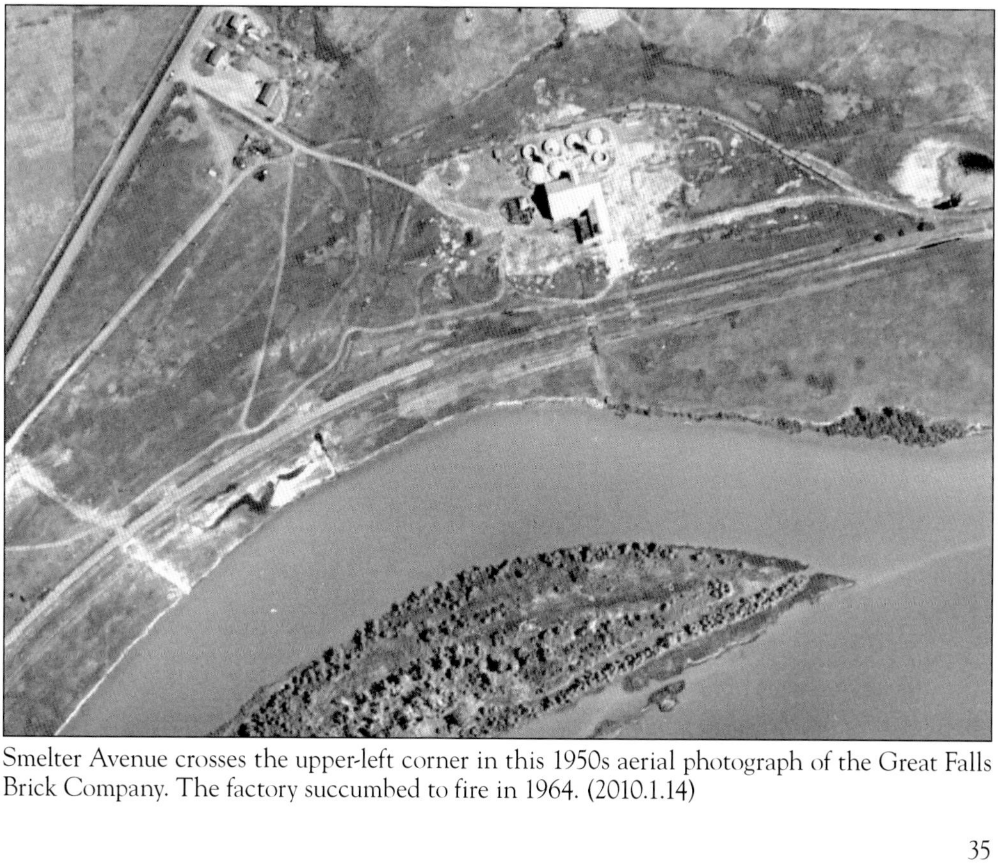

Smelter Avenue crosses the upper-left corner in this 1950s aerial photograph of the Great Falls Brick Company. The factory succumbed to fire in 1964. (2010.1.14)

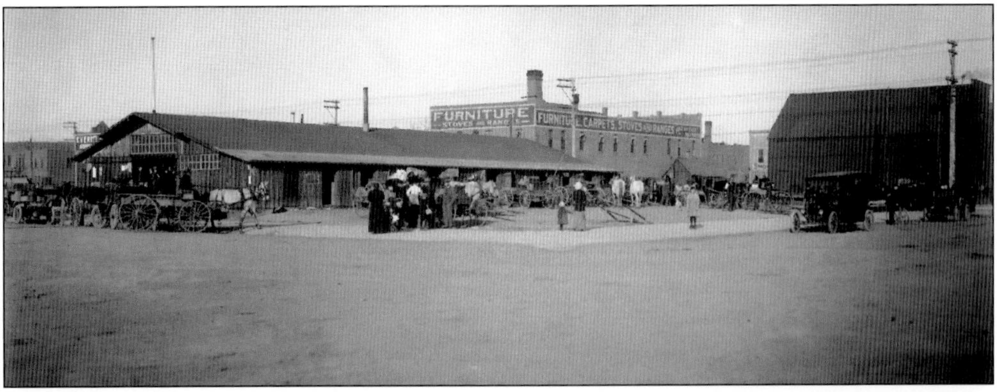

This photograph, taken about 1910, shows an open-air market in full flow. Looking northwest, this scene was taken on the corner of Fifth Street and Second Avenue South. This type of market was a perennial favorite and gave local producers an opportunity to get their produce in front of the public at a minimum of cost. Behind the market in the distance is the highly decorated Metropolitan Furniture Company with a band of advertising extending around the building. Located at 412–414 First Avenue South, Metropolitan sold furnishings for the home. C. C. Proctor was president of the company by 1910. (94.41.71)

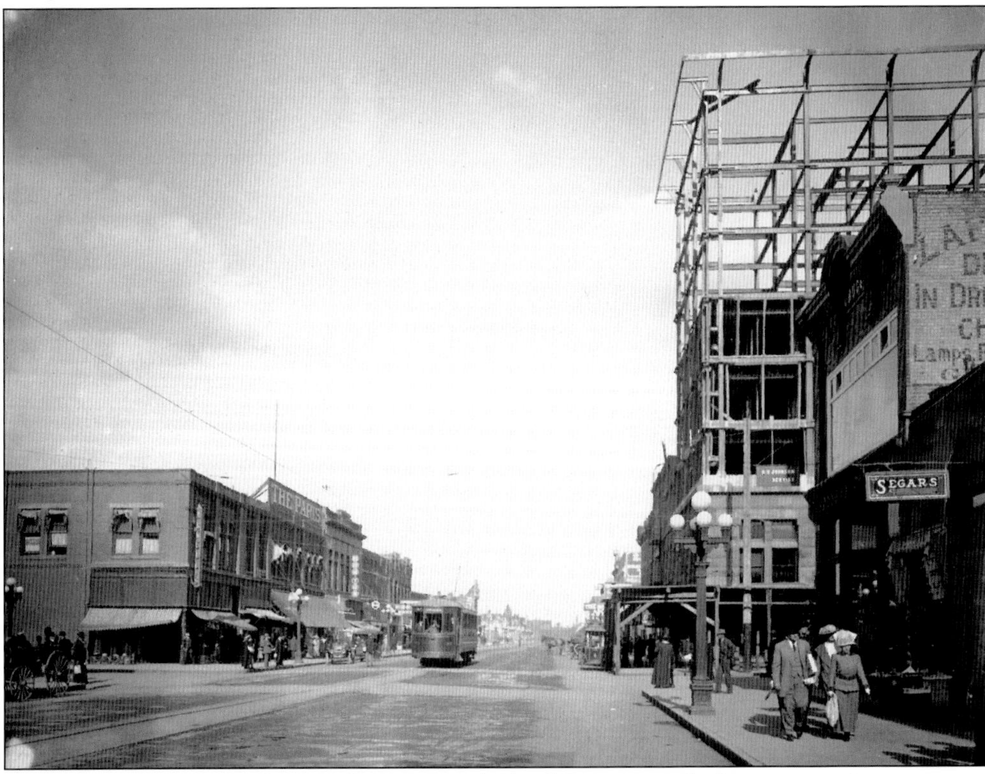

Here is the intersection of Central Avenue and Third Street, seen looking east in the summer of 1913. The Paris Dry Goods Store and the Bon Ton are adjacent on the north side of the street. On the corner to the right is LaPeyre Druggists. Just across the street, the First National Bank and its steel beams reach towards the sky. Citizens stroll lazily along the avenue, having no idea of the destructive fire that will soon change the complexion of downtown again, turning the Paris Dry Goods Store into a burned-out shell. (2007.17.820)

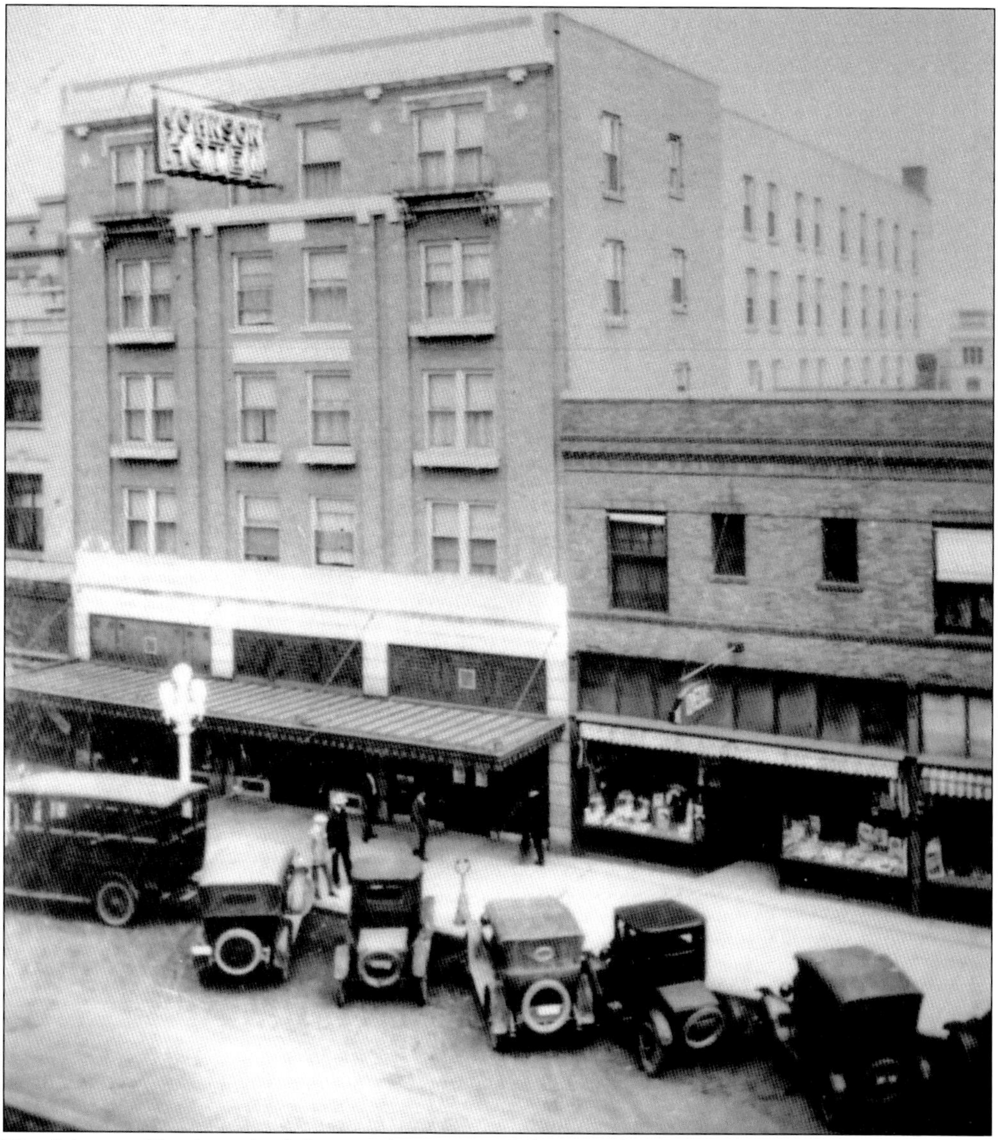

The Johnson Hotel was built by area farmer Pete Johnson after he arrived in Great Falls one day in his soiled agricultural clothes and was refused a room at a local hotel. Just prior to opening the hotel for occupancy, Johnson offered part of the first floor to host the state poultry exhibit. It was feared at the time that there was no facility in Great Falls adequate to house the show, which consisted of at least 400 poultry cages. Johnson offered the use of his new building, which would nearly be ready for occupancy by the time the poultry show opened in January 1920. Johnson understood the economic importance of having Great Falls host this show and made sure that his community, rather than some other, reaped the benefits. Pete Johnson is the tall man in the dark suit standing on the sidewalk in front of his new hotel. The large vehicle to the left is the free shuttle to and from the train station. For many years, the Johnson Hotel was a meeting place for people visiting Great Falls. Even though many residents of north-central Montana would arrange to use his hotel as a rendezvous point, they would not stay the night. Johnson overlooked this fact and allowed his hotel to be used in that fashion. He did, however, eventually set aside a part of the lobby for his paying guests. (2007.17.489)

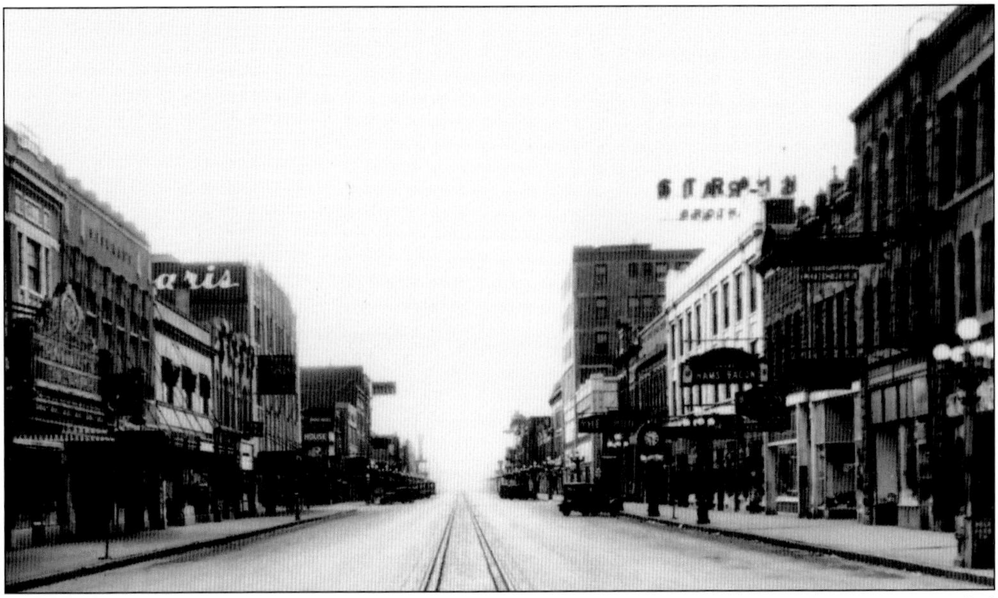

This c. 1925 image looks east on Central Avenue between Third and Fourth Streets. Angled parking was needed to accommodate the trolleys and trolley tracks in the early days. The tracks ran right down the middle of the street, and angled parking afforded enough room on the avenue to accommodate all the traffic. The Paris had built a new blonde brick store on Fourth Street and Central Avenue that boasted three levels of shopping after a devastating 1919 fire destroyed the other store. (2007.17.511)

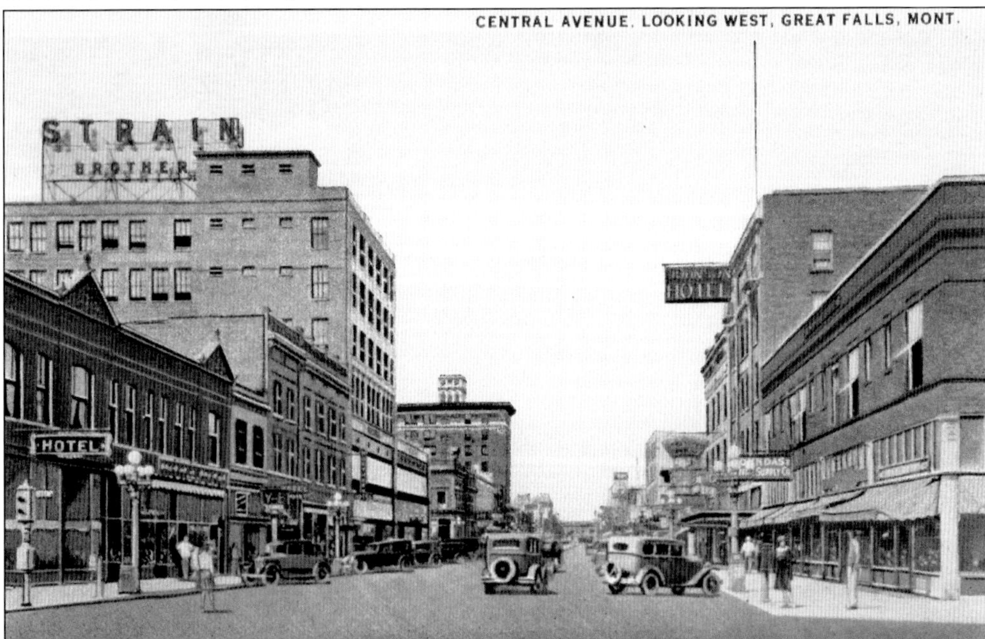

This 1920s postcard shows Central Avenue and Fifth Street looking west. The Strain brothers had developed their business into the large building on the left. The Johnson Hotel and the Dundas Office Supply are just down the street to the right. The Paris Dry Goods store can be seen on Fourth Street, just across from the Conrad Bank. (2004.84.8C)

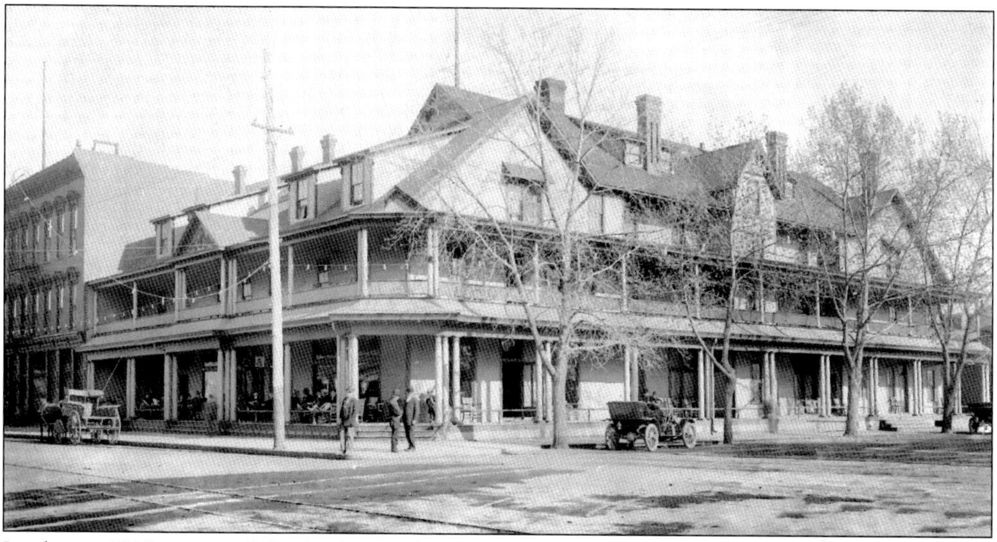

In this c. 1910 image of the Park Hotel, note the sweeping porches occupied by the travelers who favor the shady north side of the building. The trolley tracks lead east up Central Avenue. It was the era of transition from the horse and buggy (pictured on the left) to the automobile (right-center). Great Falls artist Charles Russell referred to the automobile as a "skunk wagon." (2007.17.744A)

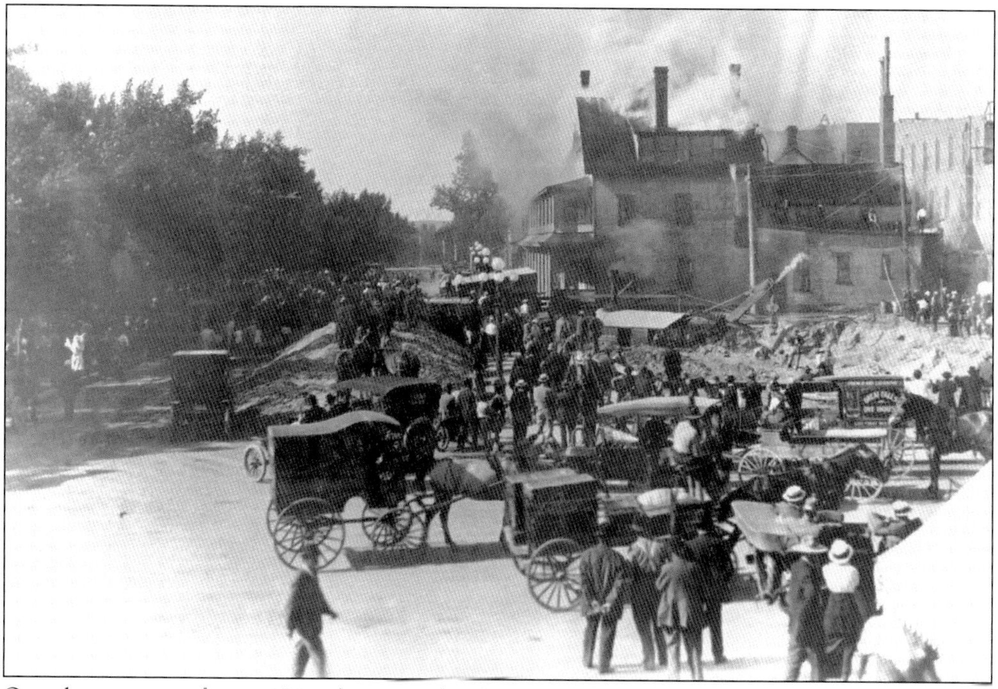

On a hot summer day in 1914, the upper level of the original 1886 frame structure of the Park Hotel went up in a blazing inferno. As soon as the ashes cooled, workers started to rebuild the damaged upper level and had it ready by the time the Territorial Golden Jubilee came along in August. The old wooden hotel was slated for demolition so that a new modern structure could be erected in its place. Much larger than the original frame building, the latest five-story Park Hotel was constructed of brick and would be a showplace for years to come. (2007.17.745)

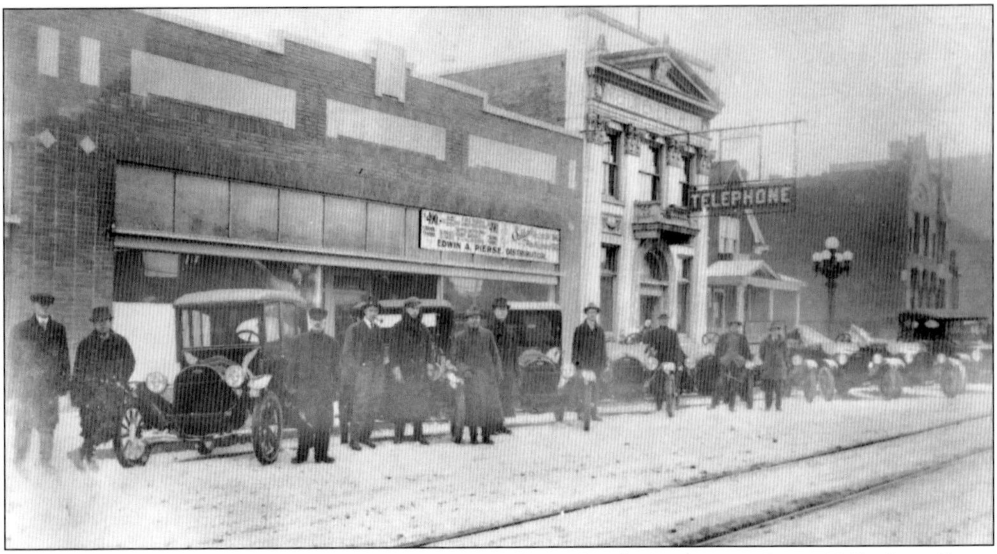

The Pierse Automobile Company was the first Chevrolet dealership in Great Falls. Its offices, showroom, and garage, located at 307 First Avenue North, opened for business in 1916. Edwin A. Pierse was the owner. Besides Chevrolet, the dealership was also a distributor for the Oakland automobile. The Chevrolet "bow tie" was proudly displayed on the sign overlooking the front of the building. The Pierse Automobile Company also sold and installed Fisk Tires. The Independent Telephone Company offices were right next door. In this image, trolley car tracks can be seen in the street in front of the businesses. (2007.17.170)

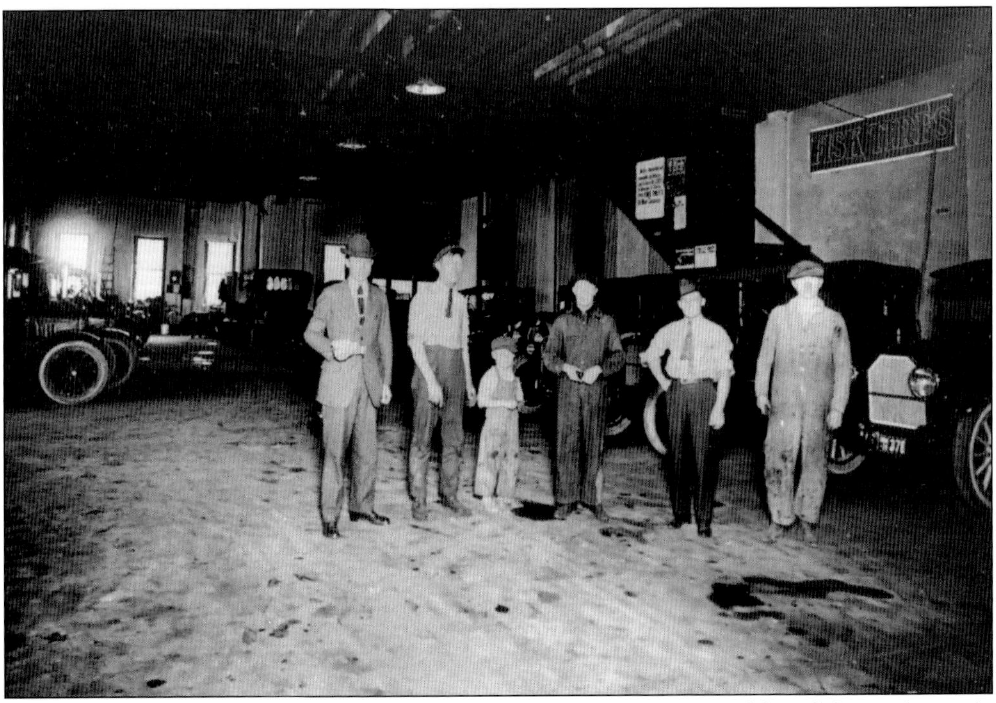

Ray Call offered the first "Drive Yourself" fleet of Model T Fords. Pictured from left to right inside the shop in this July 20, 1920, photograph are Ray Call, Al Palmluno, ? White (the boy), Emmett McGivern, Carroll Bennett, and Max Hedman. (2007.17.172)

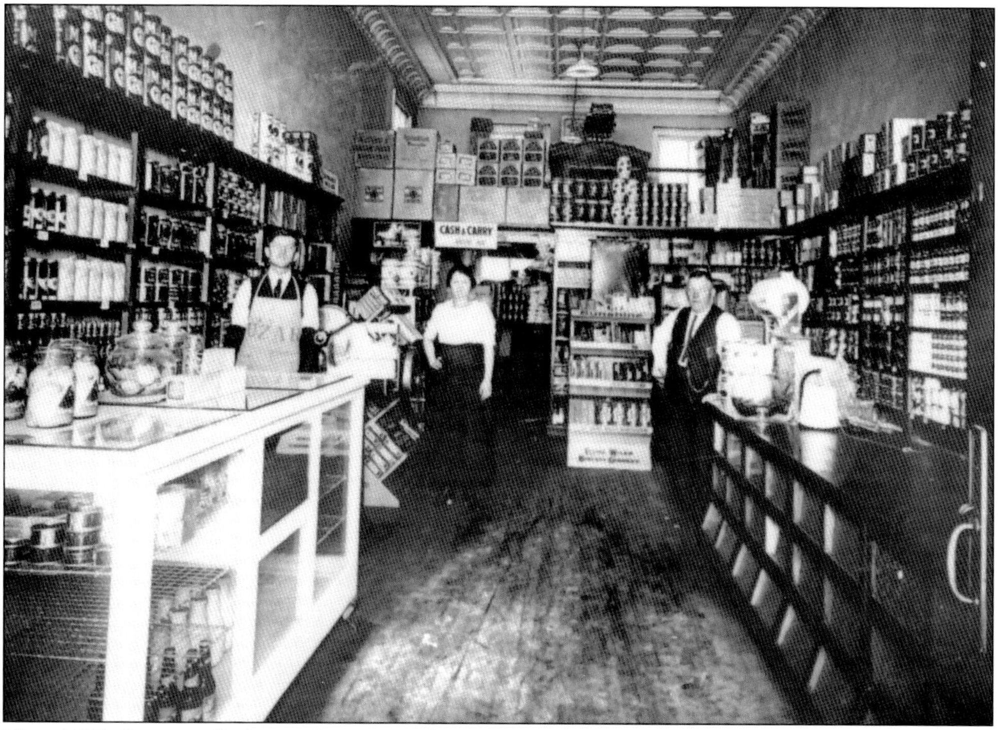

This 1925 photograph shows the Swan Thornson Grocery at 516 Central Avenue. A March 14, 1925, grocery advertisement offered sugar at 11 pounds for 87¢, Belt Valley Butter at two pounds for 83¢, and two No. 2 cans of Del Monte strawberries for 69¢. Originally, the grocery was located in Black Eagle. Thornson's store was known as the Chicago Mercantile Company and was located on Fifteenth Street close to Smelter Avenue. Its advertisements promised "groceries, dry goods, and gent's furnishings in Little Chicago." (2007.17.182)

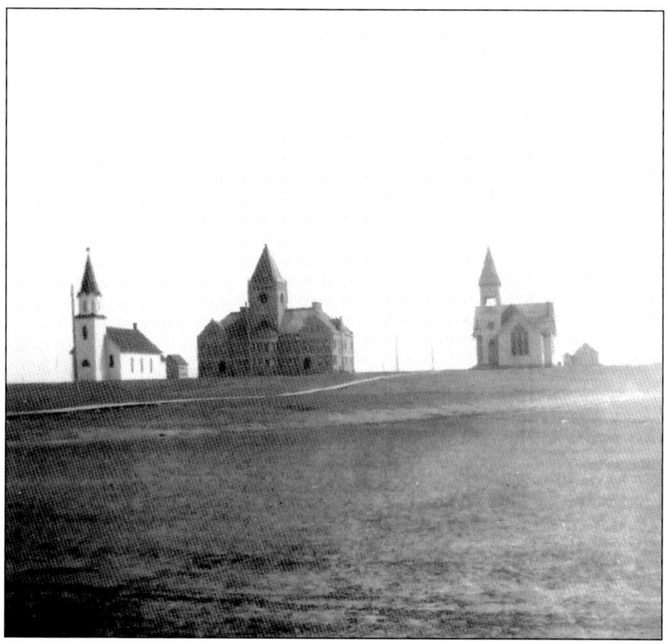

Great Falls High School is seen here flanked by Our Savior's Evangelical Scandinavian Church on the left and the Scandinavian Methodist Church on the right. Close to each church is the little rectory housing its clergy. In this photograph taken between 1905 and 1906, the development of the encroaching city is still some distance away to the west. The photographer is standing somewhere between Thirteenth and Fourteenth Streets North, at about Third Avenue North, looking south-by-southeast. (2007.17.84)

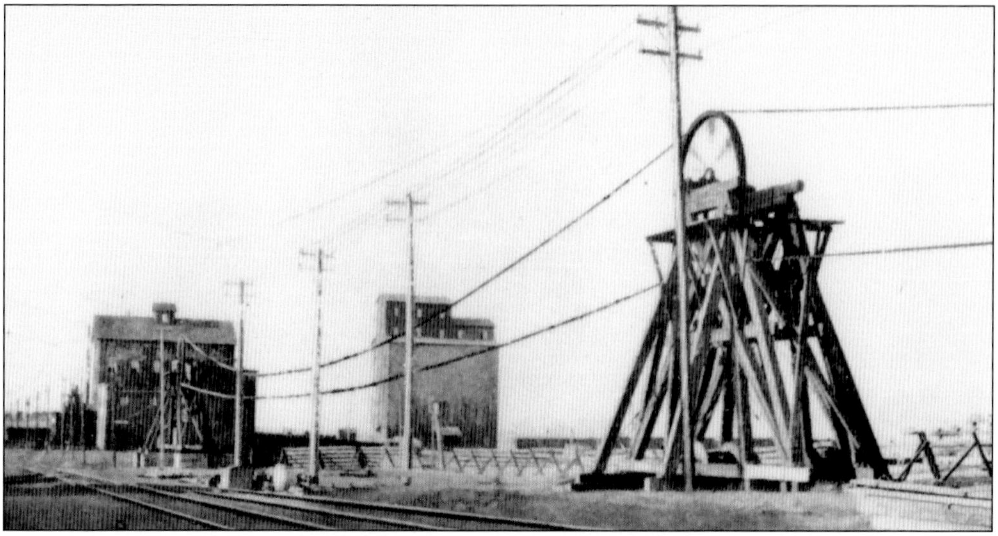

The Royal Mills, a flour mill originally built in 1892 and 1893 and located high above the Missouri River on the south bank, above Back Eagle Dam, used an energy source quite different from the normal electricity produced by powerhouses. Here a series of belts and pulleys was incorporated to make effective use of the brute physical power of the river. Energy transmitted in this way was used to turn the flour mills and grinding wheels, turning grain into flour, which was used in making bread and other edibles. By 1899, the Royal Milling Company produced half of the flour manufactured in Montana. (2007.17.793)

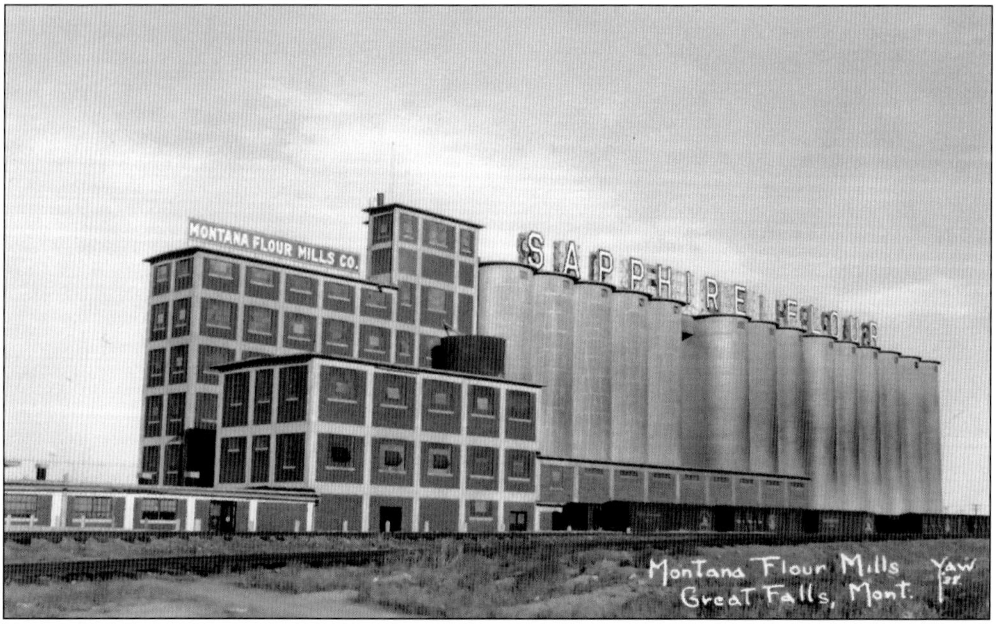

Here is the building used by the Montana Flour Mills Company, maker of Sapphire Flour, as it appeared in 1938. Incorporated in 1911, the Montana Flour Mills Company began work in this location in 1916. In later years, a neon-gas sign on top of the grain bins spelled out the name of Sapphire Flour in bright blue lights. (2006.84.16)

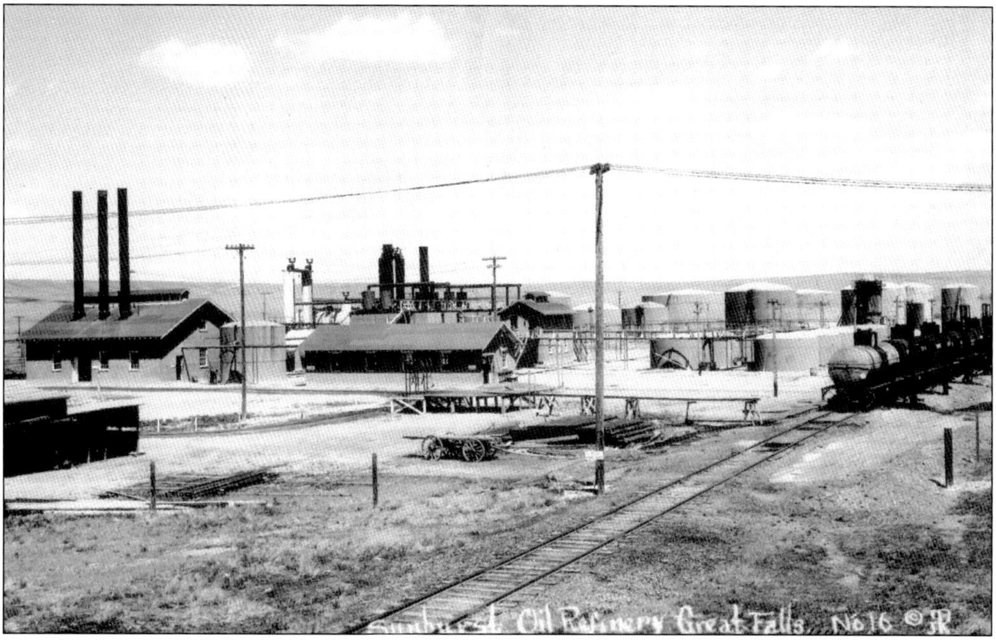

The Sunburst Oil Refinery, shown here about 1920, sat on the west banks of the Missouri River just north of the Great Falls Brewery. The oil field itself lay some 100 miles north of Great Falls. This refinery site was maintained until 1929, when a fire broke out. Operations were never resumed in Great Falls. (2008.30.19)

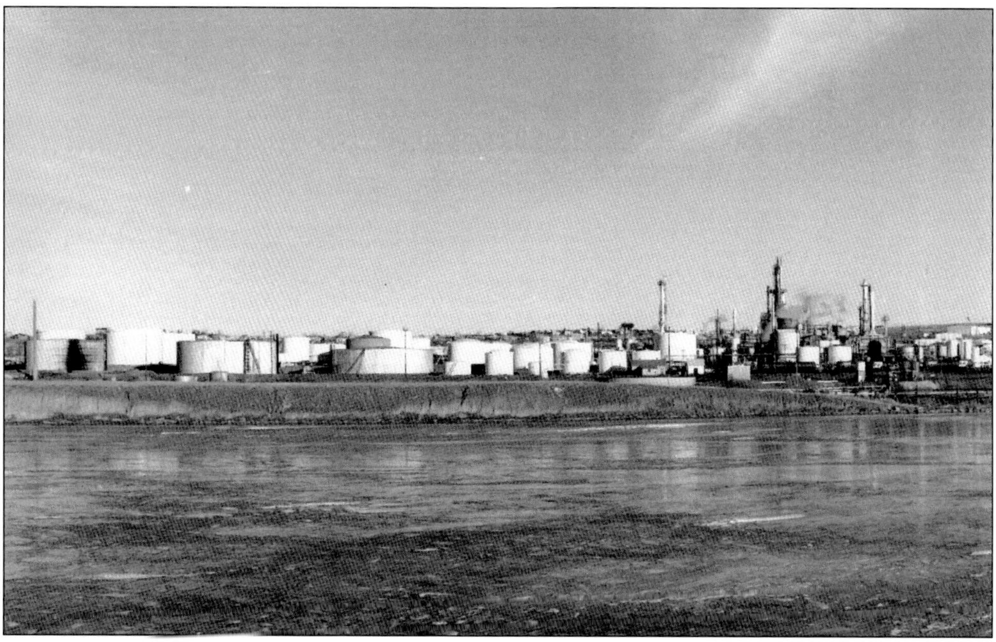

An oil-refining company has resided at the north end of the Ninth Street Bridge since shortly after the span's construction in 1920. In 1922, the American Oil and Refinery started developing its new facilities. Since then, the refinery has seen many different owners. In 1984, Holly Corporation took it over. Eventually one of its subsidiaries, Montana Refining Company, took possession. (95.100.81)

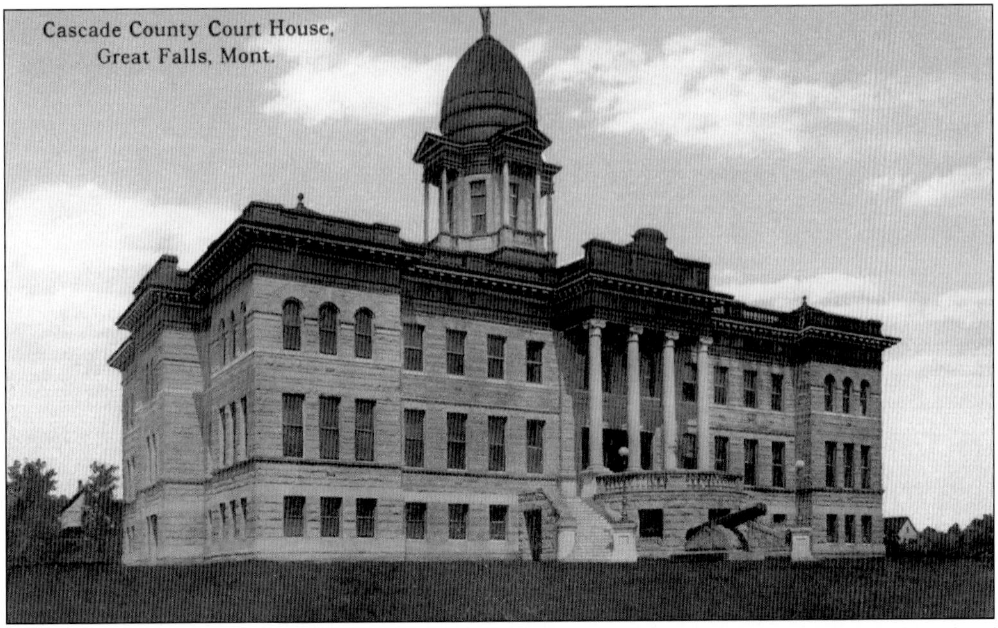

The Cascade County Courthouse was built in 1903 of native sandstone quarried just south of town. It rests on an entire city block from Second to Third Avenues North between Fourth and Fifth Streets. N. T. Lease contracted to build the courthouse in 1901. The county jail, also of sandstone, would be erected a decade later directly to the west across Fourth Street. (2010.1.15)

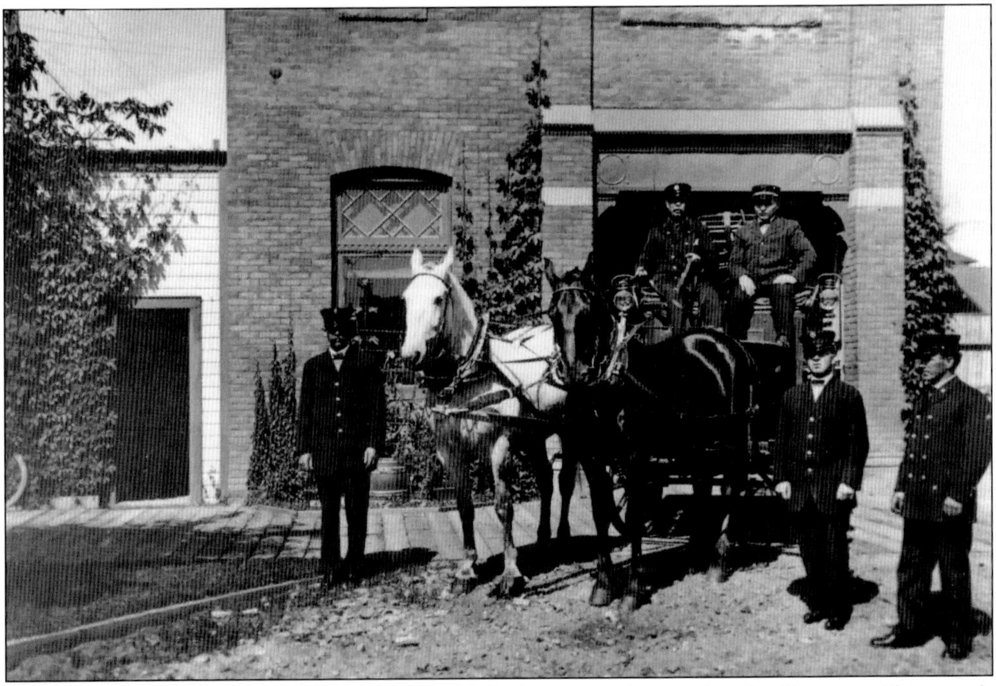

The Great Falls Fire Department maintained a firehouse on the north side of town at Thirteenth Street and Fifth Alley North. Pictured in 1912 from left to right are firemen R. E. Schreder and C. Wetherland, Assistant Fire Chief William H. Grover, hydrantman Edward Dempsey, and Capt. Alfred J. Trodick. (2007.17.61)

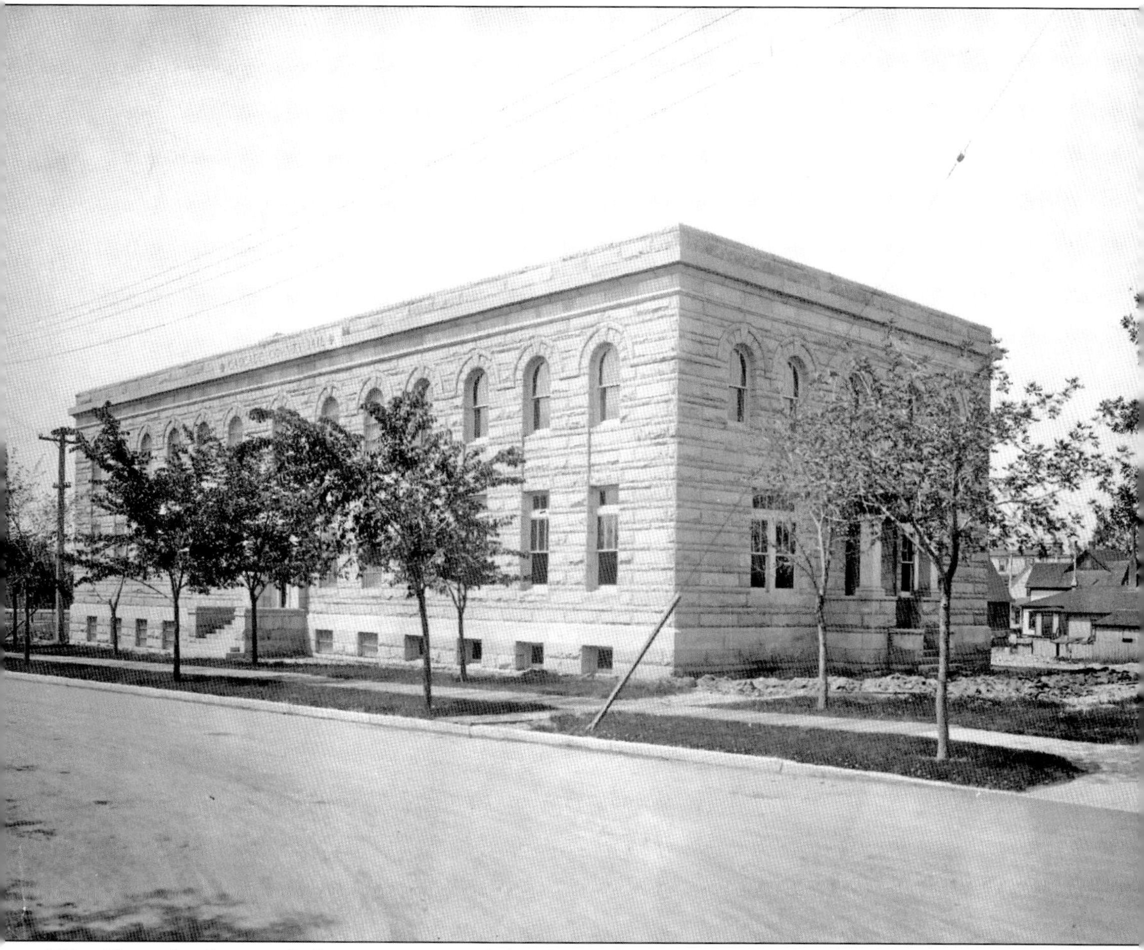

The Cascade County Jail sat just west of the Cascade County Courthouse on Fourth Street and Third Avenue North. Built using steel-reinforced concrete, it was covered with buff native sandstone furnished by the Grover and Leuchar Quarry, located just southwest of the city. The first and second jails were on Third Avenue South in the area between Third and Fourth Streets. (2007.17.242)

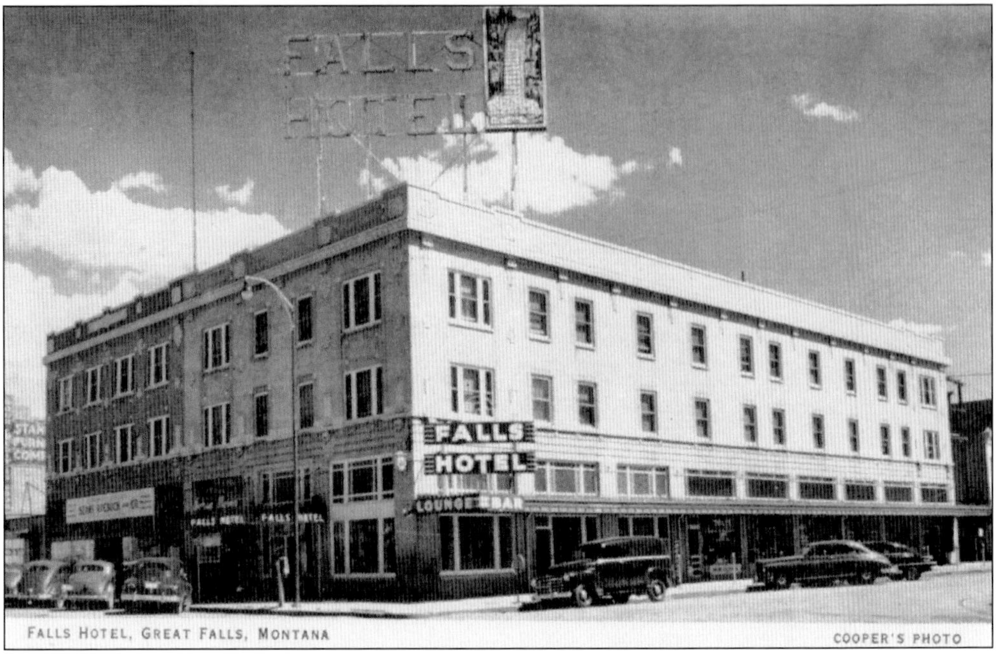

The Falls Hotel was appropriately named after the significance of the town and series of cascades on the Missouri River. Owned by Art and Dorothy Stevens, it sat on the corner of Fourth Street and First Avenue South. It was advertised as "New, Modern and Fire Proof." There was a lounge where the public could relax and unwind called the Spray Room, further evidence of the influence of the river on the business community. This undated photograph was taken in the 1940s. (98.72.156A)

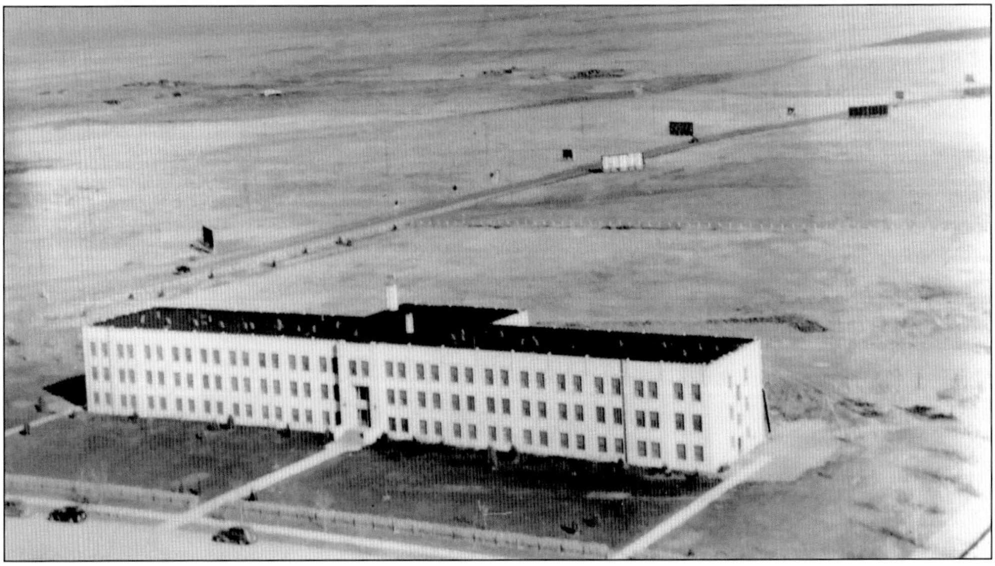

Completed in 1936, the Montana State School for the Deaf and the Blind was located east of Great Falls, on the east side of Thirty-Eighth Street North between Central Avenue and Second Avenue North. On the north (left) side of Second Avenue North in this 1937 aerial photograph is the highway to Belt and Lewistown. Notice all the billboards that flank the road, advertising to passing motorists along the busy highway. (2007.17.540)

Three

When Copper Was King

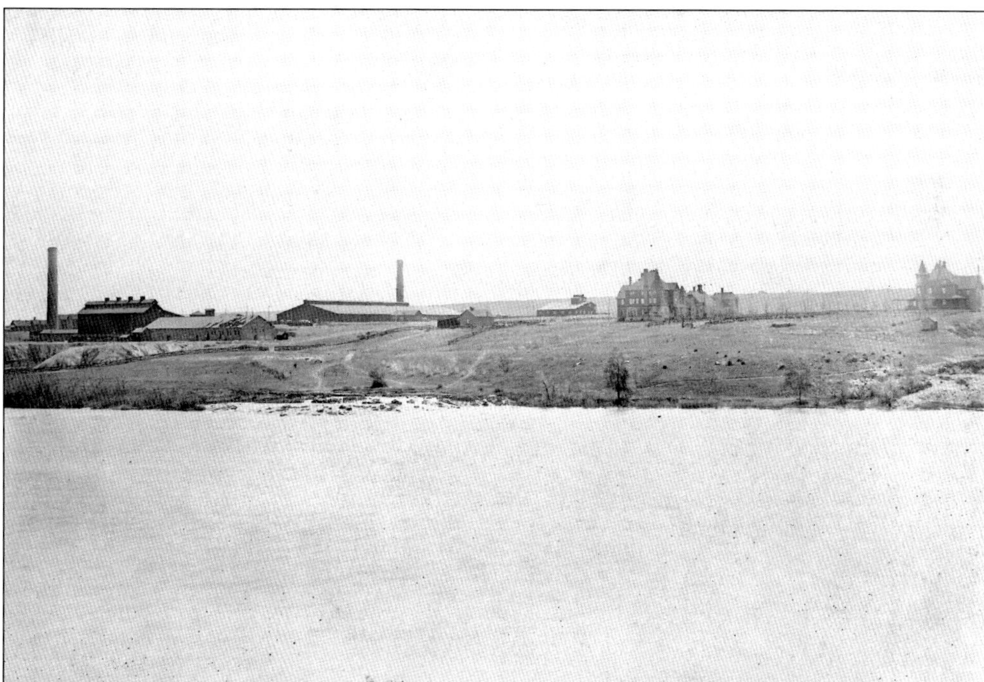

The Montana Smelting and Refining Company built its silver smelter on the south side of the Missouri River, on the higher ground at Giant Springs. Work began in 1888, and the smelter was in operation by the time Montana achieved statehood in 1889. The end of the next decade would see the price of silver plummet. By 1900, the smelter closed, and most of the equipment was moved to East Helena. (94.38.151)

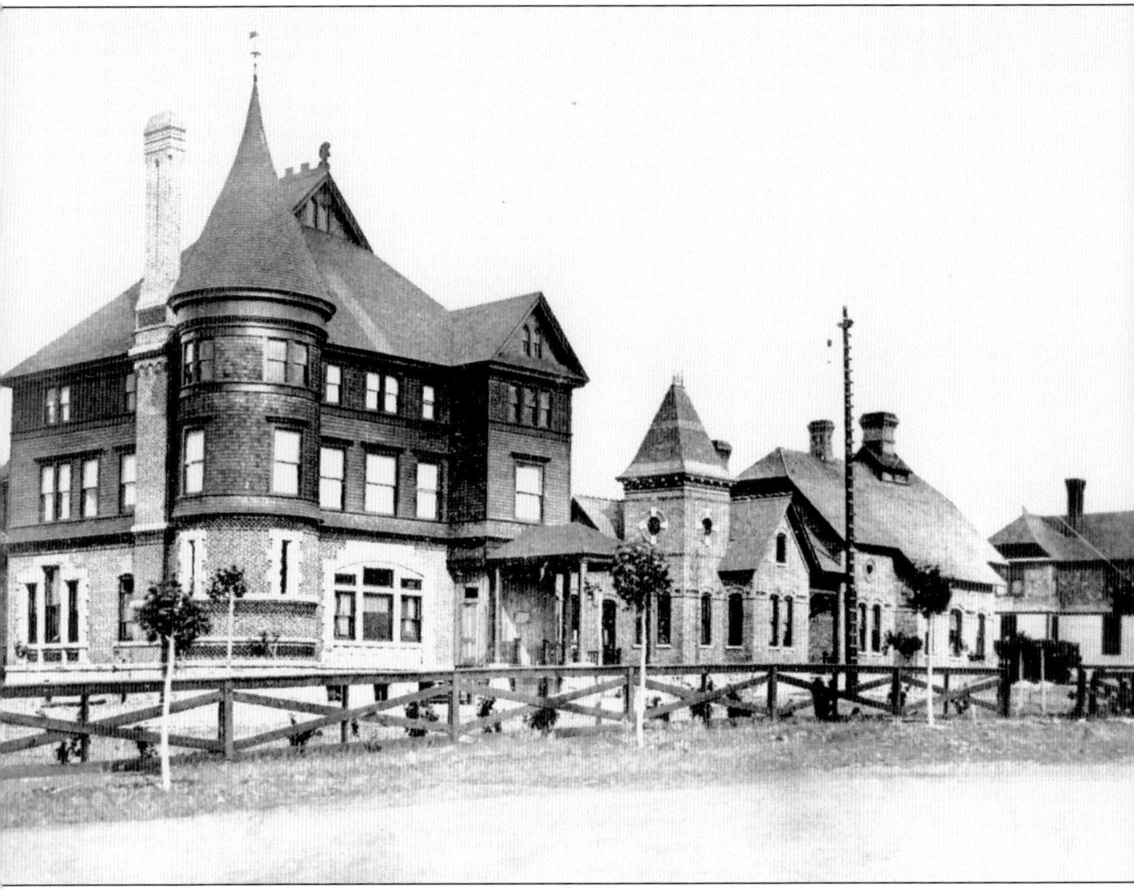

These beautiful homes built for Montana Smelting and Refining Company management personnel and their families illustrate the comfort available to upper-income inhabitants of Great Falls. Construction on what came to be known locally as the "silver smelter" began on March 5, 1888, when Paris Gibson broke ground. The facility was completed and in operation by 1889. (87.4)

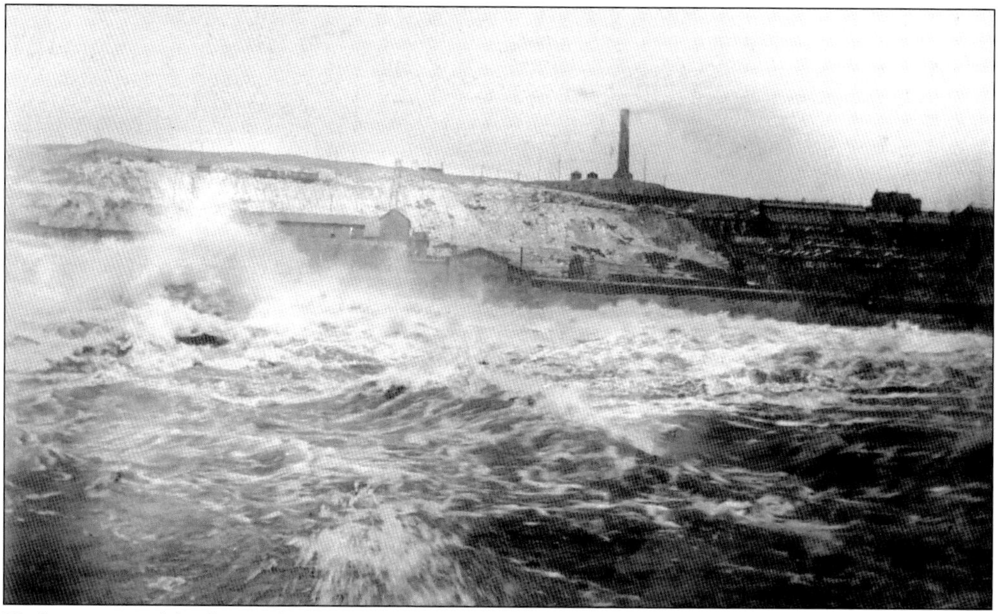

High water and high winds in 1898 provide a surrealistic view of the Missouri River near the Boston and Montana Smelter. In this picture, severe winds combine with high water to make harnessing the power of the river a most challenging task. The original 150-foot-high smokestack can be seen on the hill. (450.1)

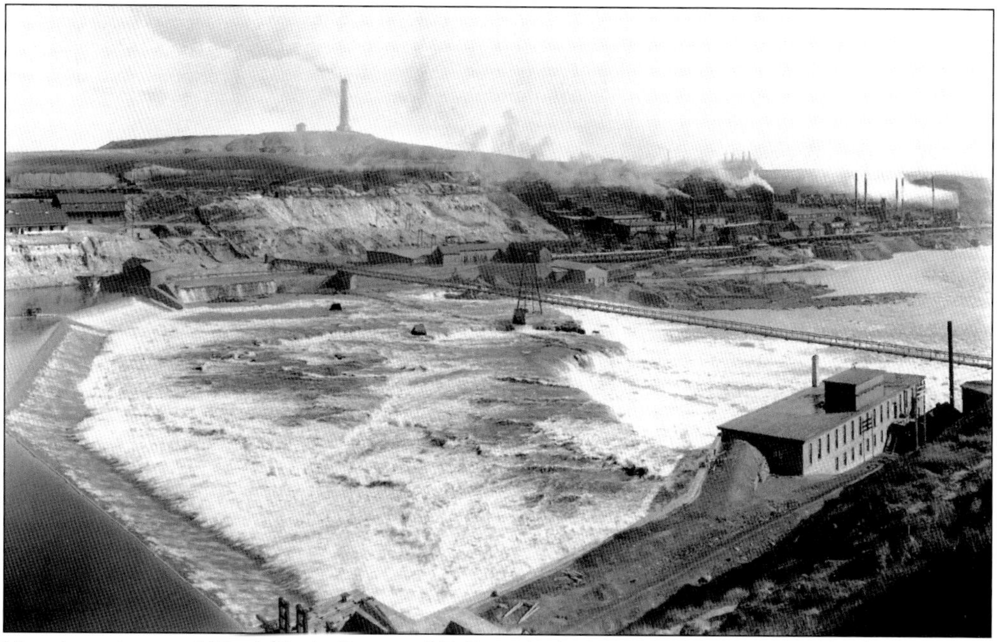

Here is an image of Black Eagle Dam and Falls with the Boston and Montana Smelter works in the background. The smaller stack, constructed early in 1891, would be removed after a much larger stack was completed almost two decades later. The footbridge was constructed at about the same time as the original smokestack. It saved workers many miles of walking over the next decade and a half, but the frail pylon center support would be no match for the devastating flood of 1908. (2007.17.795)

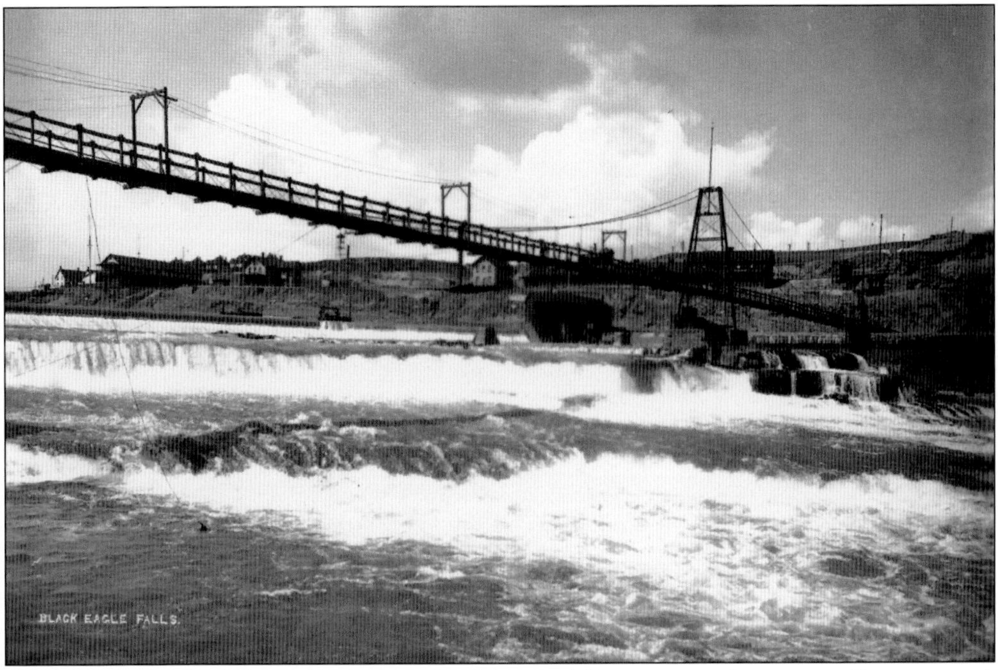

The smelter men had this walkway over Black Eagle Falls constructed to save walking to work via the other bridges, none of which would have been convenient. The Fifteenth Street Bridge was over a mile to the west. The walkway saved the men miles of walking as they made their way to and from the smelter. (2007.17.799)

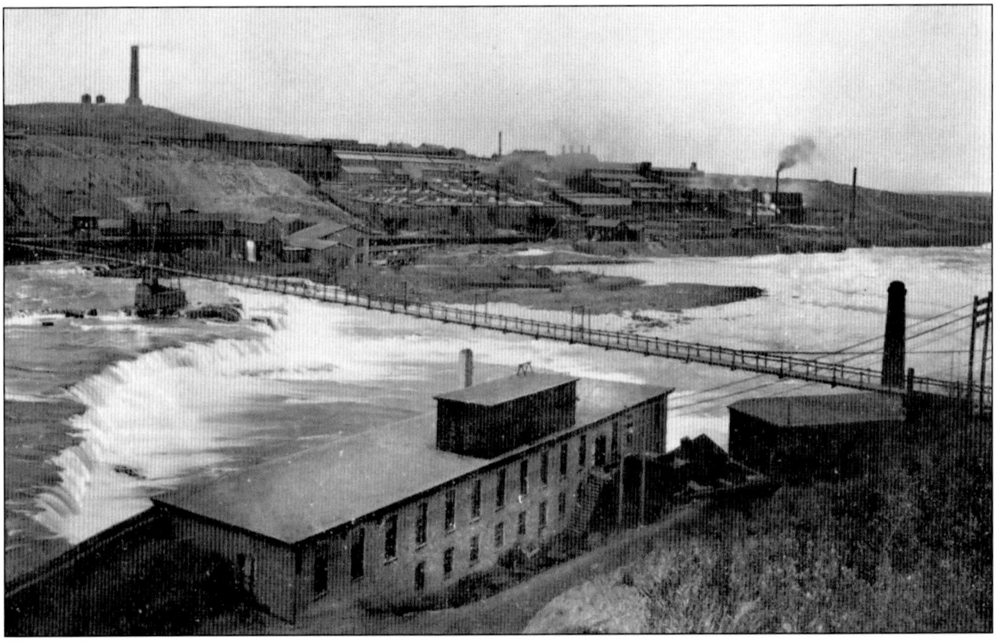

The Missouri River cascades over the ledges and rock shelves of Black Eagle Falls. The fragile, 1,200-foot-long footbridge seen spanning the river afforded not only a welcome shortcut but also gave these smelter men a view of the dam, falls, river, and smelter works unavailable to anyone else, before or since. (2007.17.273)

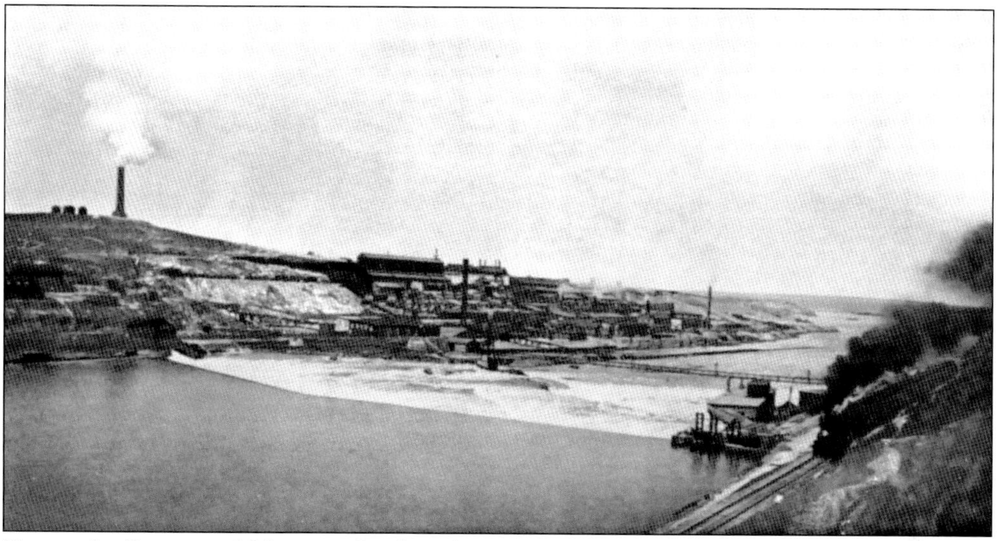

Here is the Boston and Montana Smelter about 1905. Great Falls was originally designed as an industrial town. Mining drove the future of the city in the early days, and power production was incidental. Electricity was routed from Great Falls to Helena to Butte, where it became an integral part of powering mining and smelting operations. Early documents show Butte as the destination of electrical power produced in Great Falls. (2010.1.16)

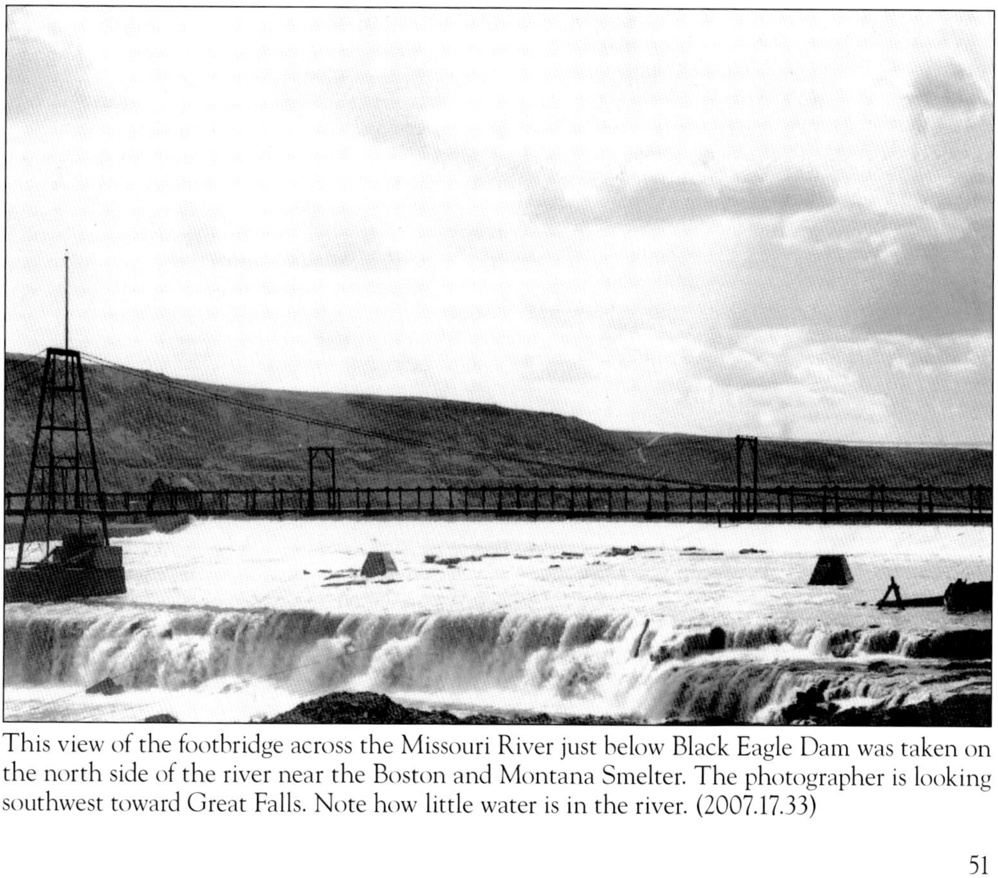

This view of the footbridge across the Missouri River just below Black Eagle Dam was taken on the north side of the river near the Boston and Montana Smelter. The photographer is looking southwest toward Great Falls. Note how little water is in the river. (2007.17.33)

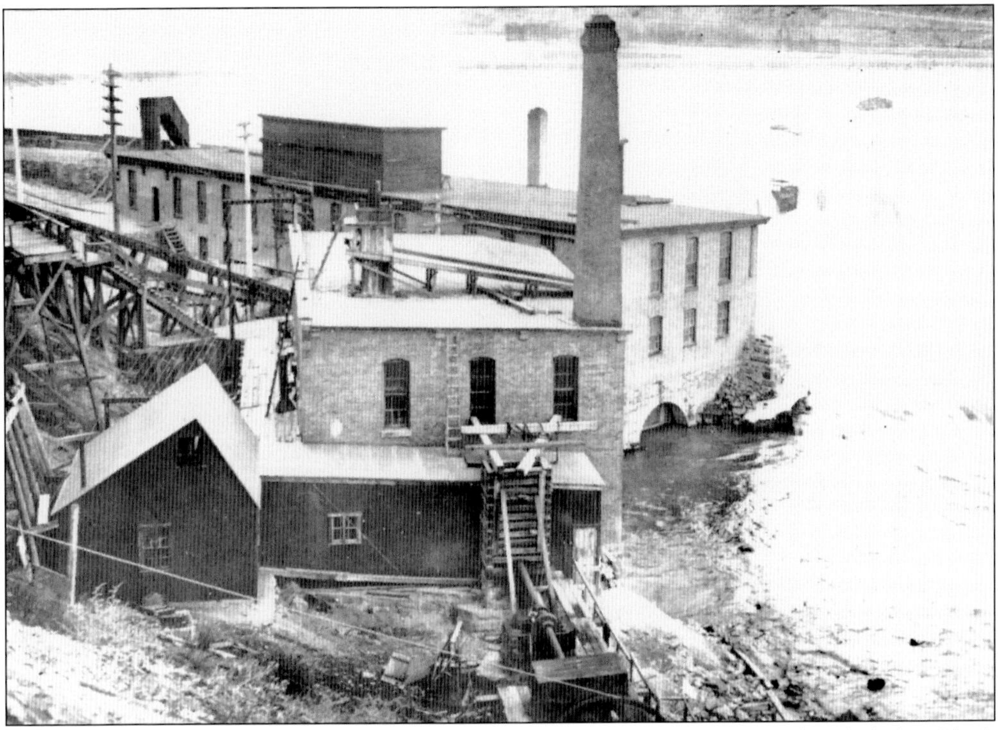

The Great Falls Water Power and Town Site Company's powerhouse immediately below Black Eagle Dam suffered extensive damage from the June 1908 flood. One of the most significant floods to hit Great Falls in its early history, it did significant damage to low-lying areas around the growing town. During the crest of the flood, water poured through the inside of the powerhouse, destroying much of the valuable facility. (2007.17.15)

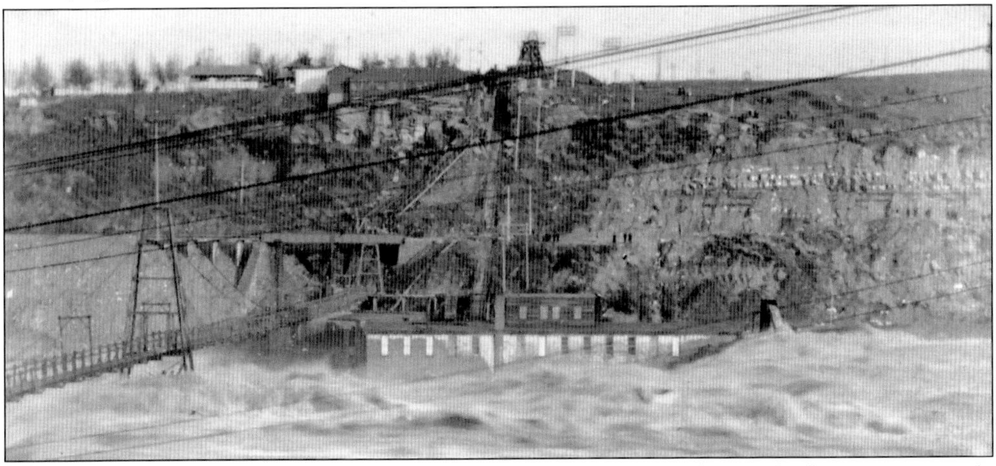

The powerhouse at Black Eagle Dam, directly across the river on the north shore, was severely damaged by the flood of June 1908. The footbridge failed not long afterwards and was swept away June 8 in the heavy current. On the steep hillside across the river, a series of cables and pulleys can be seen going up the slope from the powerhouse. This mechanical contrivance was designed to capitalize on the river's mighty current and harness the power. The series of huge belts, pulleys, and cables carried mechanical power a quarter of a mile to be harnessed at the Royal Milling Company flour mill. (2007.17.297)

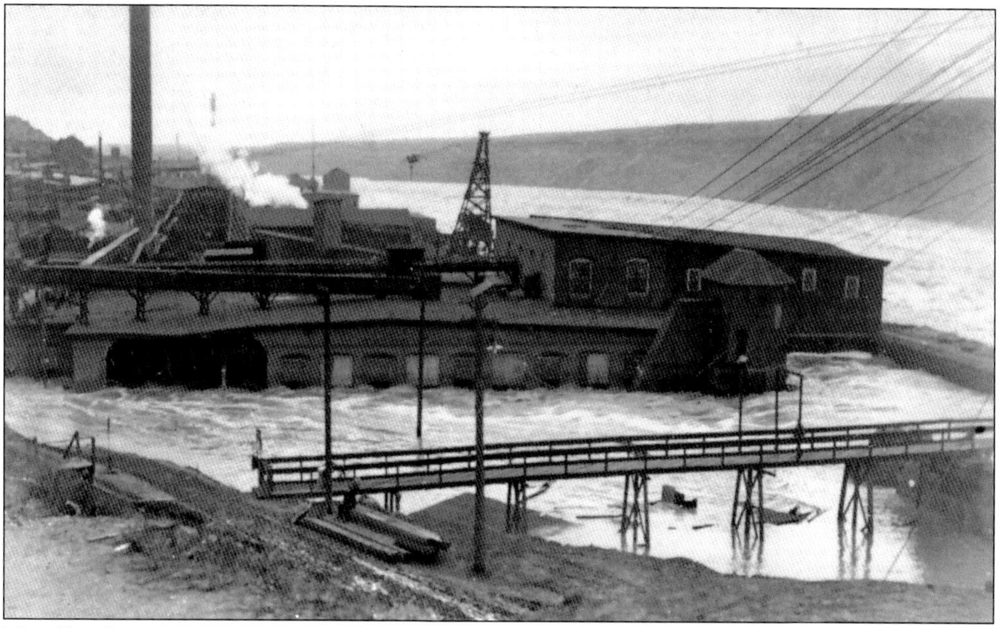

The flooding Missouri River is shown inundating low-lying smelter facilities in June 1908. The south wall (seen projecting off the right side of the building next to the river) had been breached by the swollen floodwaters and was now funneling water into the building. It would take hundreds of thousands of dollars and man-hours to restore the damage done during this event. (2007.17.286)

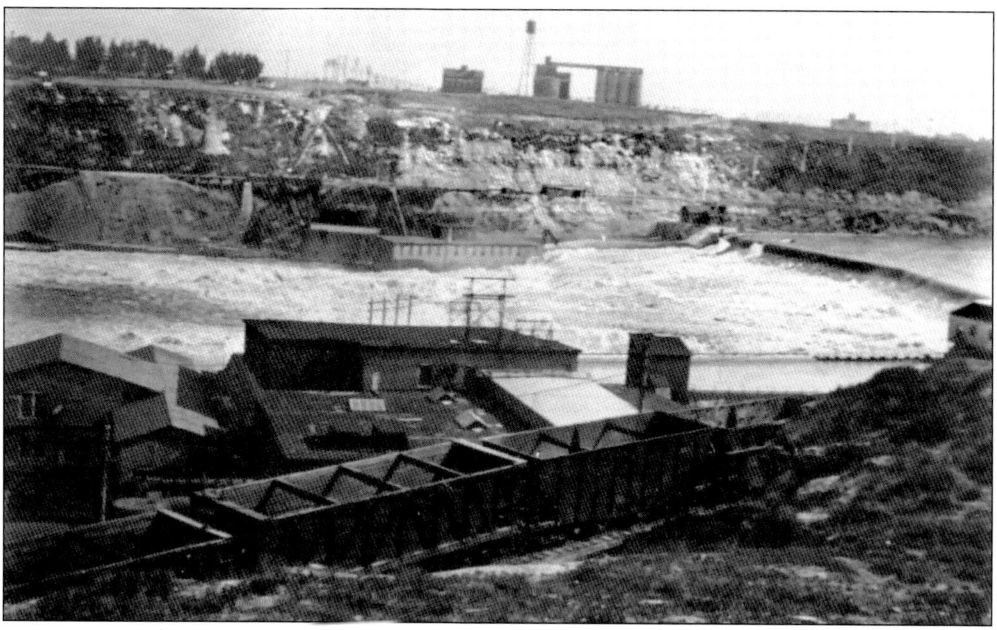

This image looks toward the south bank of the Missouri River from the spot where the smelter now stands. Black Eagle Dam is to the right. Fortunately, after the devastation caused by the floodwaters of 1908, the new powerhouse at the Rainbow site was ready to go online in 1910. Across the river, the Royal Mill stands on the right side of the horizon. On the left are the trees of Black Eagle Park. (94.45.7A)

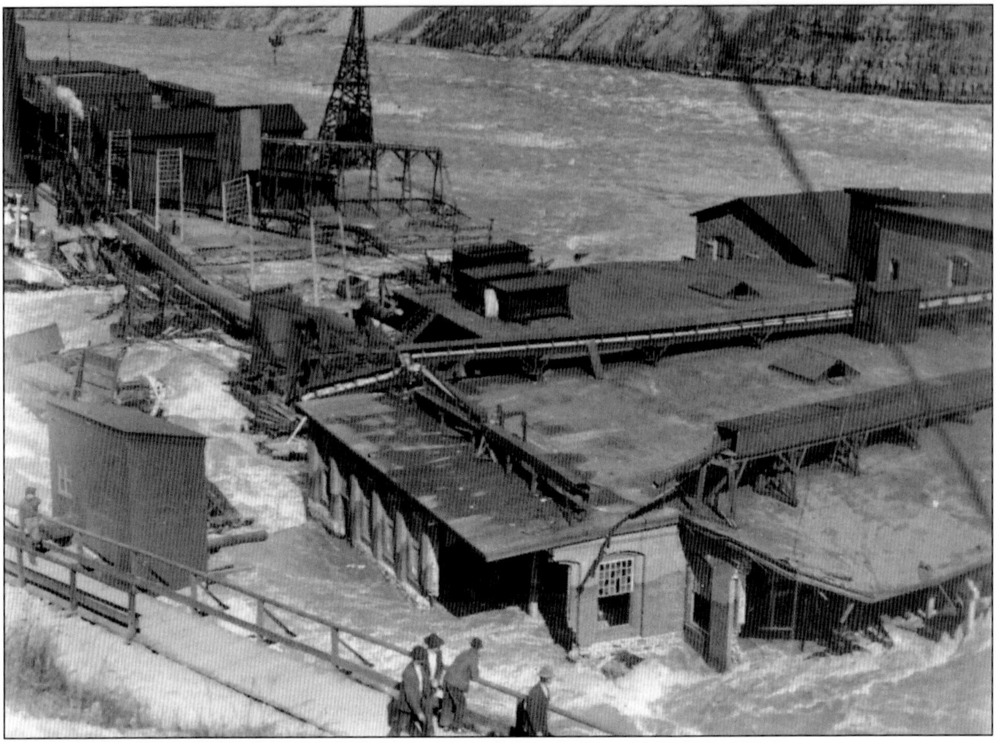

The flood of 1908 devastated the lower-lying smelter buildings along the Missouri. At one point, in an effort to divert floodwaters away from the powerhouse, a plan was made to detonate a dynamite charge in a retaining wall above the powerhouse to provide another avenue for the raging waters to return to the river and prevent further damage to the powerhouse. (2007.17.294)

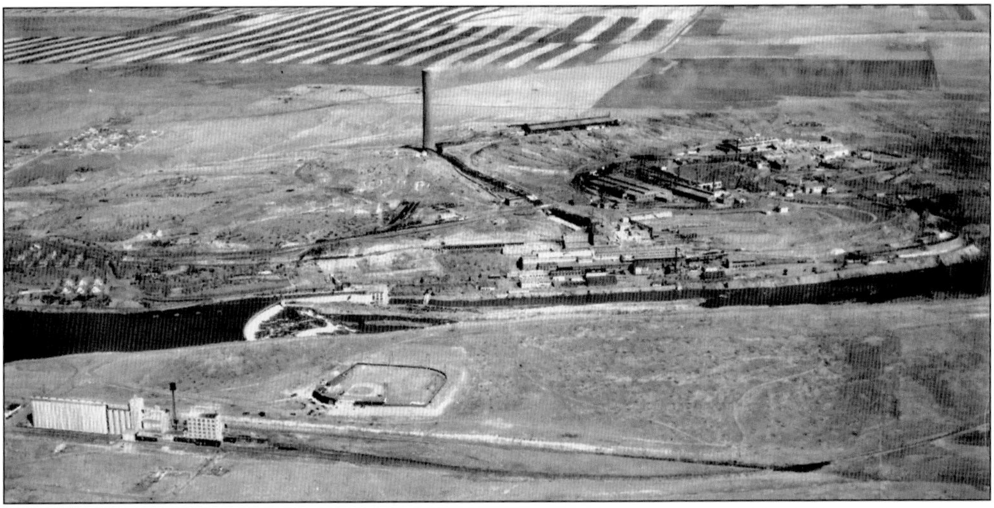

This c. 1940 photograph of the Anaconda Company Smelter works and Black Eagle Dam shows that Black Eagle Park, on the south side of the river just to the right of the baseball field, has deteriorated into oblivion. The new ballpark diamond is visible just to the north and east of the General Mills grain elevators and flour mill. It took 250 pounds of ore to produce the 12 ounces of zinc and 1.75 pounds of copper to make the 2.5 pounds of brass necessary to make one trumpet. (2007.17.317)

Work is well underway on the giant Anaconda Company smokestack in this photograph taken on May 18, 1908. The stack is at the 65-foot level in this photograph and would climb another 441 feet before completion. Bricks for the stack, made of local shale, were produced at a brick plant west of the smelter works. (2007.17.275)

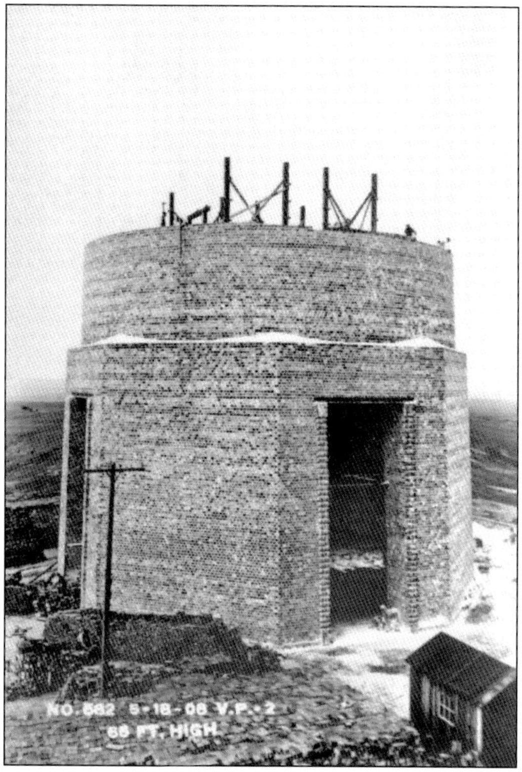

In the image below, the new Anaconda smokestack races skyward in the early summer of 1908. To its right is the diminutive smaller smokestack built in 1891. Upon completion of the "big stack" in 1908, the two stood together for a few years, but the fate of the smaller stack was sealed when the new stack became operational. The smaller stack was demolished in 1915. (2007.17.274)

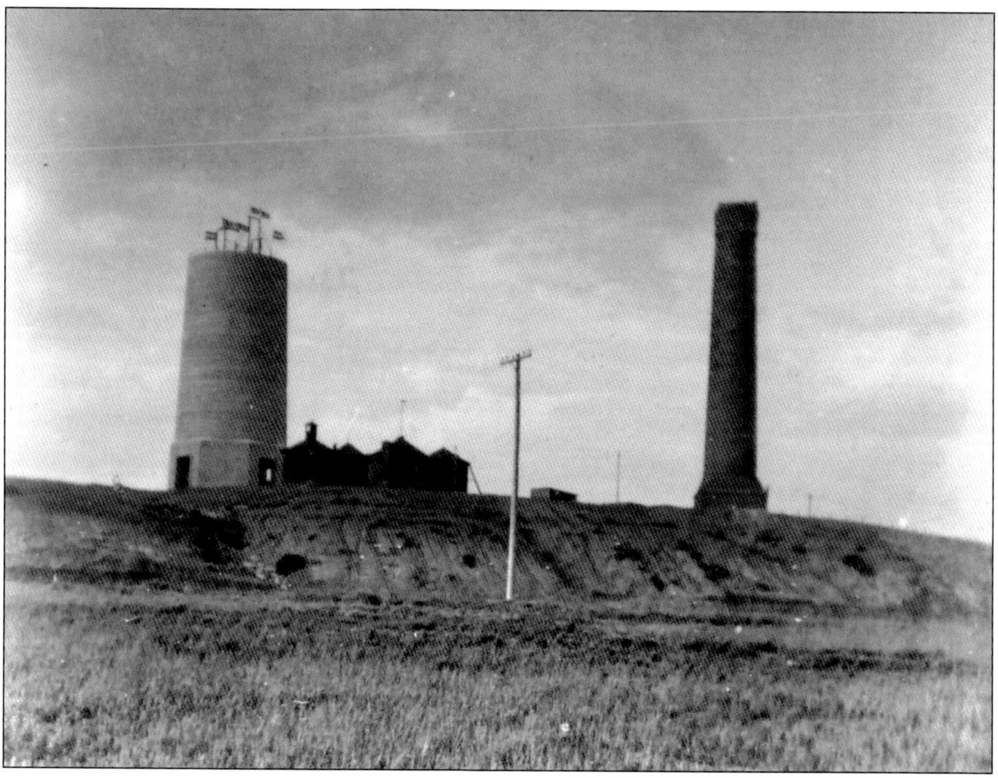

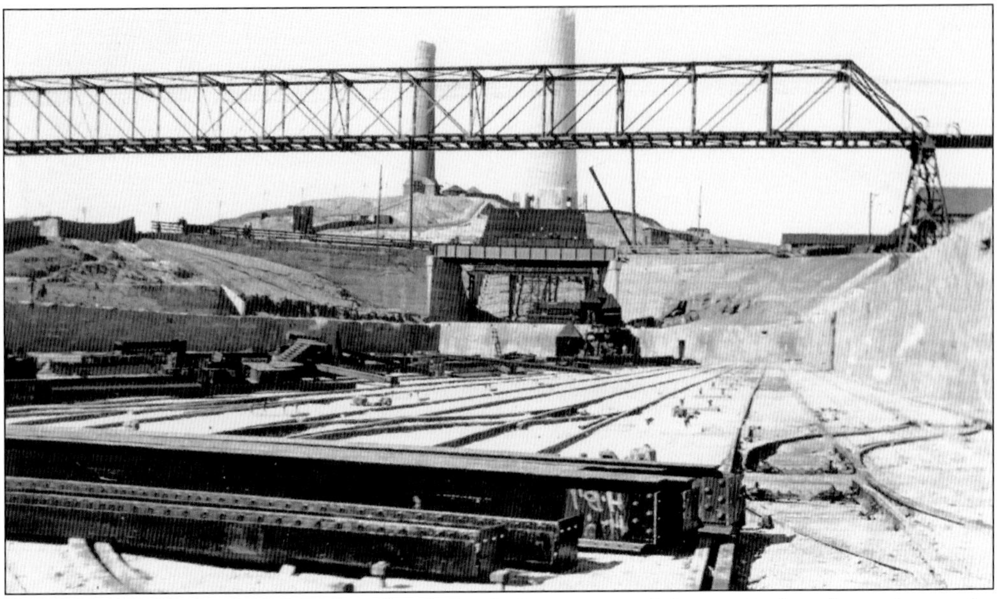

Construction of the dust chamber that helped clean some of the particulate from the smoke feeding the enormous Anaconda smokestack was well underway in this 1908 photograph. The 478-foot-long and 176-foot-wide dust chamber was filled with thin wires at 2.5-inch intervals. As the smoke passed through, the particles of ash collected on the wires and fell into hoppers on the floor, where they could be removed. (2007.17.272B)

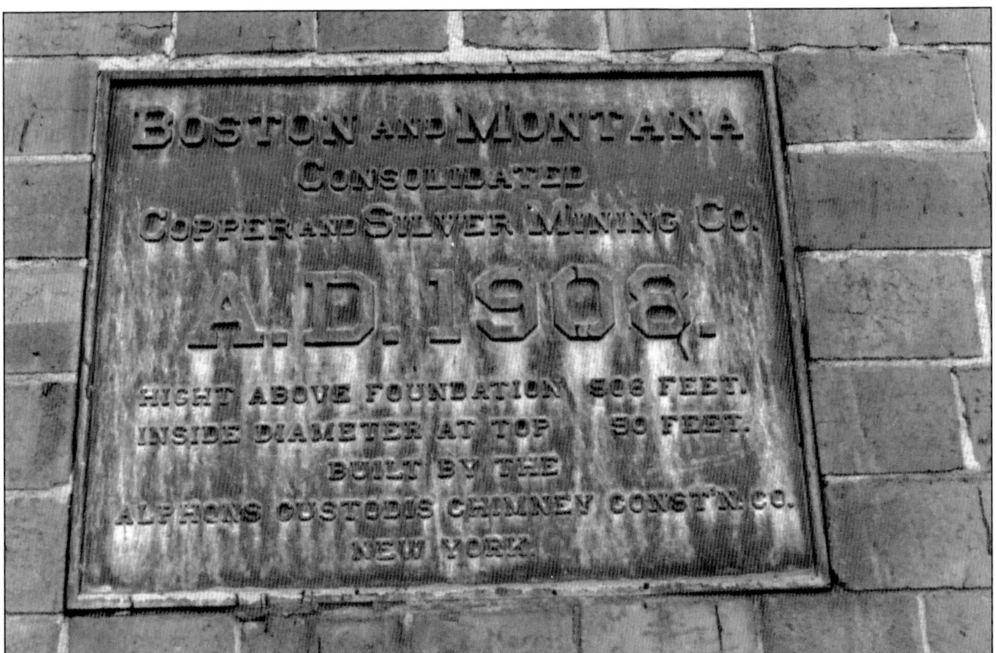

This nameplate was affixed to the newly completed stack. The first brick was laid on April 7, 1908, and the final brick was put into place on October 23, 1908. The entire stack, comprised of 5.7 million individual bricks, took only six and a half months to build. (2000.2.6)

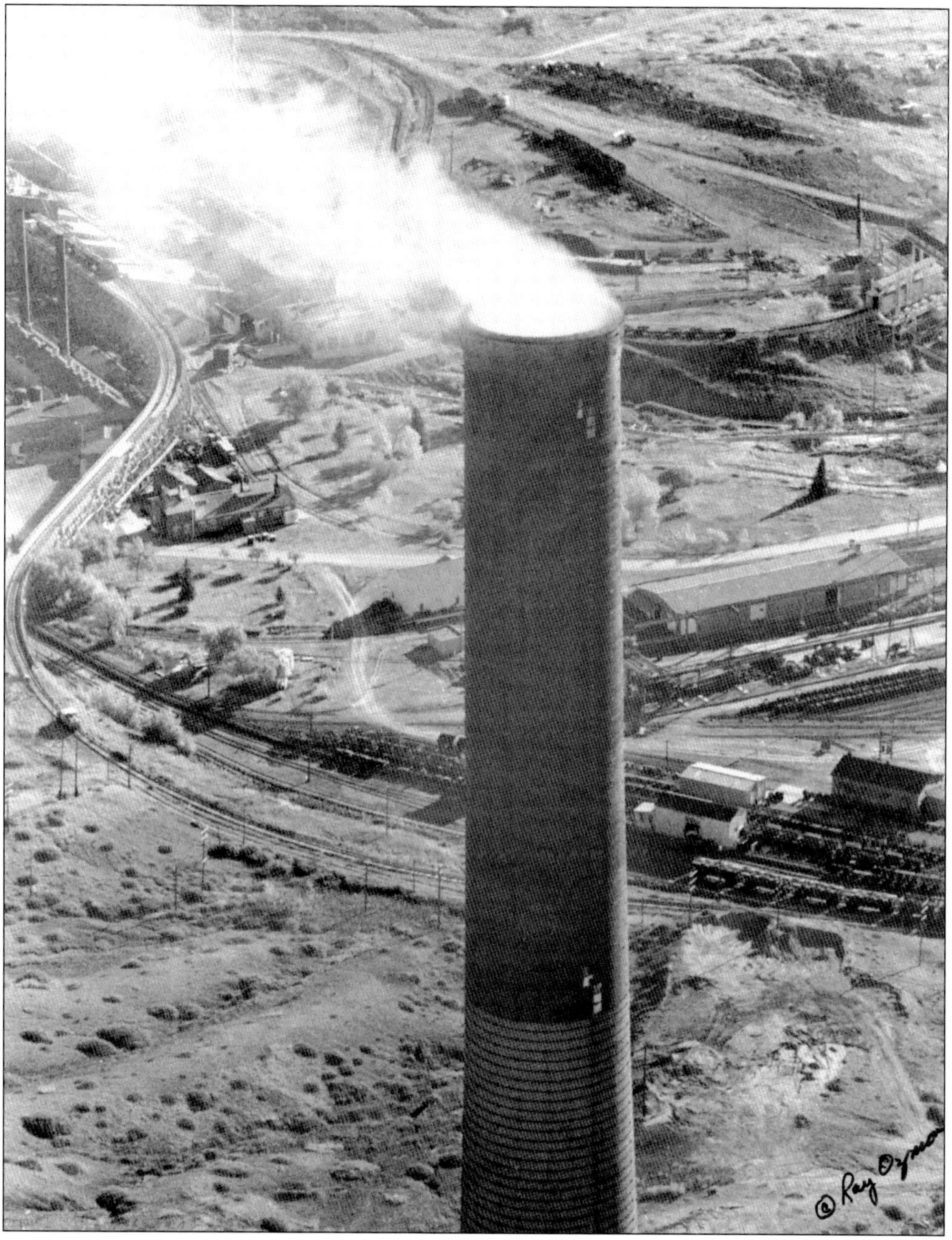

Here is a bird's-eye view looking down the barrel of a 506-foot smoking gun. The top of the stack was 50 feet wide at the opening, and the stack had 18-inch-thick walls. The outside diameter at the base of the stack was 78.5 feet, with a wall thickness of 6 feet. (Ray Ozman photograph.)

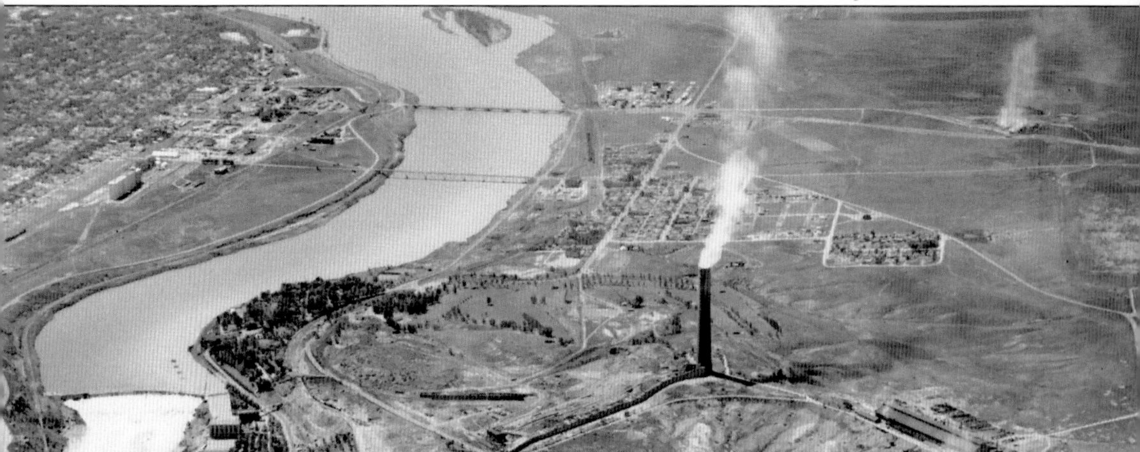

This *c*. 1950 aerial view shows Black Eagle Dam, the Anaconda Smelter and smokestack, the town of Black Eagle, and part of the north side of Great Falls. Smoke pours forth from the 506-foot-tall stack. A second source of smoke, to the right and beyond the stack, is the location of the city dump, where there seemed to be a perennial fire burning. (94.41.75)

Four

Hydroelectric Power

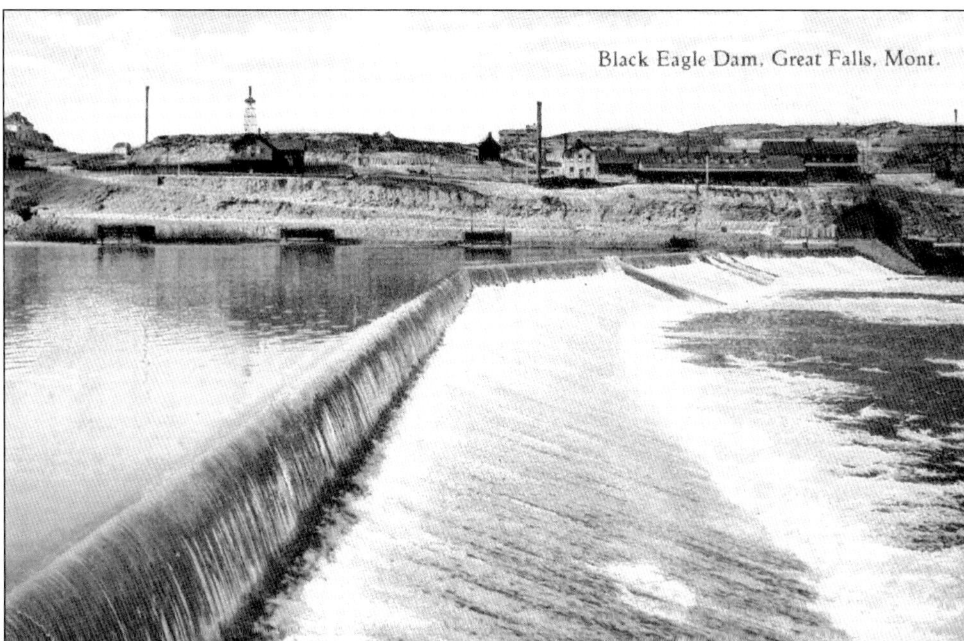

The first hydroelectric dam on the Missouri River was constructed at Black Eagle Falls near the town of Great Falls. The primitive rock-and-timber structure served the purpose of raising a pond behind it that could be used to provide the necessary water pressure to produce electricity. In 1916, this powerhouse put out only 3 megawatts of electricity. After rebuilding and modifications, it eventually put out 18 megawatts. (2010.1.17)

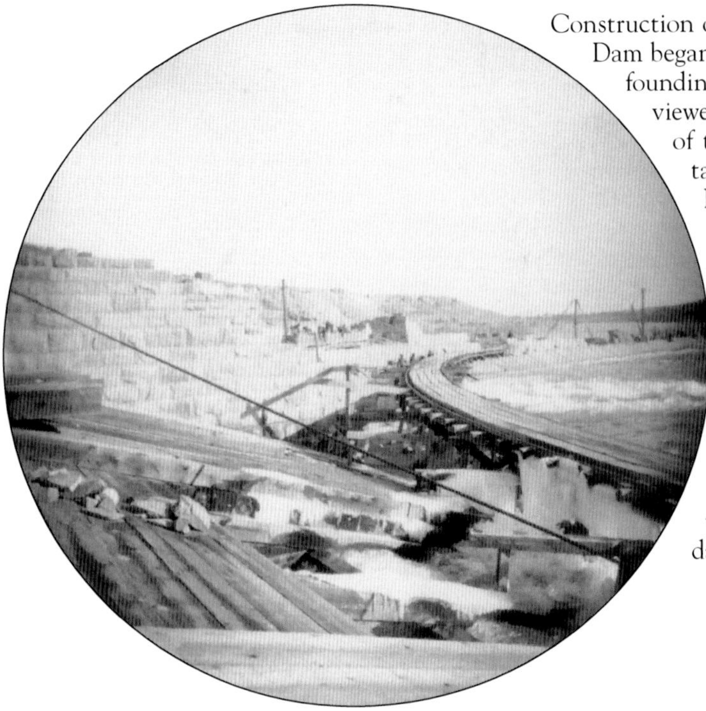

Construction of the original Black Eagle Dam began in 1890. When the town's founding father, Paris Gibson, first viewed the falls, he was reminded of the development that had taken place on St. Anthony Falls on the Mississippi River in his hometown of St. Paul, Minnesota. Gibson recognized the potential for hydroelectric development. By December 8, 1909, engineers envisioned the proposed placement of dams, and an engineer's profile of the river showed the most probable sites for dam placement. (94.38.43)

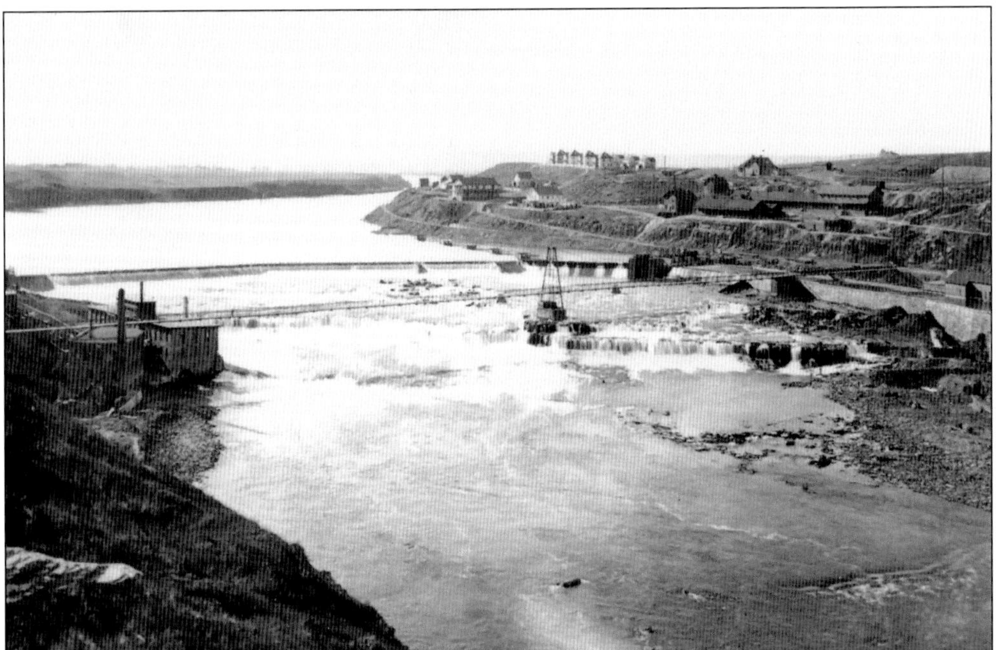

Black Eagle Dam was the first hydroelectric dam of its scale on the free-flowing Missouri River. The fact that hydroelectric power was generated in Great Falls and that more hydroelectric dams were in the planning stage gave rise to the town's nickname, "Electric City." This term showed up as early as 1900 and was certainly synonymous with what Great Falls was about to represent: wholesale electrical generation on a scale heretofore unknown in the world. (2007.17.9)

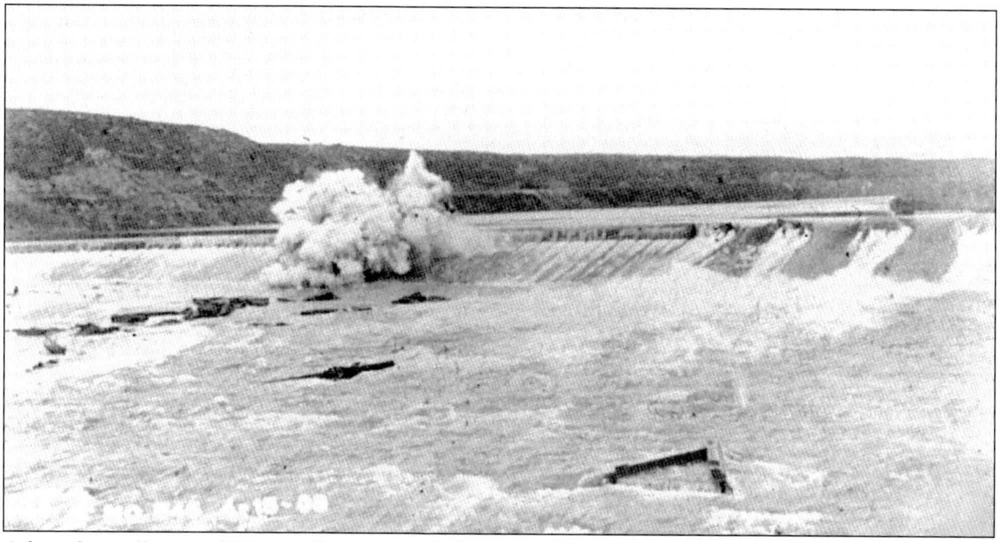

After the collapse of Hauser Dam near Helena on the Missouri River, a wall of water headed downstream toward Great Falls. Dynamite was set off on the face of the original Black Eagle Dam on April 15, 1908, in hopes that by blowing away a large portion of the dam, the floodwaters could pass through more easily. Two men drowned in the attempt to dynamite the dam; one was trying to remove flashboards from the dam's face, and another worker went under after his boat capsized. (96.98.11)

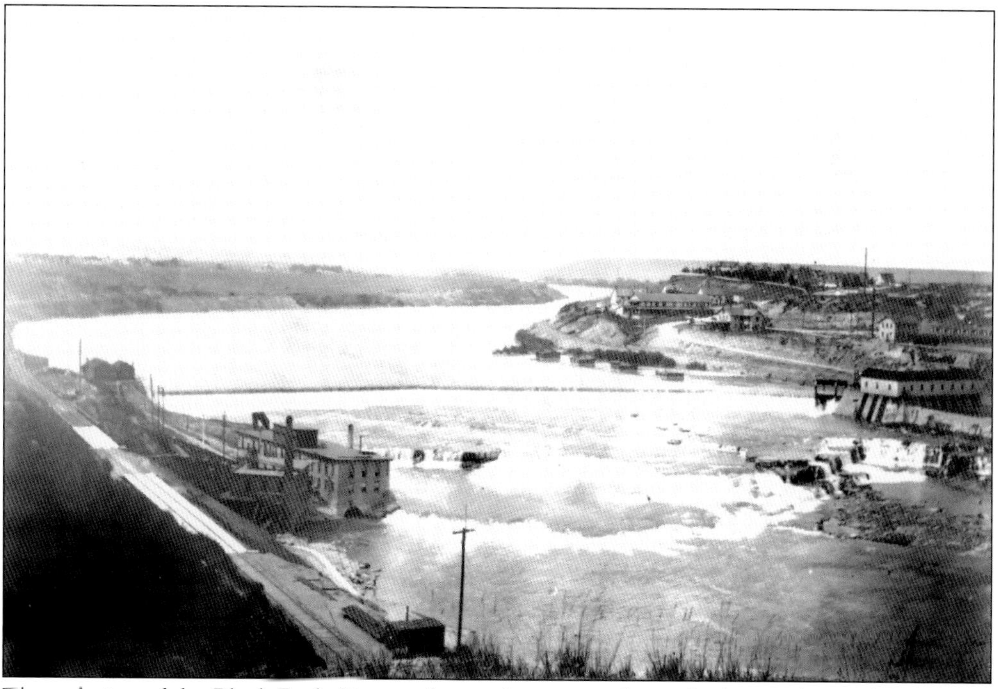

The redesign of the Black Eagle Dam and powerhouse was driven by lessons learned during the catastrophic 1908 flood. Early stages of development can be detected taking place across the river on the right. As time passed, power generation would take place on the north bank, and the powerhouse structure on the left would become history. A completely new dam would be built in 1926, thereby burying the existing dam structure in its pool. (2007.17.290B)

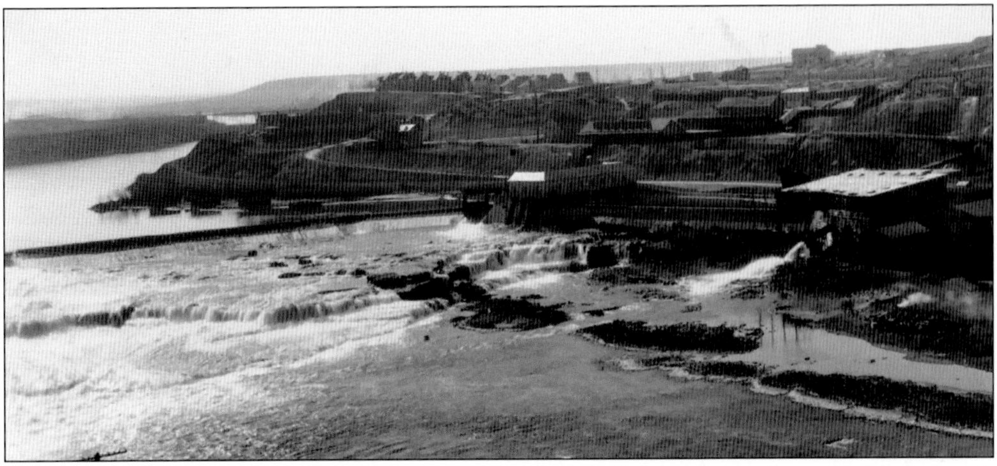

The Black Eagle Falls and Dam are shown here around 1926. Construction of a new dam a few yards downstream from the original 1890 structure resulted in greater control over reservoir levels. The new powerhouse was moved across the river to the north side and a more controlled environment, resting within the fenced boundary of the Anaconda Company properties. (2006.84.23)

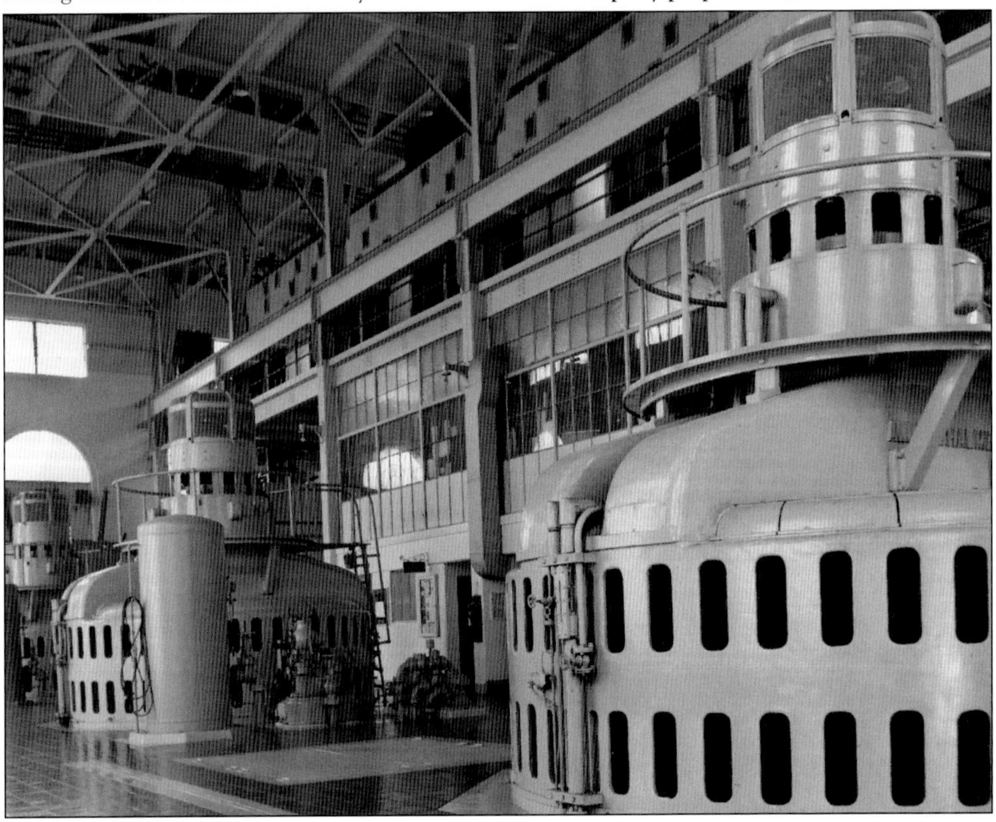

The Black Eagle Dam today has three Allis-Chalmers three-bladed propeller-driven generators capable of turning out six megawatts each—18 megawatts in all. This gives this dam the smallest electrical generating capacity of any of the five Great Falls plants. The dam could not have been built any higher without adversely affecting the city, due to other infrastructure (such as sewer outlets) within the proximity of the pool behind the dam. (2003.33.26)

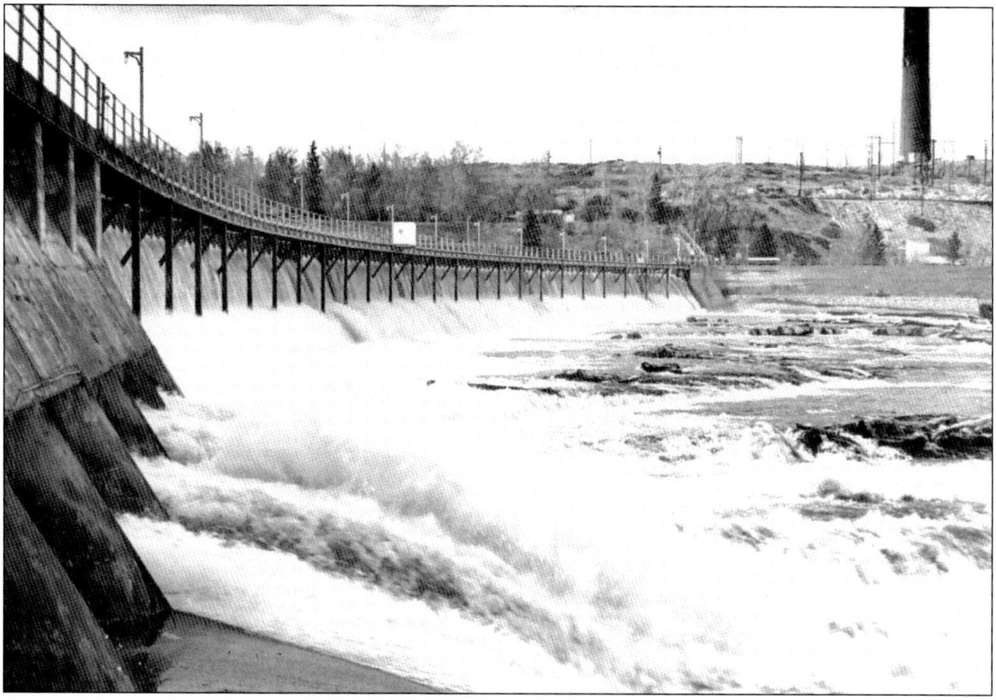

In 1926, the Black Eagle Dam was completely rebuilt downstream from the old 1890 superstructure. This modern replacement boasted eight floodgates and a fenced walkway complete with rails for heavy maintenance work. This dam is essentially the same today as it was 85 years ago. (2003.33.14)

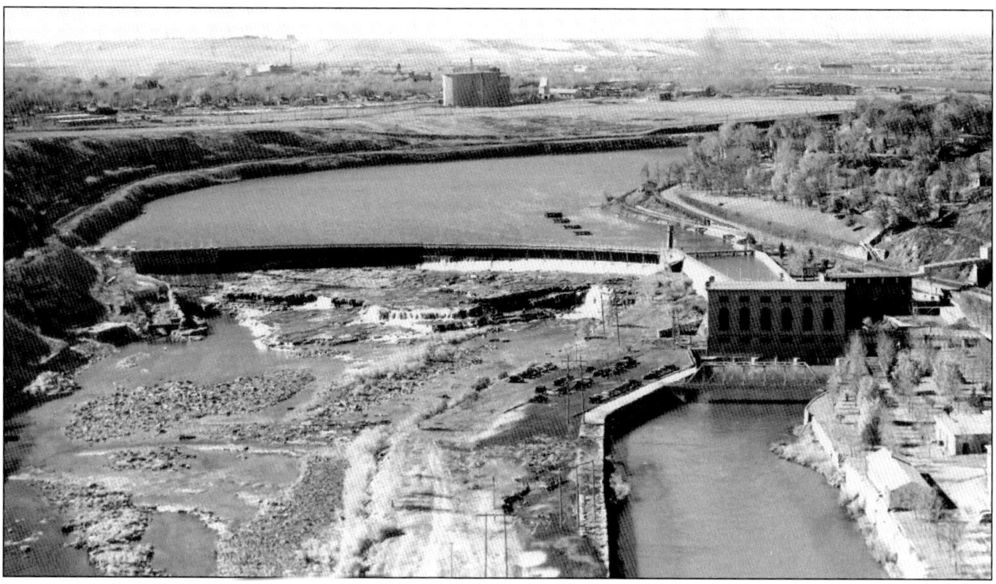

This picture of Black Eagle Dam was taken during minimal stream flow that resulted in a very noiseless waterfall. Dams on the Missouri River near Great Falls were reluctant to send water over the top. When necessary, most of the river was routed through their powerhouses and turbines during low water, resulting in dry falls. Electrical generation for public use, however, took precedence over aesthetics. (94.38.209)

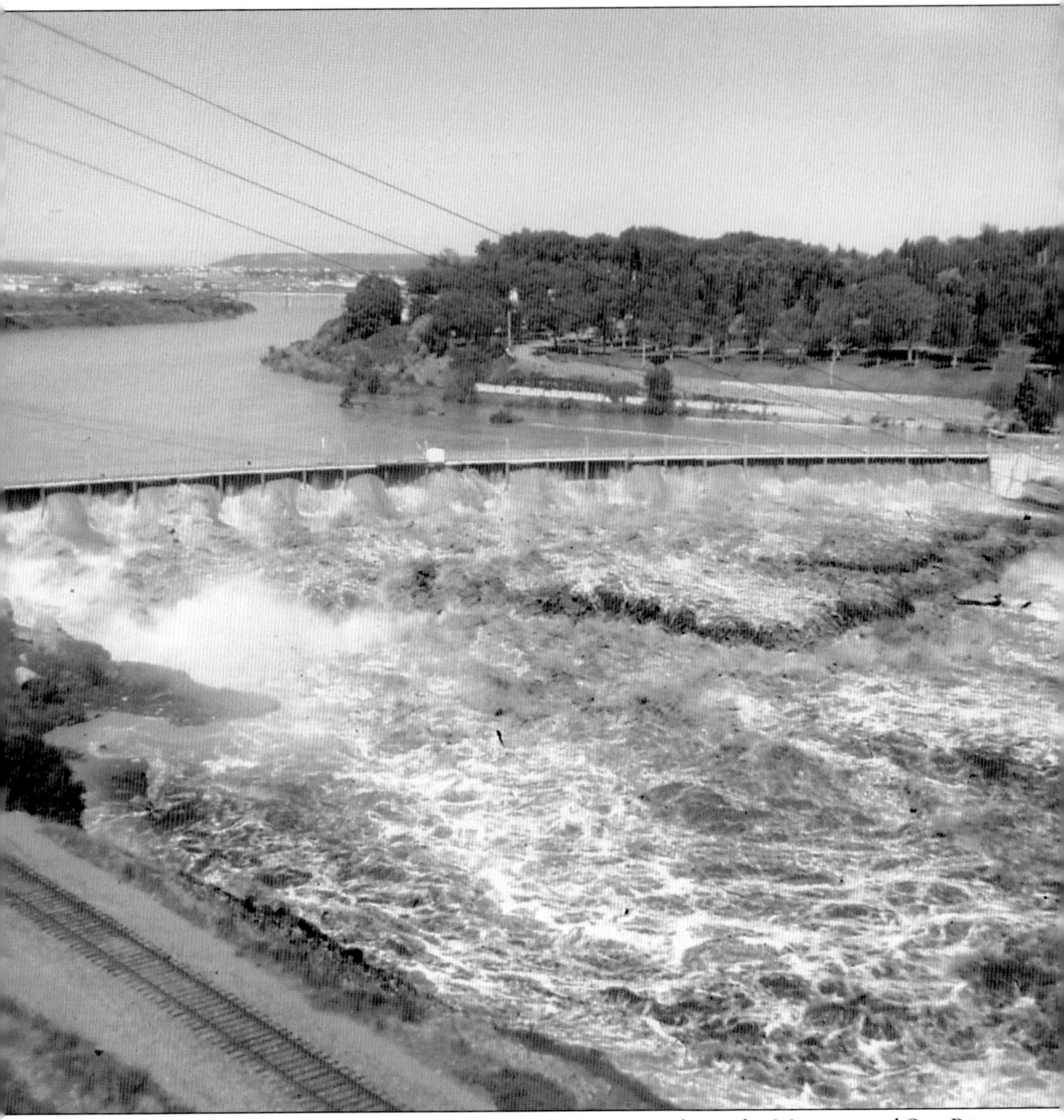

During the flood of 1975, an enormous head of water came down the Missouri and Sun Rivers, which joined at Great Falls. Here the floodwaters almost overwhelm Black Eagle Dam at Black Eagle Falls. Being the smallest of the five dams at Great Falls has not seemed to affect Black Eagle's resilience. Over the years, the dam has withstood pounding after pounding from raging floods, enormous spring runoffs, and the tremendous hydraulic energy forces associated with these events. (2010.1.18)

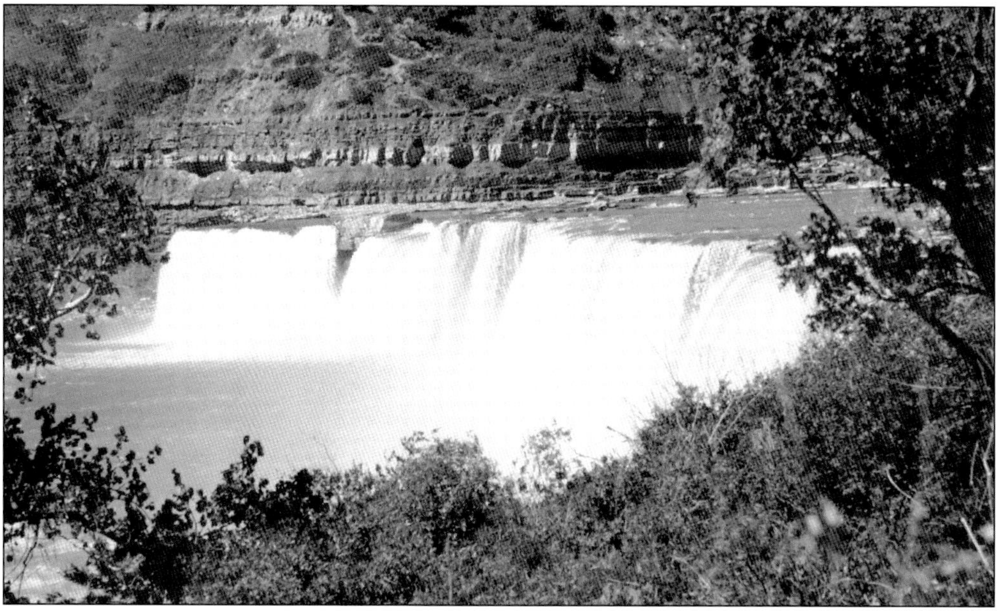

Rainbow Falls is seen here from the north shore. Meriwether Lewis was trapped on the north side of the river upon his arrival here. Discovering this falls on June 14, 1805, he compared it to what he had witnessed the day before while viewing the Great Falls and called this falls "pleasingly beautiful," while the Great Falls was "sublimely grand." (2003.33.21)

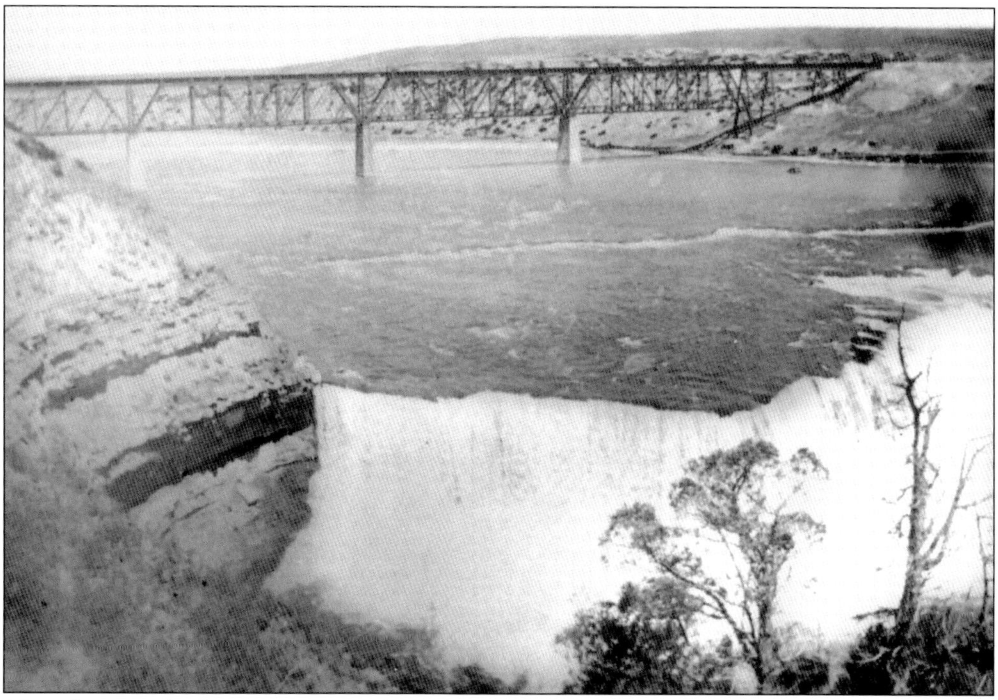

This photograph shows a portion of Rainbow Falls with the Great Northern Railroad trestle (built 1902) in the background. Just beyond the trestle is 6-foot Colter Falls. This falls would soon be covered by the pool that would form behind Rainbow Dam after its completion in 1910. (2007.17.17)

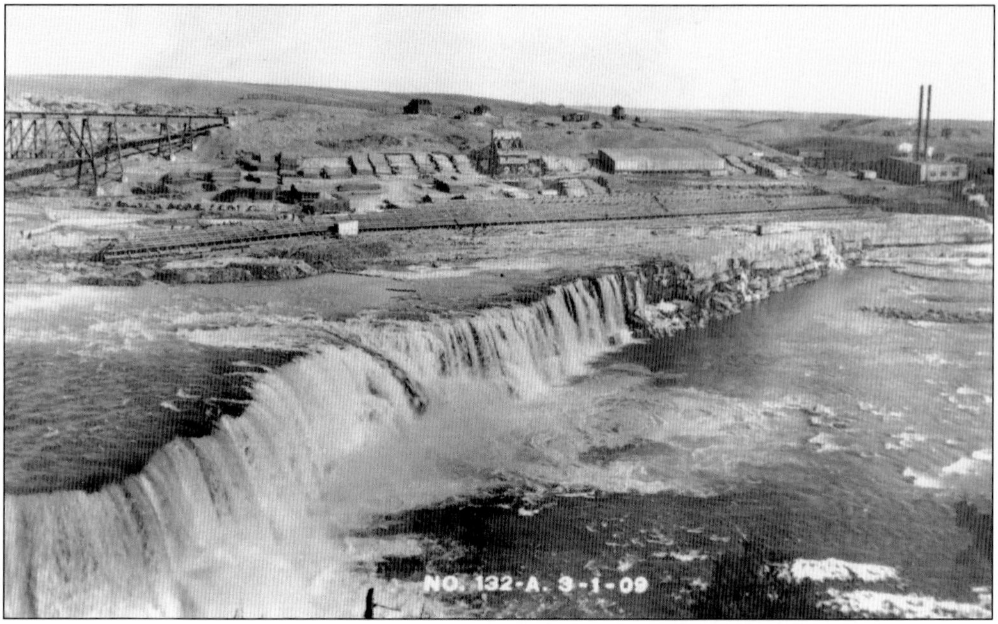

In 1909, a series of coffer dams were created at Rainbow Falls to push the Missouri River from one side of its bed to the other in order to keep the current away from the construction area. Here workers are laying the main forms and preparing for the main body of the dam. (2007.17.19)

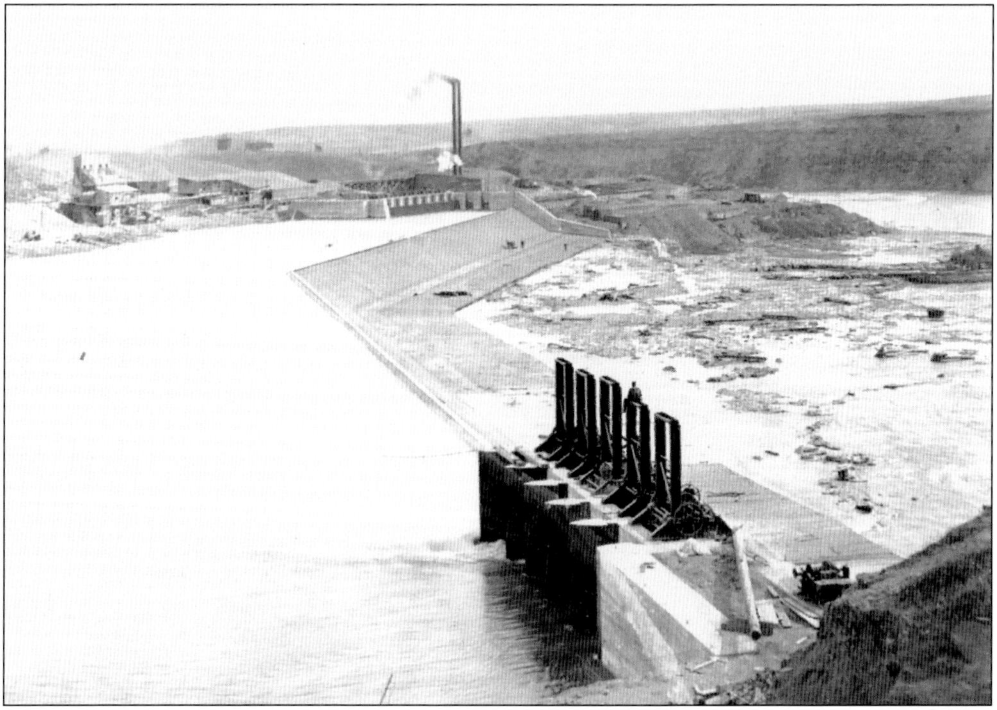

Rainbow Dam was constructed in 1909 and 1910. The waste gates are at bottom right. Each gate is 8 feet wide and 10 feet high, and all are set in heavy concrete masonry. They can discharge 9,000 cubic feet of water per second under full pool conditions. Each of the five gates is manually operated with a heavy hand-operated mechanism. (2007.17.23)

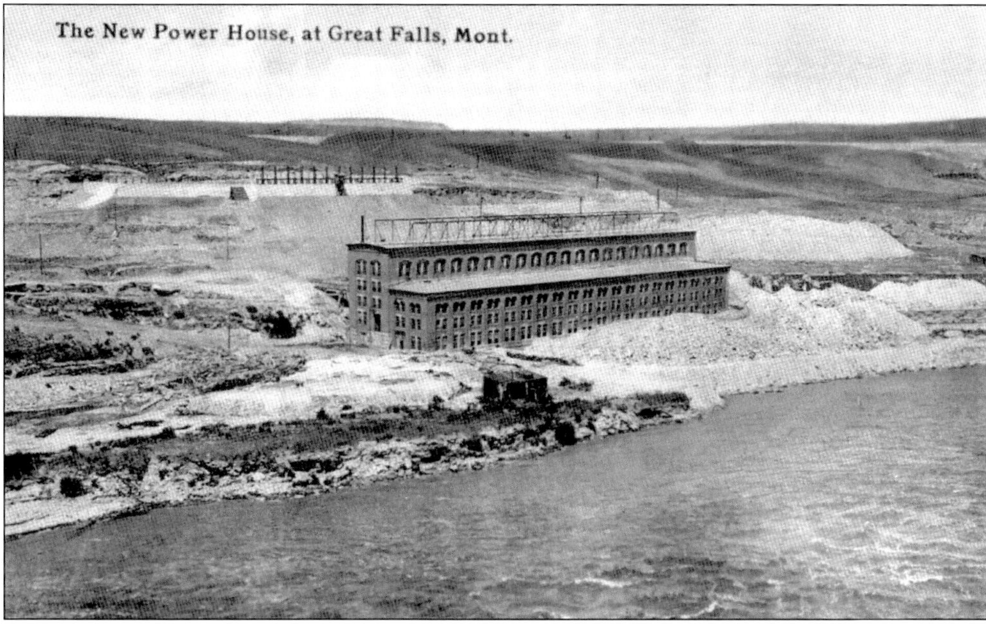

The powerhouse for Rainbow Dam is shown here under construction. Two steel penstock tubes, each 15 feet, 6 inches in diameter, run 2,499 feet from the dam to the reservoir behind the powerhouse. The powerhouse is 326 feet long and 80 feet wide. The generating room, closest to the river, is a single story high. The switch and high-tension rooms closest to the regulating reservoir are two stories high. The water is carried this far downstream to make more efficient use of the gravitational effect on the increased drop in elevation that is afforded by piping the water around Crooked Falls. (PC85.8.1056)

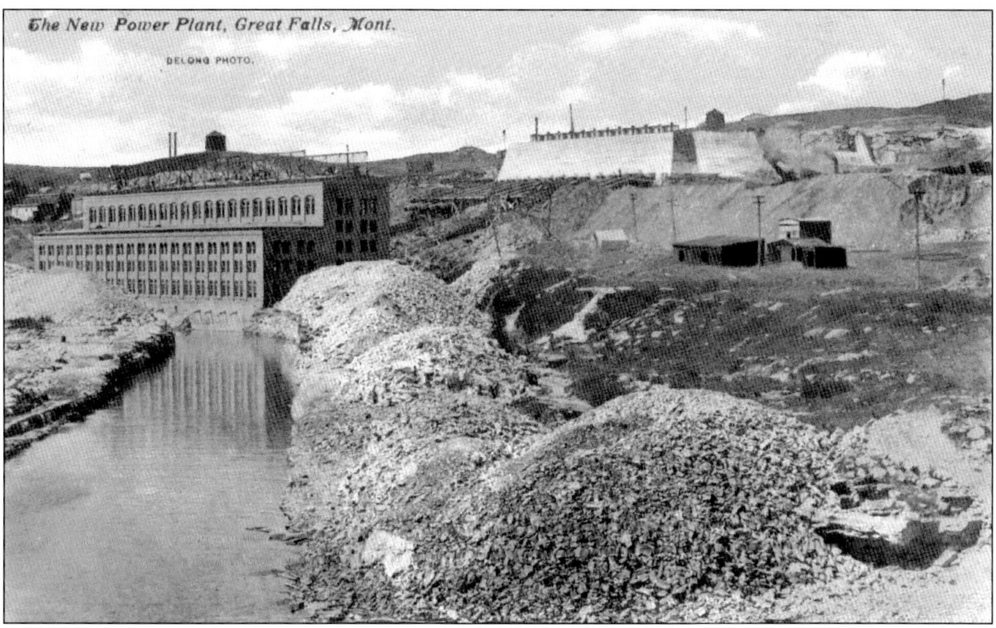

Rainbow Dam powerhouse had a channel excavated to accommodate the outflow of water from its massive generators. Five years later, a channel was also excavated at the Great Falls. (PC26.20B)

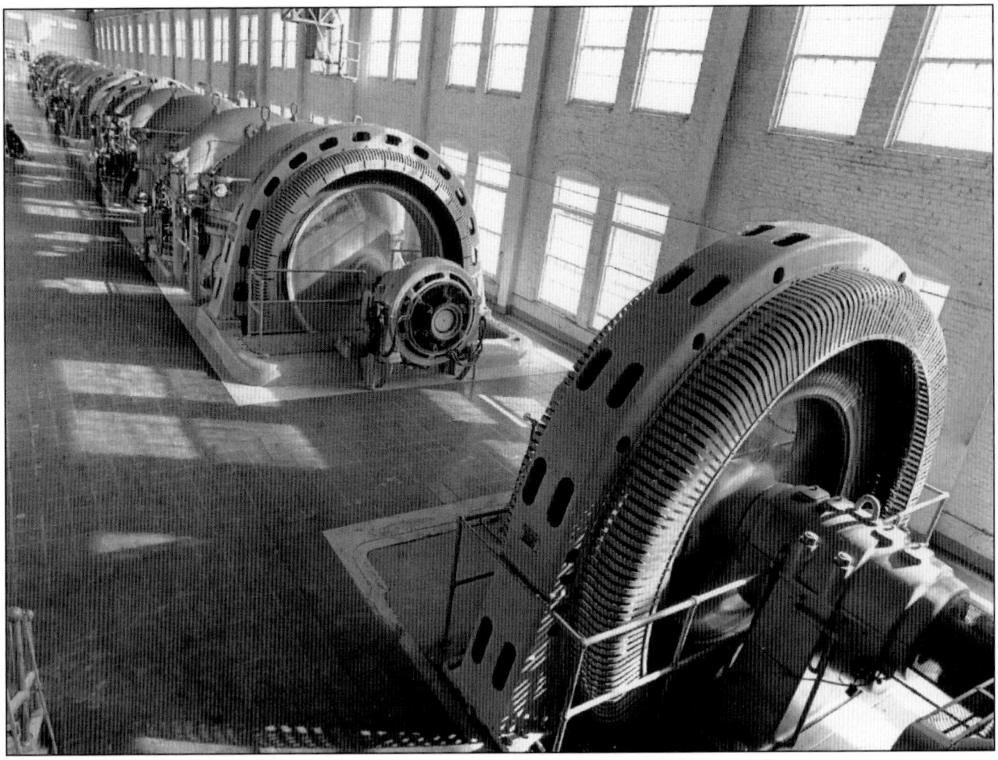

Here is the massive battery of turbines at the Rainbow Dam powerhouse. These turbines received their water from the dam almost half a mile upstream. Adding the various elevations of the dam, the drop at Rainbow Falls, the drop at Crooked Falls, and the drop between Crooked and Rainbow Falls, the water pressure was equivalent to a combined drop of 108 feet. Originally six General Electric generators were installed. Later, two Westinghouse generators were added. The total energy produced at Rainbow Dam and its powerhouse is 35 megawatts. (2003.33.23)

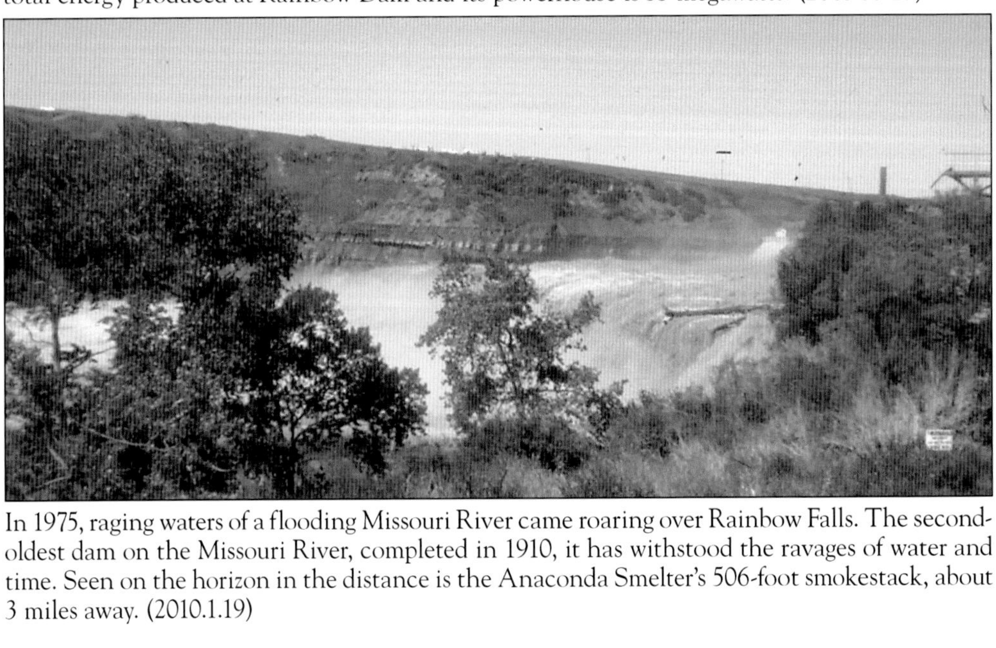

In 1975, raging waters of a flooding Missouri River came roaring over Rainbow Falls. The second-oldest dam on the Missouri River, completed in 1910, it has withstood the ravages of water and time. Seen on the horizon in the distance is the Anaconda Smelter's 506-foot smokestack, about 3 miles away. (2010.1.19)

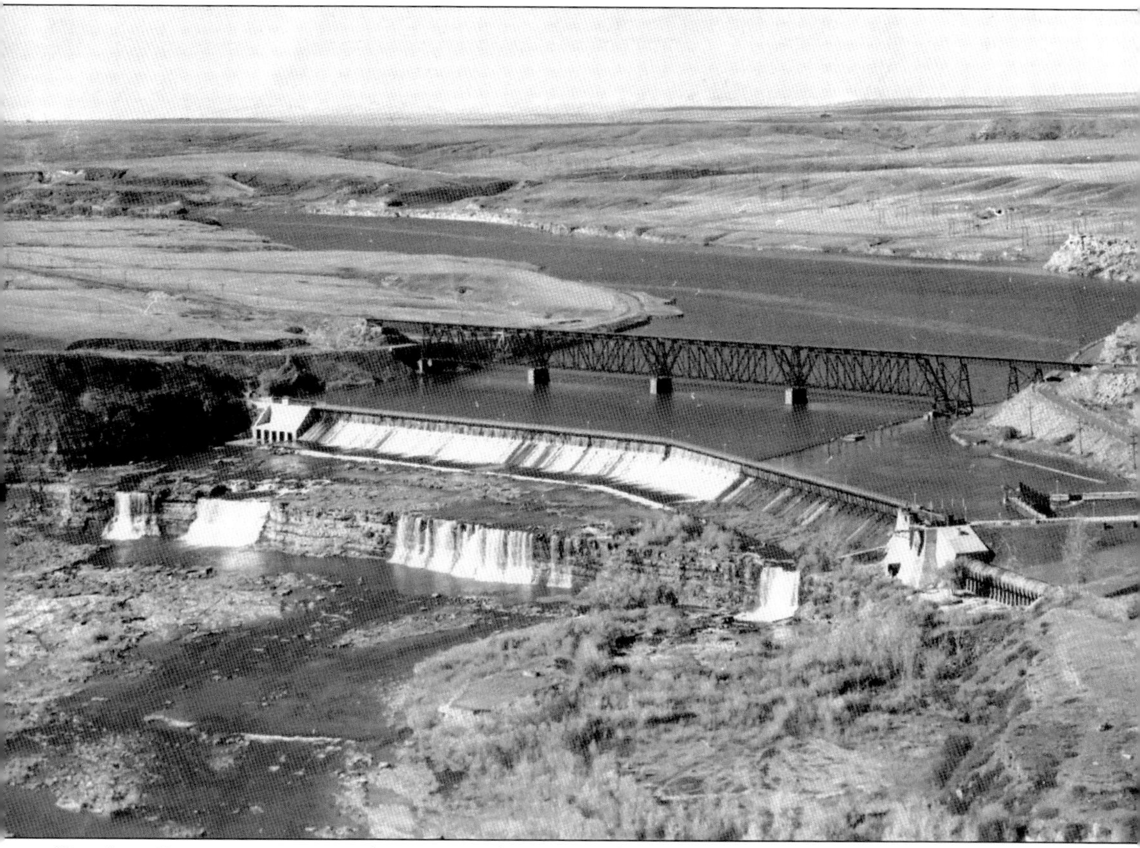

Rainbow Dam was constructed in 1909 and 1910. It is the longest of the five dams at 1,146 feet, is 67 feet wide at its base, and has a 49-foot-wide apron on the downstream side to direct the flow of water as well as to protect the riverbed. The crest of the dam sits 26 feet above the streambed. It is unusual in that the powerhouse is located about half a mile downstream, and the water is carried there via steel tubes. The reason for this unique design was to take advantage of the 19-foot drop at Crooked Falls and the additional drop in the riverbed. This additional drop provided more energy at the generators, as water pressure is always improved by an increase in elevation from the source—in this case, the level of the pool behind Rainbow Dam. (2007.17.882)

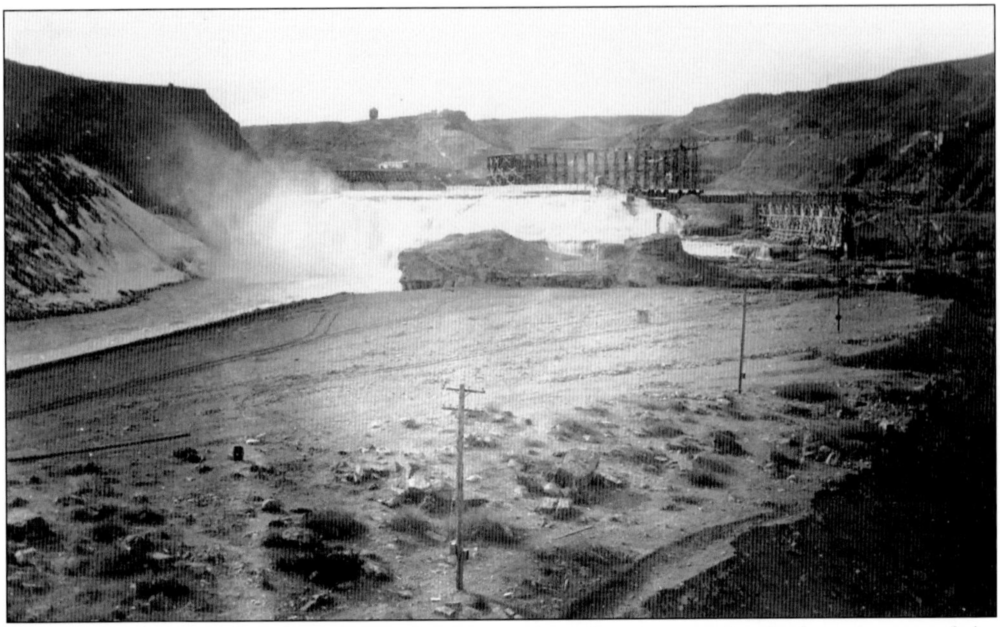

Even as the dam was being constructed, plans were underway to make the best use out of the island created by the channel leading from the generator powerhouse. Leveling was done, but before that could be accomplished, tons of large boulders had to be dealt with. Once the channel was constructed, access to the island would be a problem. A causeway between the powerhouse and island was constructed for heavy vehicle traffic. Pedestrian access for the public would come later. (94.38.39)

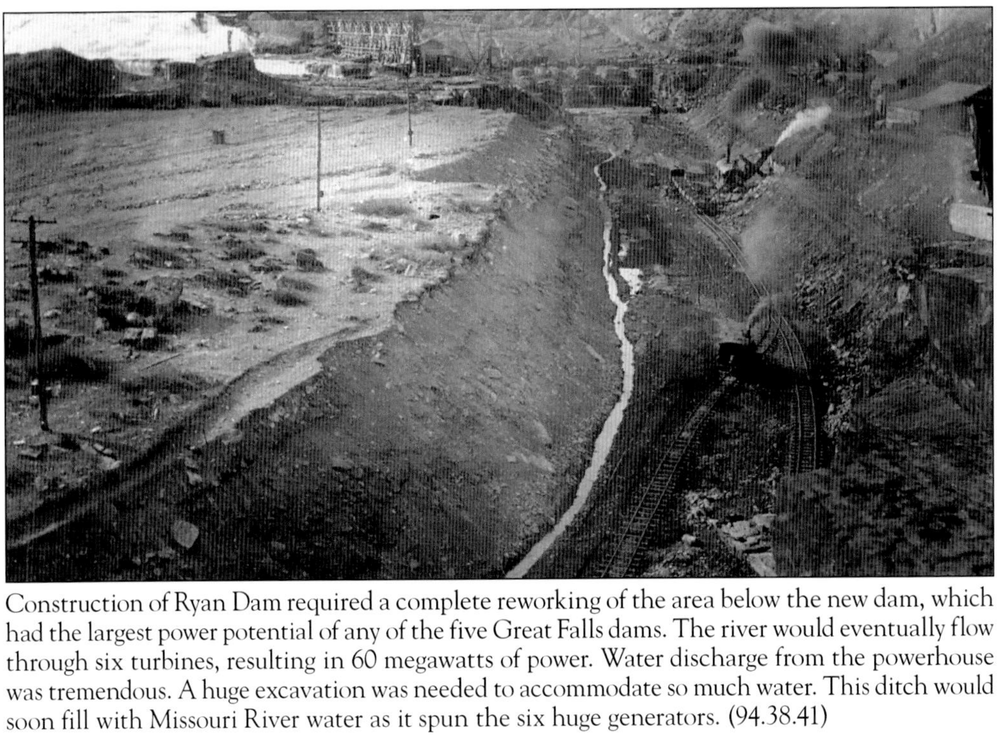

Construction of Ryan Dam required a complete reworking of the area below the new dam, which had the largest power potential of any of the five Great Falls dams. The river would eventually flow through six turbines, resulting in 60 megawatts of power. Water discharge from the powerhouse was tremendous. A huge excavation was needed to accommodate so much water. This ditch would soon fill with Missouri River water as it spun the six huge generators. (94.38.41)

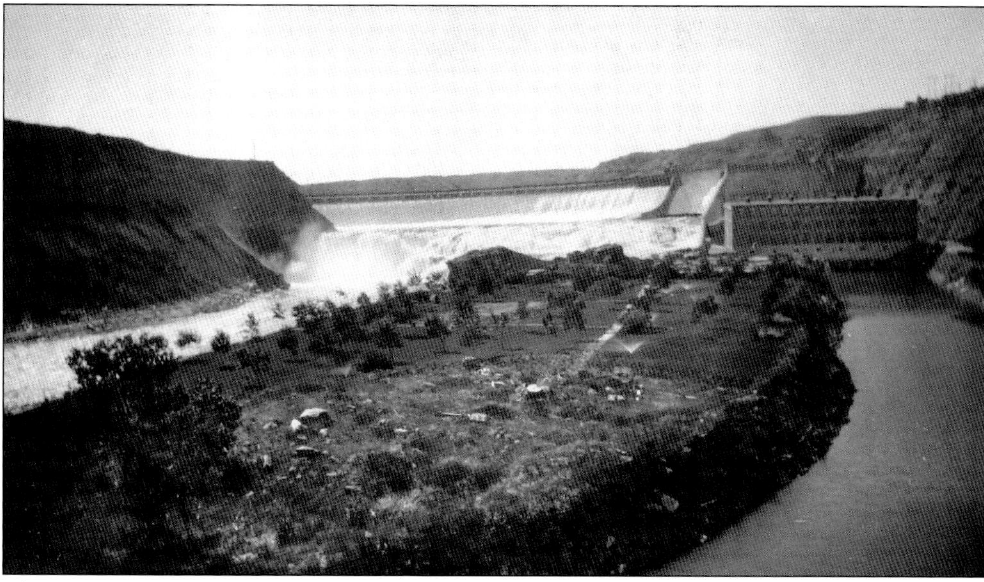

This image captures the Great Falls of the Missouri, Ryan Dam, and Ryan Island. At the time of this photograph, the island was still in its infancy, and the landscaping and other improvements were underway. The Montana Power Company put considerable time and money into creating a comfortable space for the public to enjoy the scenic Missouri. Sprinklers are in place, and water is pouring out onto the new lawn. Trees were planted to lend an air of beauty to the site. (2000.46.53)

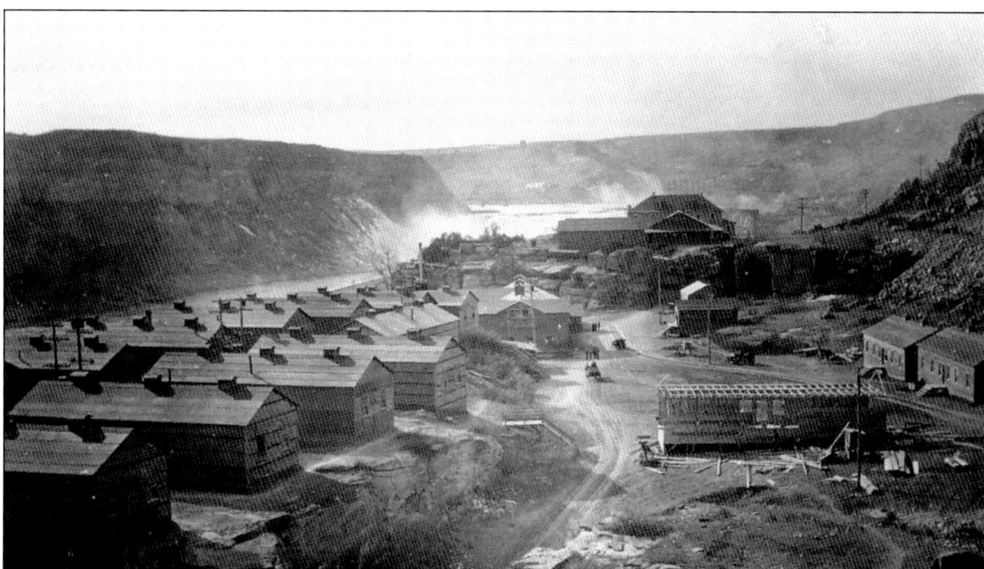

Ryan Dam was built with a workforce of 650 men. Ground was cleared and leveled. Barracks were constructed. Initial phases of construction started in 1913 and continued until the dam's completion in 1915. In this 1915 photograph, notice the large number of barracks constructed to provide temporary quarters for the workers. (94.38.40)

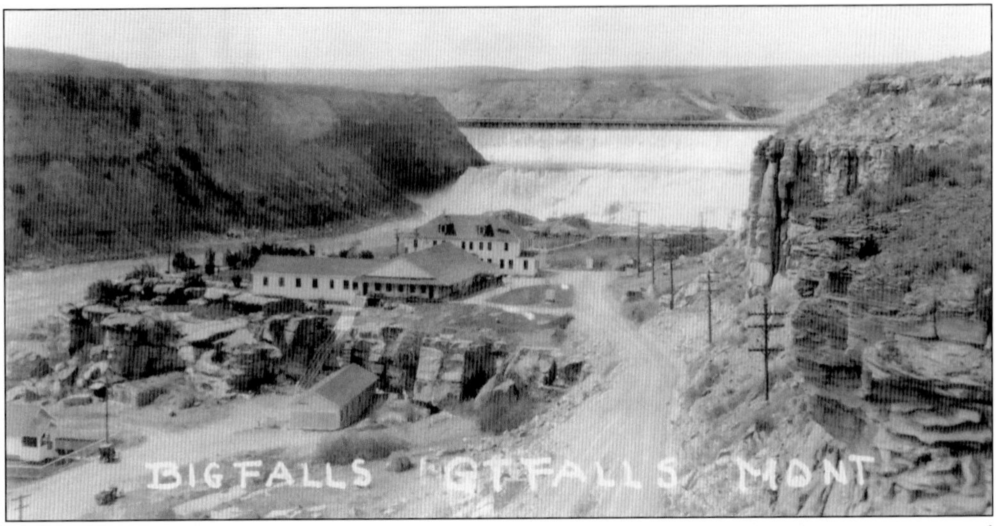

During the construction of Ryan Dam, some of the low-lying areas below the dam were converted from primitive river bottom to a more improved grade where temporary buildings could rest. These buildings served various purposes, such as worker housing, shops, and outbuildings; there was even a large kitchen and dining hall built to serve the workers. A large administrative building housed power company officials and others needing temporary accommodations. In March 1913, actual construction got underway. The concrete plant was located 1,500 feet above the dam, and 3-foot-gauge tracks for dinky engines and hopper cars were placed along the dam's upstream face. (92.1.52)

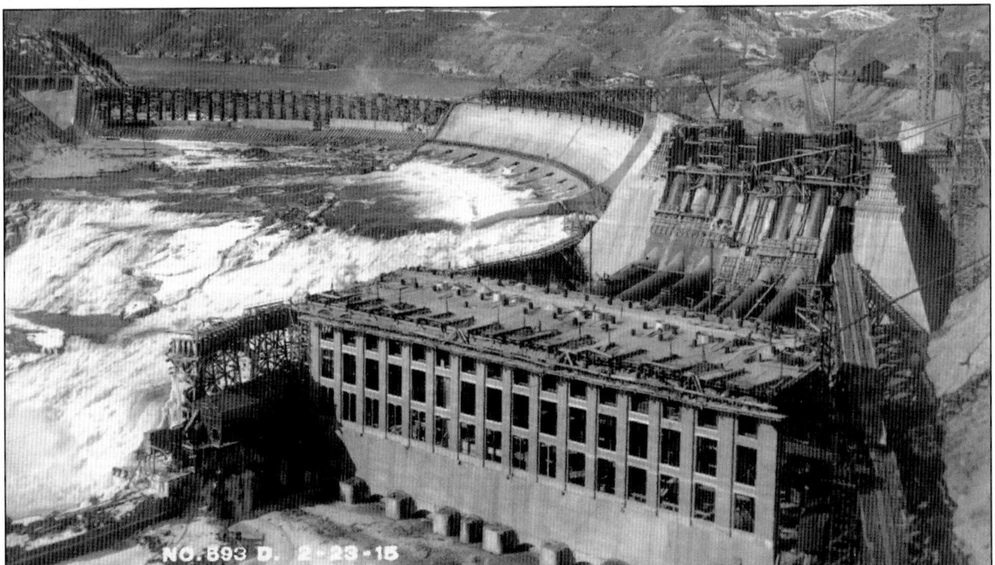

The Volta (Ryan) Dam is shown here under construction at the Great Falls of the Missouri. The original name given to the dam was "Volta" for Alessandro Volta, the Italian who had given his name to the unit of electromotive force called the "volt." The name of the dam would be changed in 1929 to "Ryan Dam" to honor the former president of the Montana Power Company, John D. Ryan. Six ducts led from the intake area to the powerhouse and are visible in this photograph. Note the rails where a small locomotive was employed to make the tough task of moving tons of concrete easier. (2007.17.7)

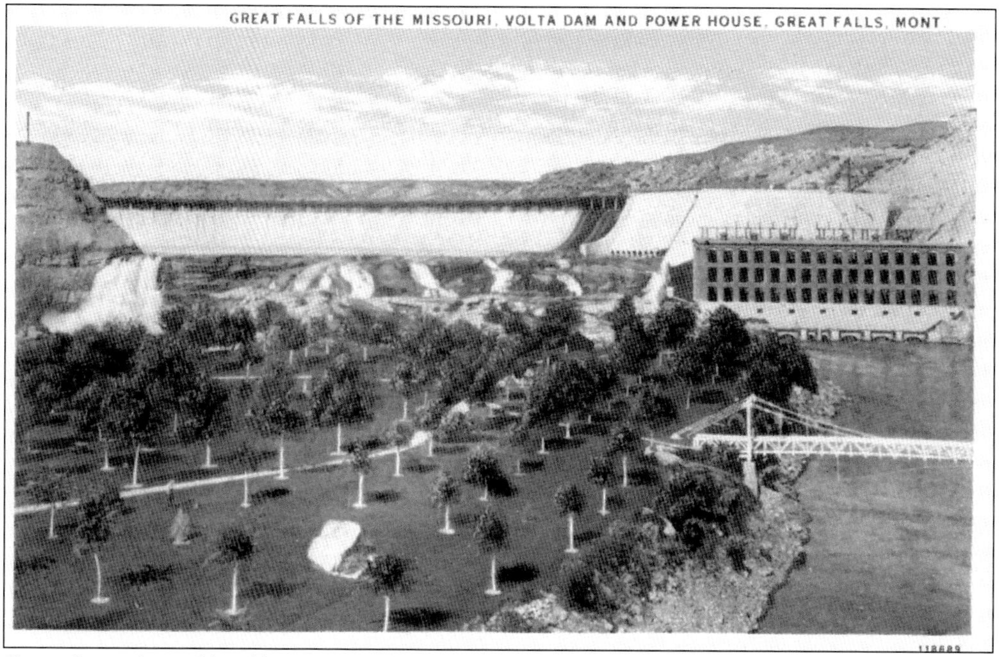

Once the rocks and boulders were laid, topsoil was hauled in. Landscaping came next, with trees, shrubbery, and lawns, and then a picnic shelter complete with tables and benches. Additional tables and benches would be built and strategically placed across the island for summer use by the public, along with restroom facilities and a modern electric kitchen. (2010.1.20)

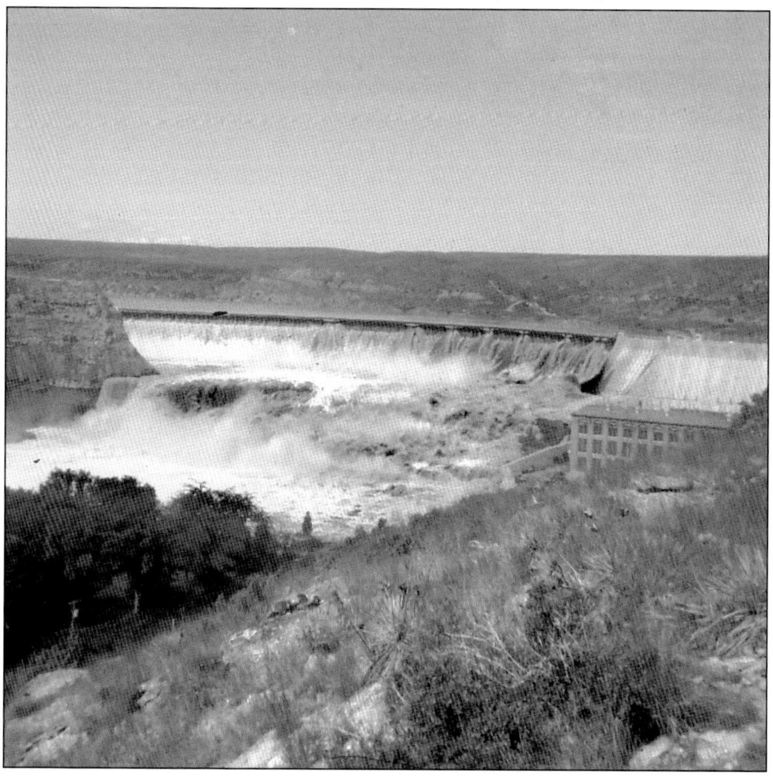

The huge volume of water cascading over the Ryan Dam at the peak of the June 1975 flood is representative of what many June floods were like. Although not as bad as earlier floods, there was still considerable lowland flooding and damage into the millions of dollars. (2010.1.21)

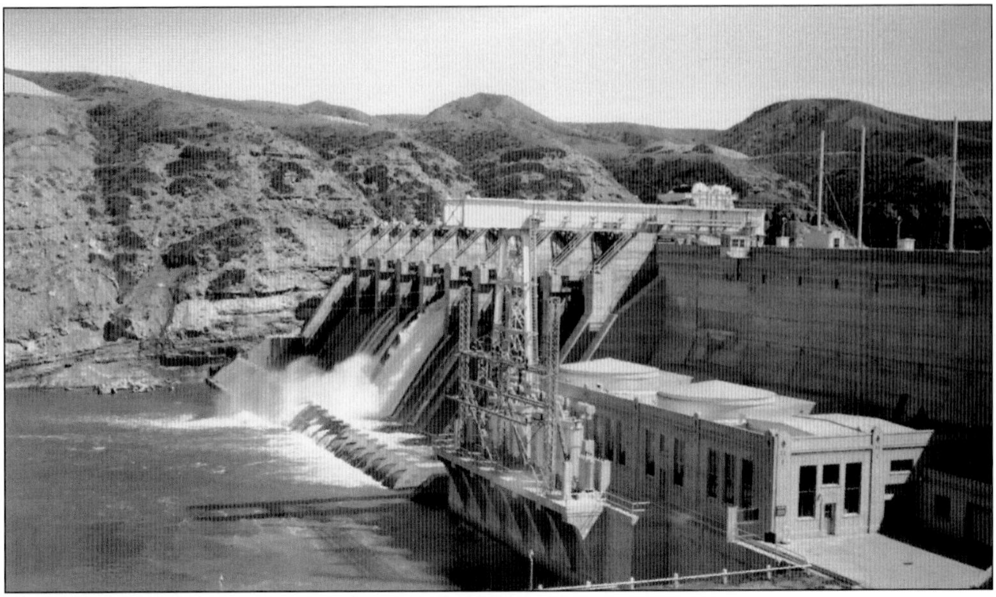

Morony Dam is the furthest downstream of the five Great Falls hydroelectric plants. It is located only 12 river miles downstream from Black Eagle Dam, 18 miles by car. Morony Dam was named after John G. Morony, one of the men who spearheaded the merger of Montana Power Company in 1912. The 842-foot-long dam, built in 1930, is 96 feet above the streambed. The elevation of a full pool behind the dam is 2,887 feet above sea level. This dam produces 48 megawatts. (2006.84.73)

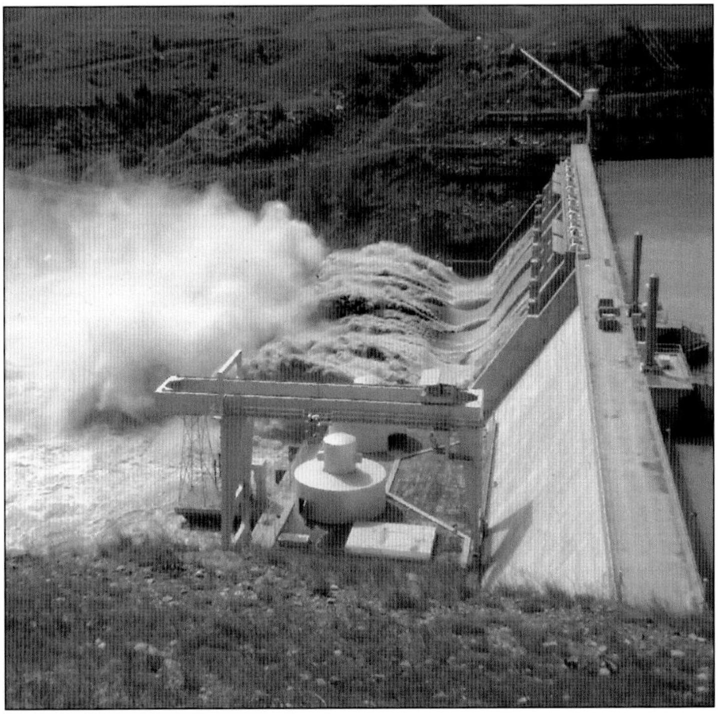

Cochrane Dam, completed in 1958, is shown discharging a huge volume of water as it tries to dissipate floodwaters from the enormous runoff and flood of June 1975. Cochrane Dam is named for Harold Cochrane, an early power company engineer who supervised the design of the Rainbow and Morony Dam power plants as well as the redesign of the Black Eagle power plant. The 856-foot-long dam is 100 feet above the streambed. It produces 60 megawatts of power. (2010.1.22)

Five

From Here to There

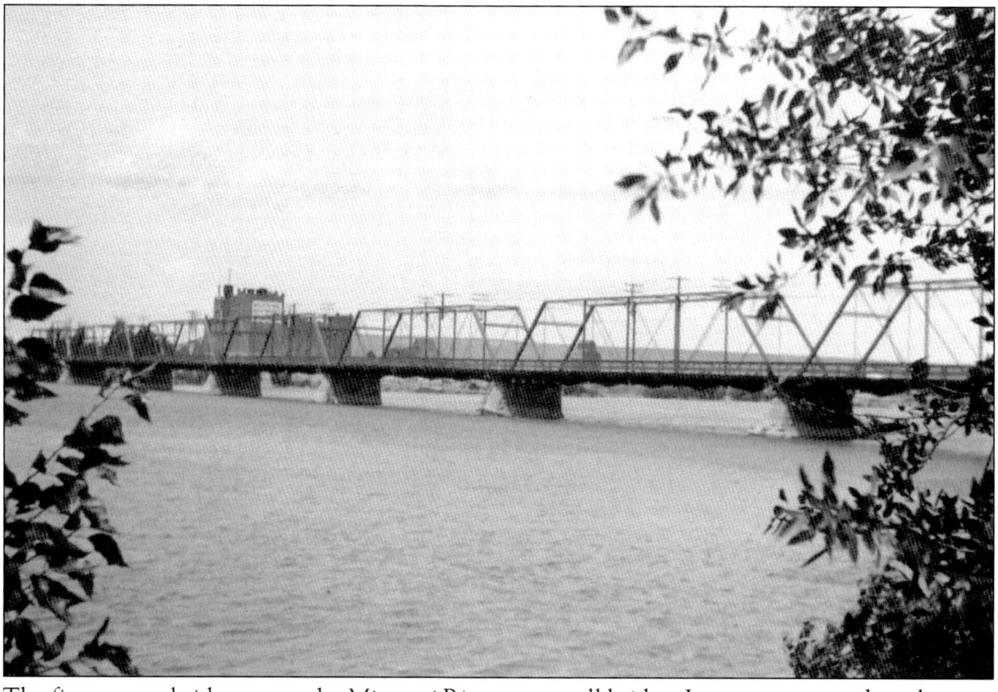

The first wagon bridge across the Missouri River was a toll bridge. It was constructed on the west end of First Avenue North and connected Great Falls to the West Side. It was completed in 1889, two years after the railroad came to Great Falls. At the time, west Great Falls was beginning to rapidly develop where the Great Northern Railroad had its yards. (PC92.1.158)

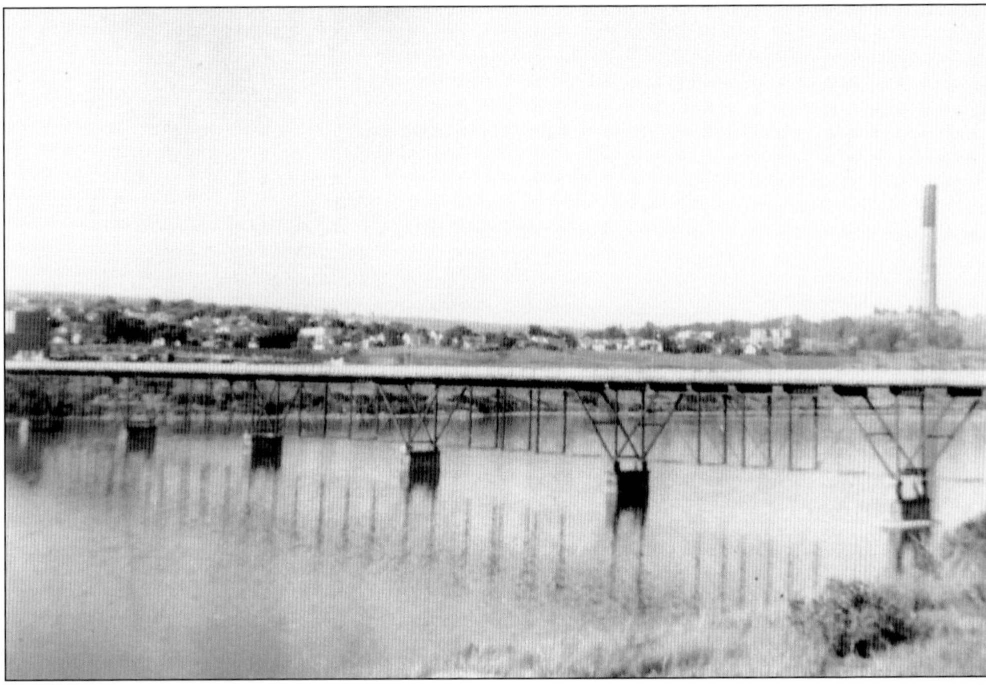

On Tuesday June 12, 1891, the county commissioners awarded the contract to construct the Fifteenth Street Bridge, connecting the city of Great Falls to what would become Little Chicago (later renamed Black Eagle) and the Boston and Montana Smelter and north Great Falls. The Wrought Iron Bridge Company of Canton, Ohio, agreed to build the bridge for $35,000. (1989.63.21)

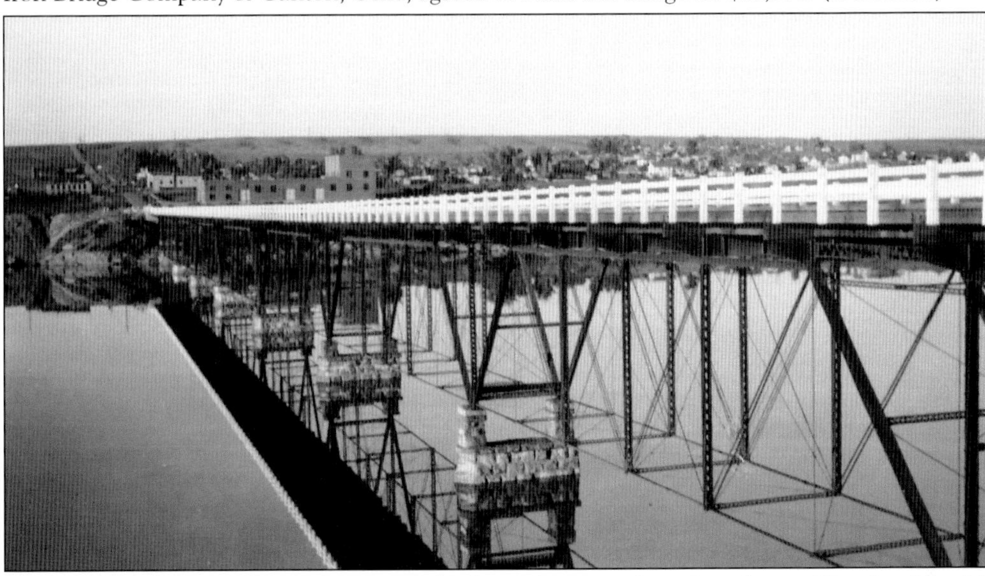

The Fifteenth Street Bridge was given its final test for strength and rigidity on Tuesday, May 10, 1892. Testing consisted of driving 10 teams of horses hauling 30 to 35 tons of dirt out onto the bridge. Each span was tested and measured separately. It was found that the larger spans only settled a quarter of an inch. Shorter spans settled three-eighths of an inch. Engineer Parker regarded the test as totally satisfactory. After the bridge was completed, it measured 1,060 feet long and rested on nine piers. (188.1)

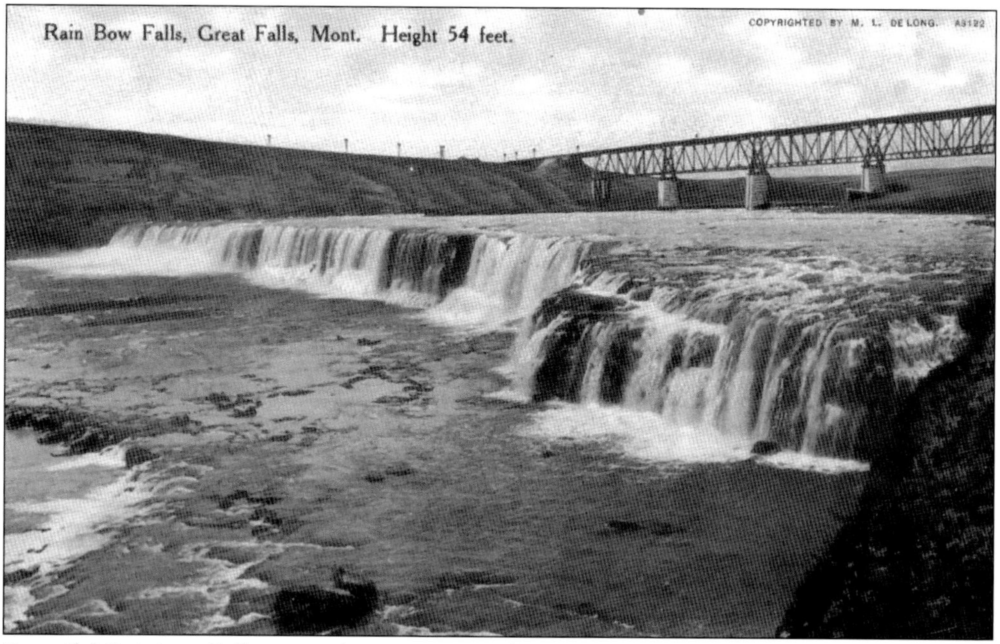

Beautiful Rainbow Falls is seen here some time between 1902 and 1909. The Great Northern Railroad moved its right-of-way from west Great Falls, where it originally entered the city in October 1887, primarily to save time and fuel. By moving the right-of-way east several miles, the railroad avoided several steep grades, including the grade down Watson Coulee in west Great Falls, a second incline near the Great Northern section house at Portage, and a third at a long, steep hill near Fort Benton called Government Coulee. (2010.1.23)

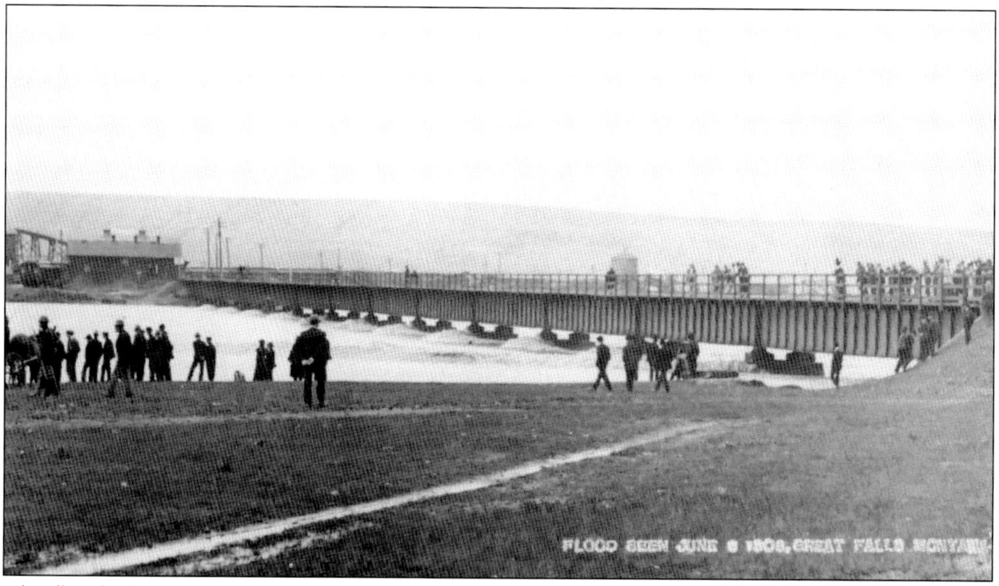

The flood of 1908 almost reached the bottom of the Great Northern Railroad Bridge just below Broadwater Bay. The tops of the bridge supports were about 9 feet above the normal surface of the Missouri at this point. Broadwater Bay starts at the upstream portion of the bridge. Here a large crowd has gathered to witness the excitement created by the extensive flood. Brave souls tempted fate by going out onto the bridge itself, evidently confident that it would not fail. (94.38.273)

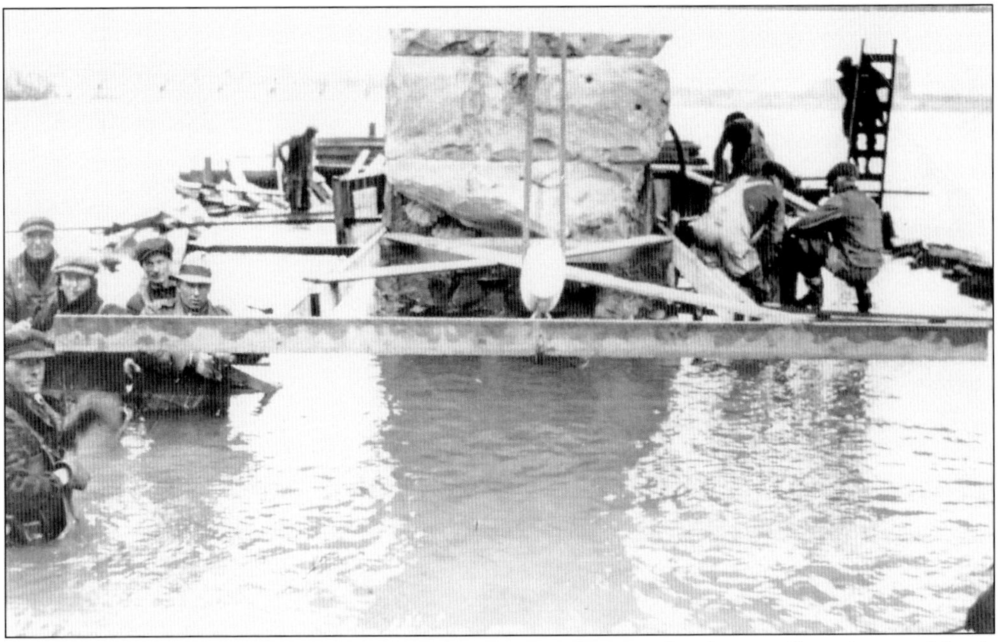

Workmen stand in the Missouri River as they prepare footings for the new First Avenue North Bridge in 1919. The waters of the Missouri are never warm at this latitude, but in the winter, spring, and early summer, they can be especially cold. Spring runoff consists of melting ice and snow from the mountains to the Southwest. These men must have been hardy to be able stand in that cold water for hours at a time. (2007.17.833A)

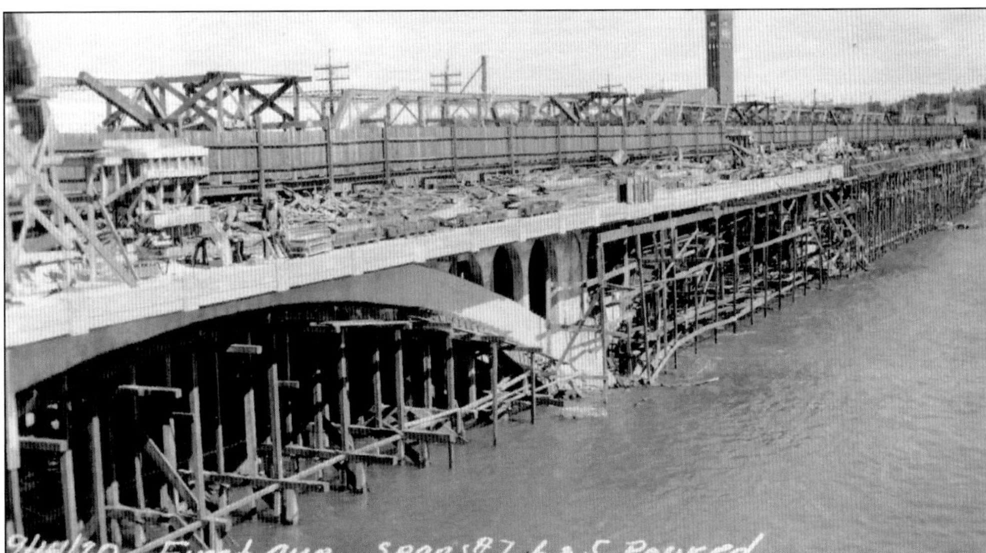

Construction of the new First Avenue North Bridge and its series of arches is seen in this September 1920 photograph. As the steel-reinforced concrete set, the forms could be dismantled and moved on to be reused in the next section. Construction began in 1919, and the bridge was completed in 1920. (2007.17.829A)

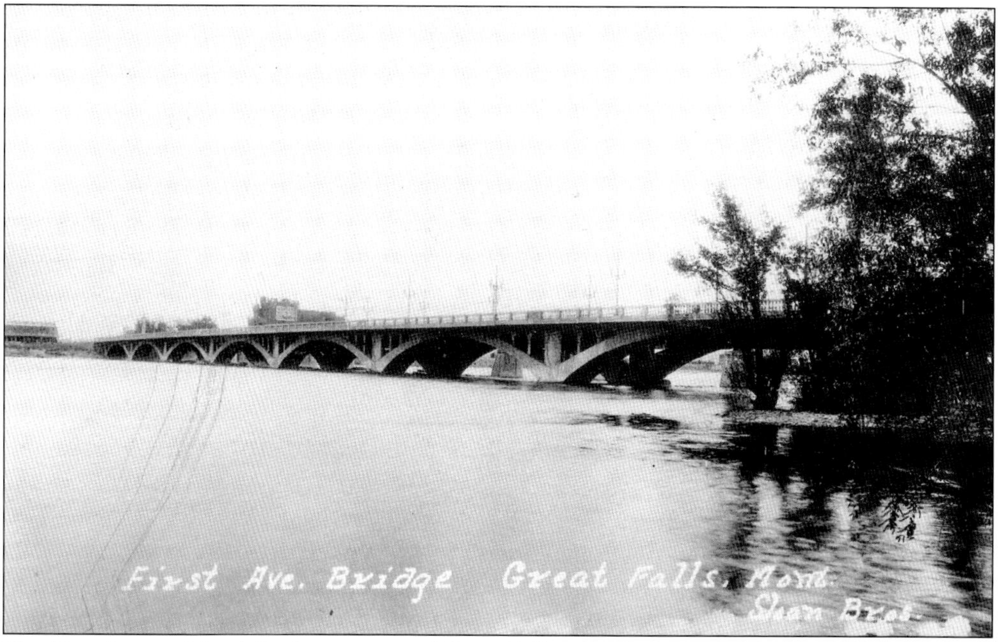

The First Avenue North Bridge connected Great Falls with the West Side. It replaced an original frame toll bridge. Construction began in 1919 and was completed in 1920. It was the first of two bridges in Great Falls to employ beautiful arches in its design. The other arched bridge was the Tenth Street Bridge, also built in 1920. Both of these bridges used steel-reinforced concrete in their design and were designed by the same architect, George Shanley of Great Falls. The Montana Brewing Company can be seen on the west bank, just to the right of the bridge. (PC92.1.102)

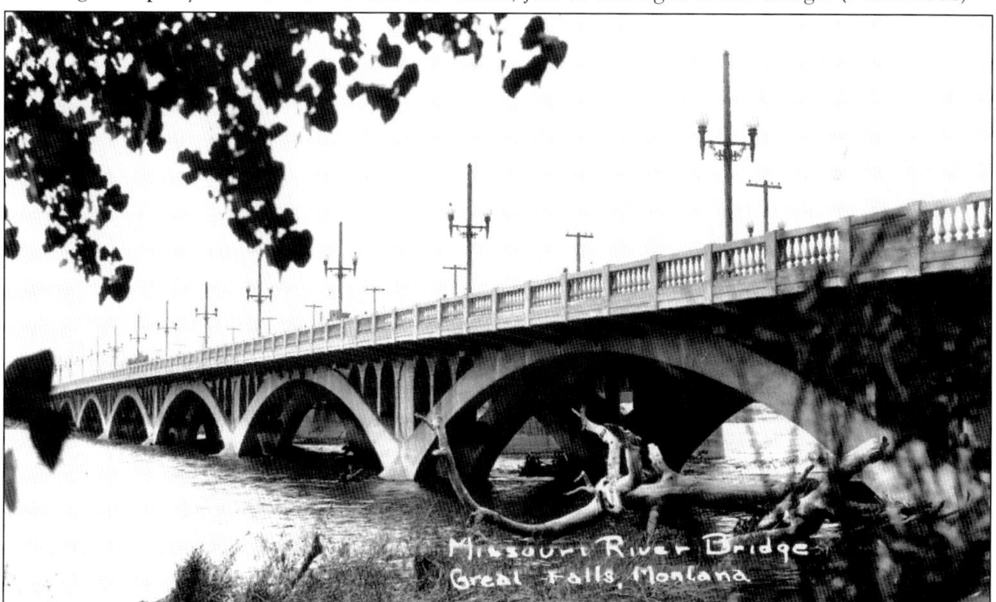

The graceful arches of the First Avenue North Bridge, framed by the leaves of nearby cottonwood trees, lend a romantic appearance to this photograph. Both this bridge and the Ninth Street Bridge were under contracts won by the Porter Brothers Company of Spokane, Washington. This bridge cost $232,000, while the Ninth Street Bridge cost somewhat less. (2006.84.19)

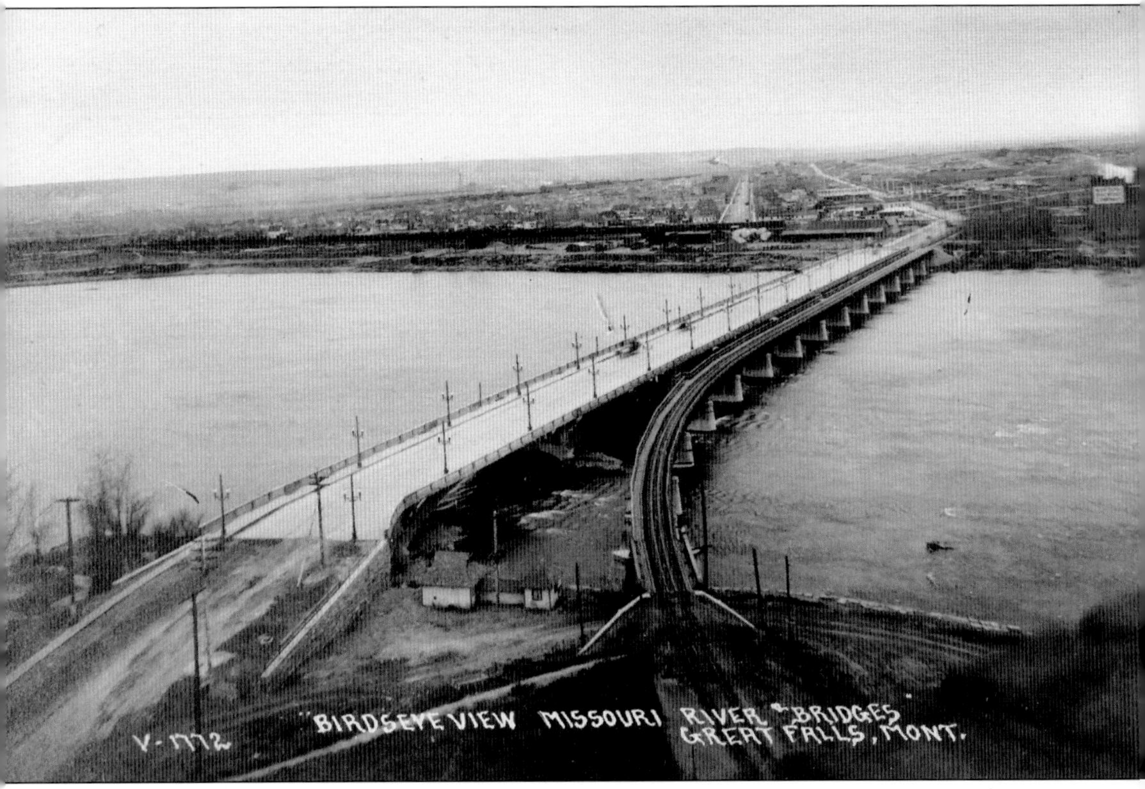

Looking west across the Missouri River from the Milwaukee Railroad tower provides a nice panorama of west Great Falls in this undated postcard view. The Montana Brewing Company is visible on the far bank on the extreme right. (PC92.1.101)

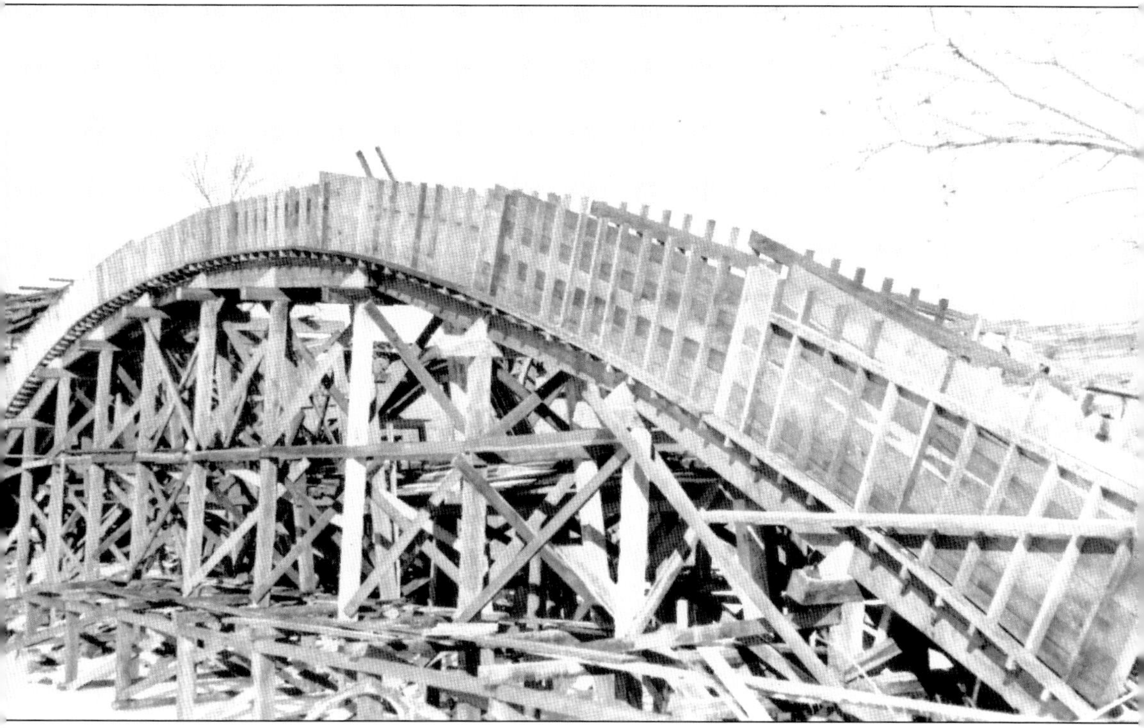

The skill and workmanship used to develop the concrete forms for the Tenth Street and Central Avenue West Bridges is remarkable. Notice the huge amount of dimension lumber as well as timbers and planking that goes into creating the forms for just one arch. Once the concrete has set, the form has to be dismantled, and work begins on the next section. (2005.11.11)

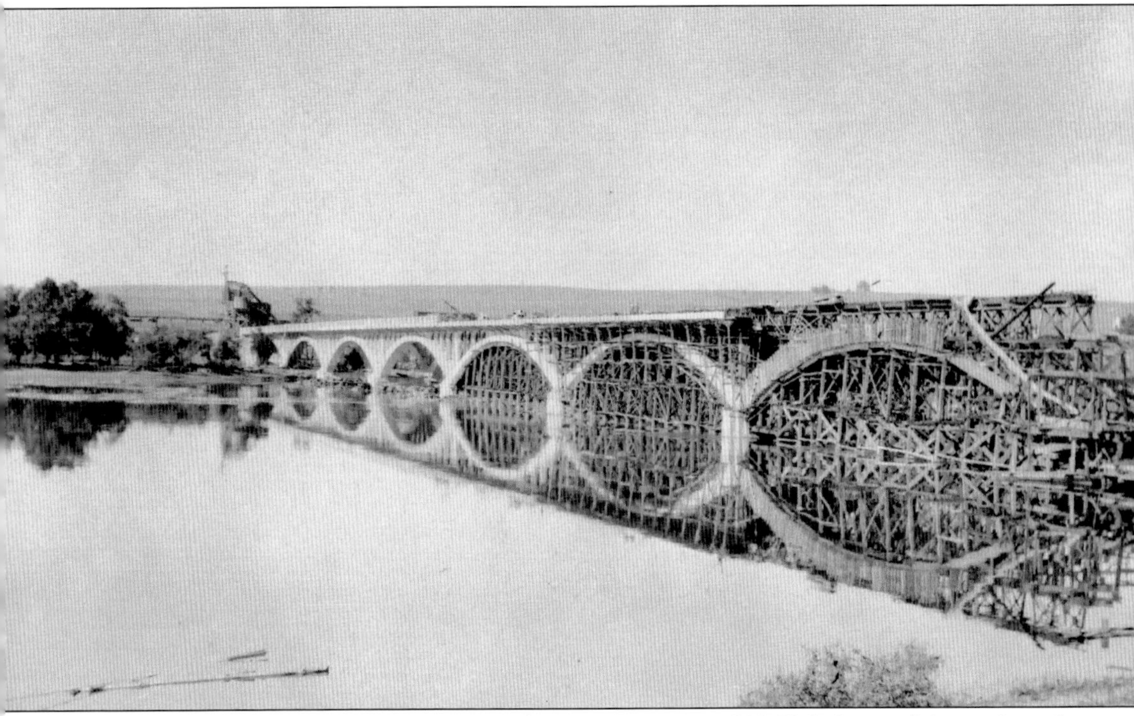

The Tenth Street Bridge is shown here under construction in 1920. To help speed the work on this bridge, builders incorporated railroad delivery of large amounts of concrete to the site, shortening construction time considerably. This area of the river formed into a reservoir, as it is backed up behind Black Eagle Dam for about 2 miles. Before these waters became a quiet reflective pool, the river ran as a series of cascades and rapids. (2005.11.12)

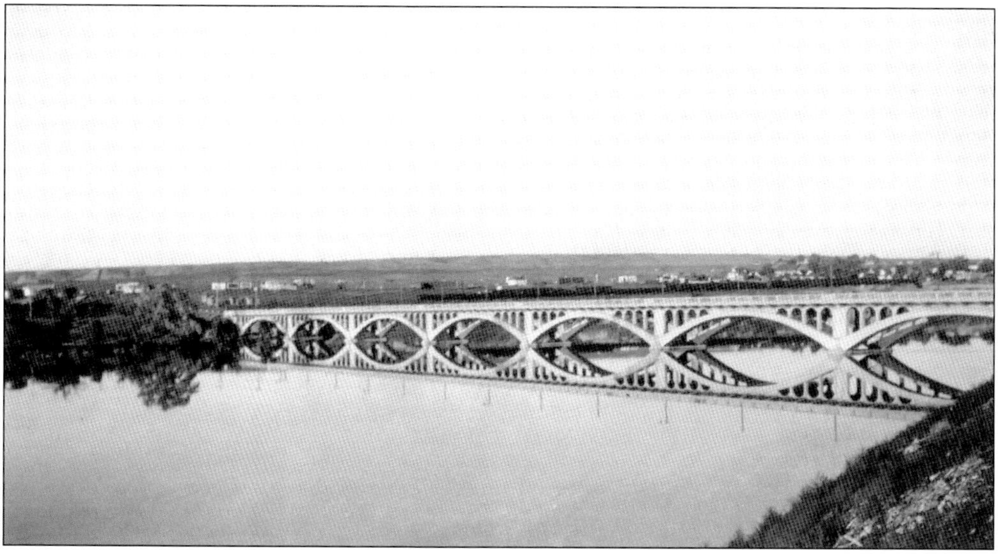

The Tenth Street Bridge brought traffic on U.S. Highway 87 from the northern reaches of the state, such as Fort Benton and Havre, as well as the burgeoning grain lands north of the city. Built in 1920, its graceful arches reflected beautifully against the placid waters of the Missouri. Black Eagle can be seen in the background on the right. (188.2)

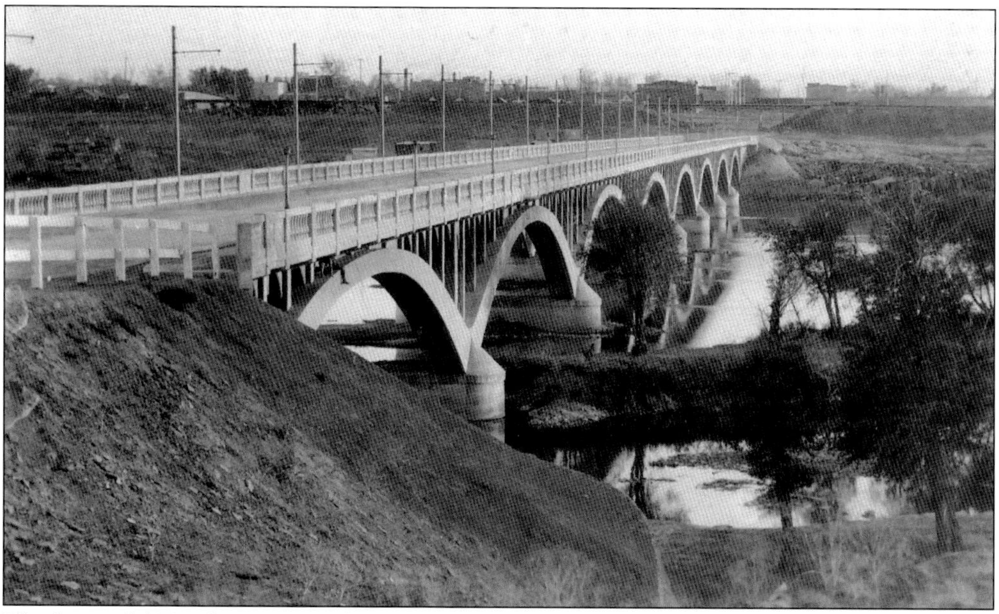

The beautiful Tenth Street Bridge was completed in 1920. In order to construct this bridge, workers first had to build a railroad trestle across the river to carry the concrete and steel. Seven concrete piers were then constructed using a powerful pile driver. A concrete mixing plant was constructed on the north side of the river, kept supplied by a temporary railroad spur from the smelter. Anywhere from 40 to 400 men worked on this bridge. Some 1.25 million feet of lumber was required, as well as 350 tons of reinforcing steel. It took 11,000 barrels of cement and 8,500 cubic yards of sand and gravel. These beautiful arches are reminiscent of an age when aesthetic qualities in construction remained an important part of design and engineering. (PC92.1.41)

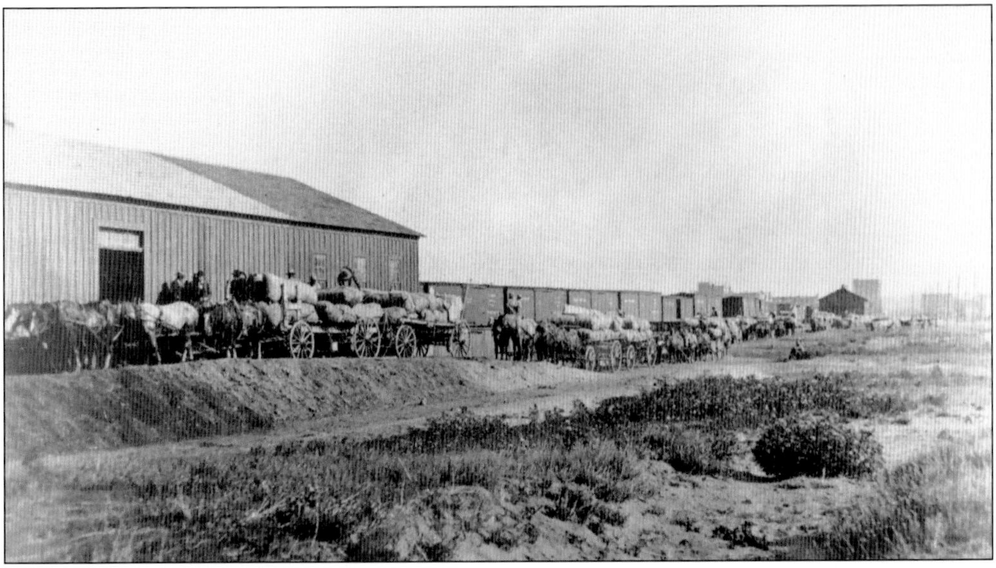

Here is the Great Northern warehouse on July 15, around the year 1890. A large amount of wool was coming into Great Falls as a result of changing agricultural practices on the upper Great Plains. The winter of 1886–1887 had decimated the cattle industry in Montana. Many of those who stayed in ranching forsook cattle for sheep. The sheep population would continue to grow, and by 1900, an estimated six million were on the range, making Montana the nation's top wool-producing state. (2007.17.306)

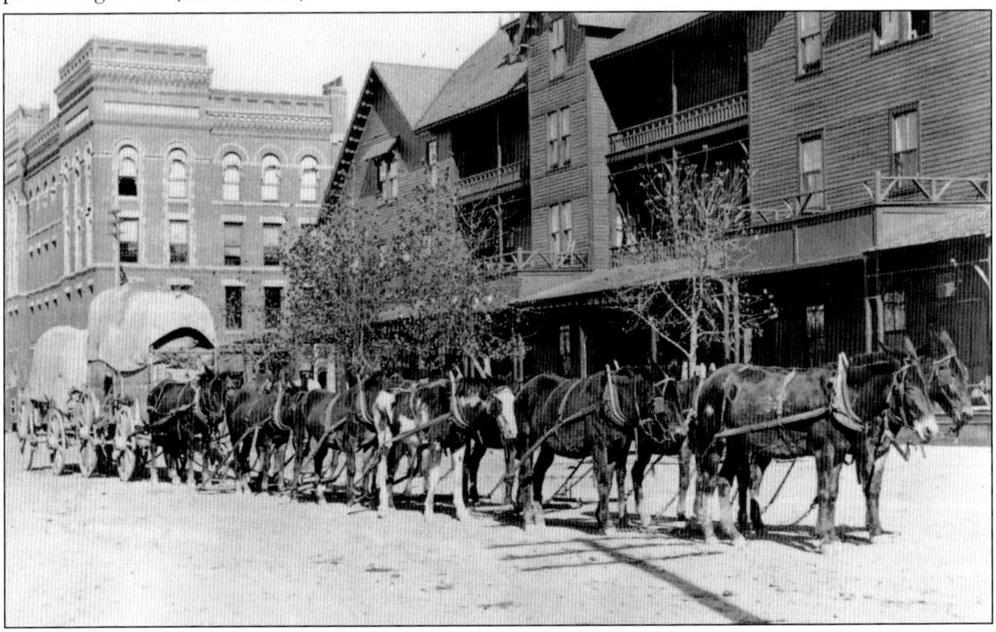

This freight outfit at the corner of Central Avenue and First Street looks ready to head out of town. The big building on the left is the original Park Hotel, opened by founding father Paris Gibson and H. O. Chowen on September 1, 1886, at a reported cost of $50,000. Notice that the freighter is using mostly mules in his 12-animal team to do the hauling. The wagons are hooked in tandem, a common practice of the day. One outfit could haul a lot of trade goods or freight and still be handled by one driver. (2007.17.529)

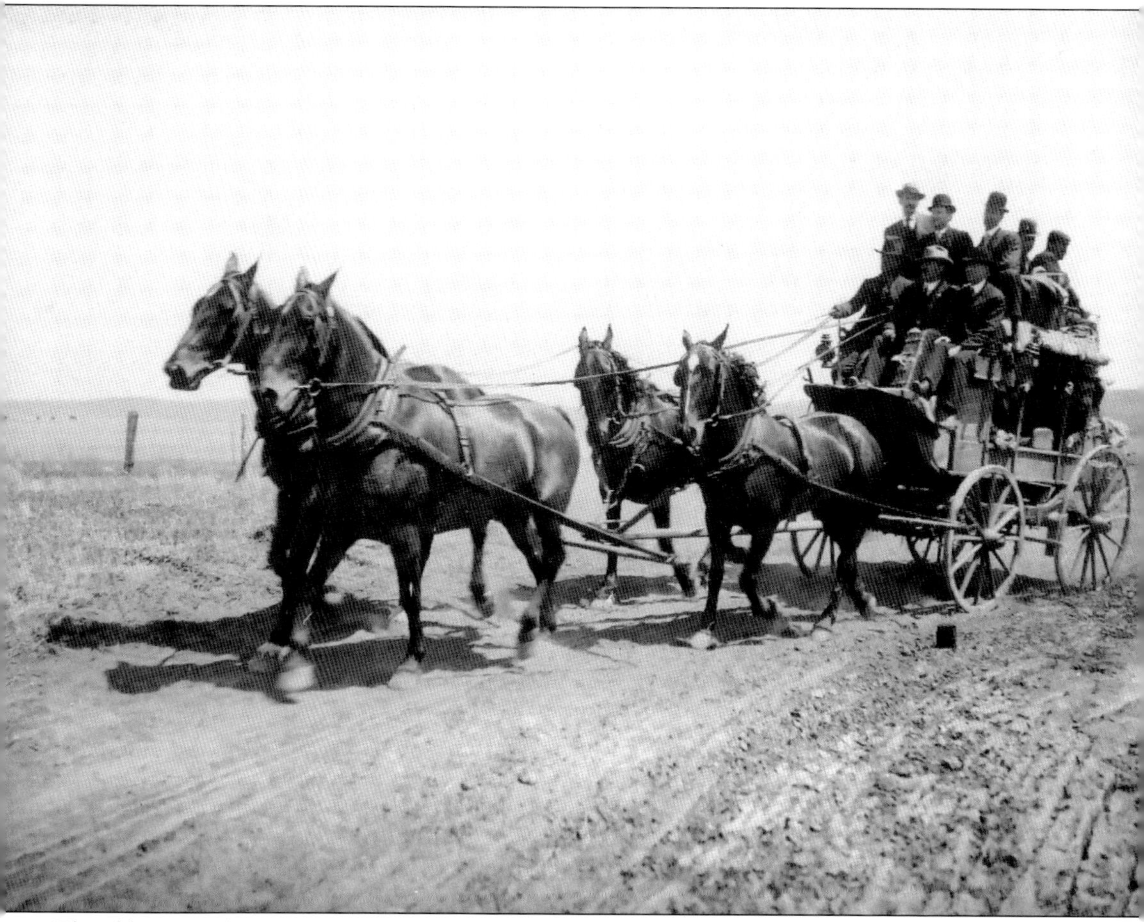

The old Concord stage runs between Great Falls and Lewistown in this undated photograph. The stage driver needed to be ready to travel in any weather—and in Montana, that could mean a variety of things. He had to handle the team and his passengers in blistering heat, insects, intense cold, driving rain, snowstorms, and the unending Montana wind. Another stage line ran between Fort Benton and Helena on the old Military Wagon Road. It had stops at a number of places, but those drivers had to know how to see in the dark, since it ran all night. This mode of travel ran well into the 20th century. (2005.26.13)

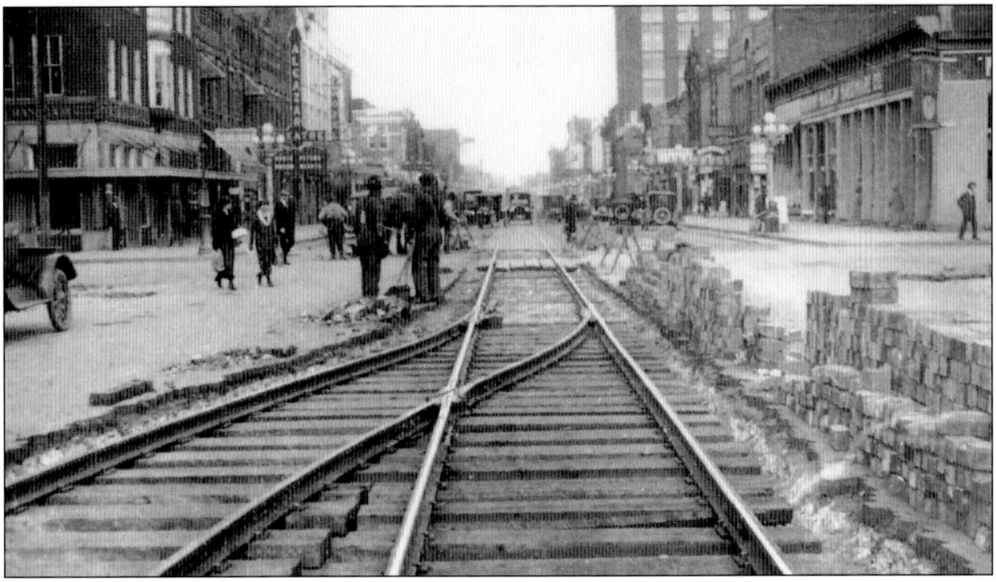

Great Falls was very innovative in its approach to ridding itself of muddy streets. In 1910, The Kettle River Company provided creosoted wooden-block paving to the city. People from all over the state came to Great Falls to see the paving and bring home the latest ideas to their communities. Here some of the paving has been taken up as workmen repair a section of street railway track. At the time, the Kettle River Company of Minneapolis, Minnesota, claimed to be the largest manufacturer of creosoted products in the world. Paris Gibson, of course, came from Minneapolis–St. Paul. (2007.17.506)

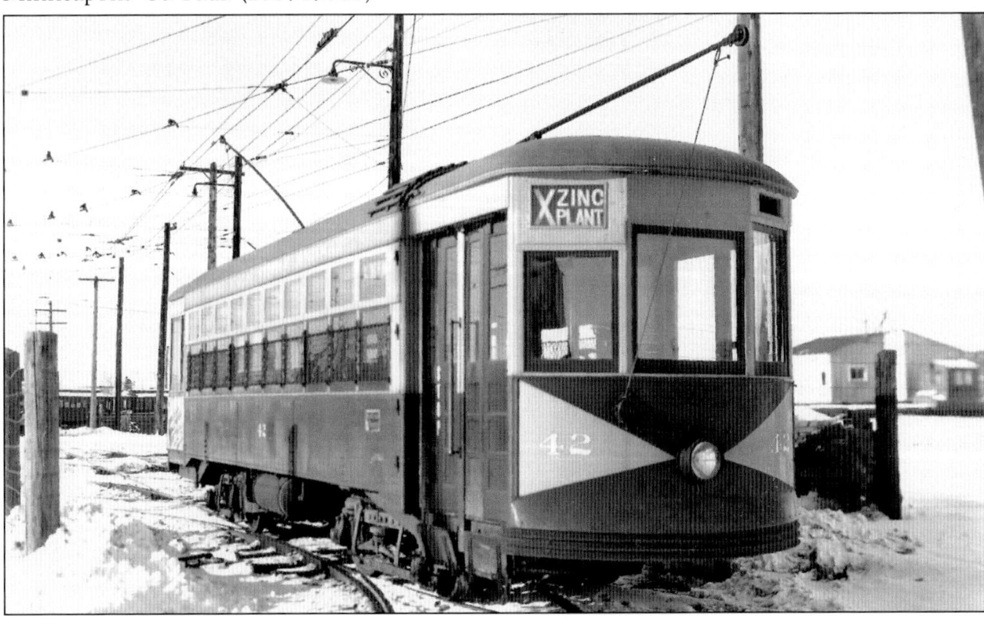

As soon as Black Eagle Dam started producing electricity in December 1890, the city electric streetcar system was operational. It was formally opened to the public in March 1891. A round trip from downtown to Black Eagle Dam and back cost 20¢. Eventually 27 cars and 18.6 miles of track served the city. On December 1, 1931, the trolley system was retired and replaced by a bus line operated by Great Falls Coach. (133.1)

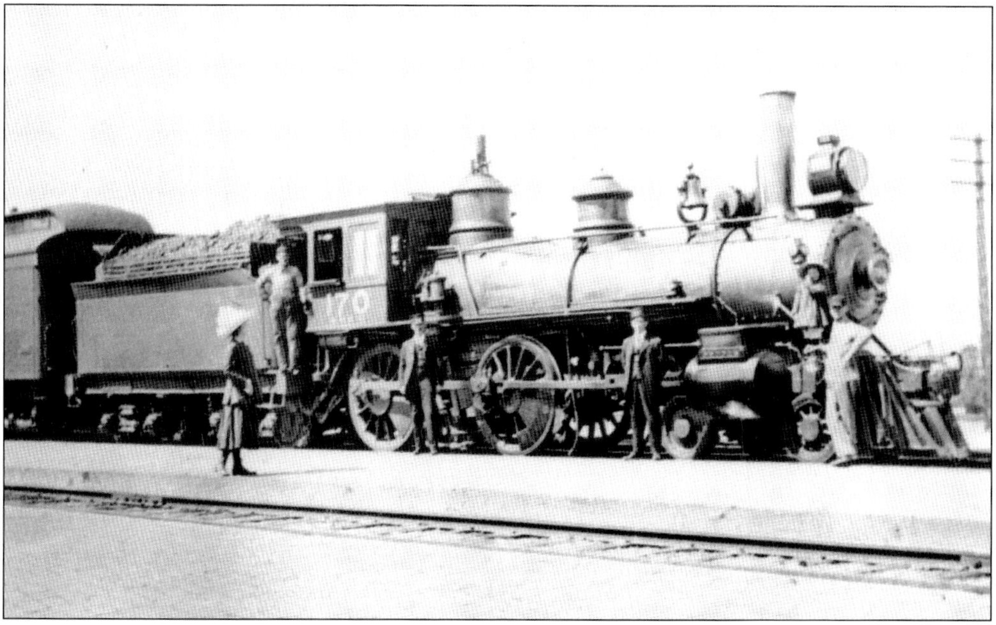

Here is Great Northern locomotive no. 170, under control of Engineer James C. Sanders, seen posing with his two daughters on May 29, 1911. They are in front of the Great Northern depot in downtown Great Falls. The new Union Station opened in 1910. The new brick structure was an impressive sight as it overlooked the extensive brick paving between the station and the tracks. (2007.17.351)

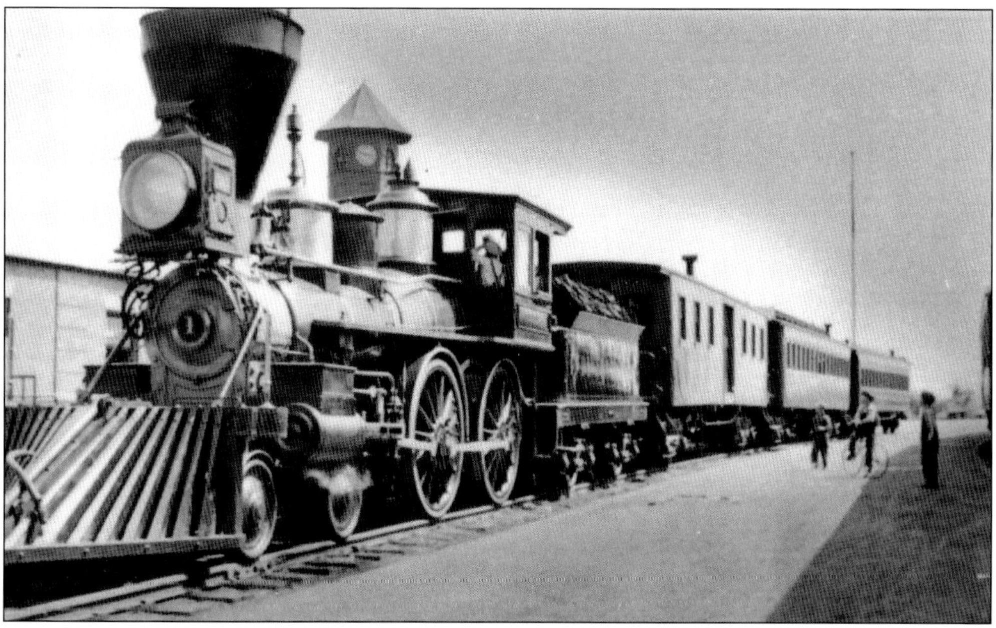

Traveling across the Northwest in 1920 was engine no. 1, the *William Crooks*, built in 1861 for the St. Paul and Pacific Railroad, a precursor to the Great Northern Railroad. James J. Hill, president of the Great Northern, named the engine for his chief engineer. Here it waits in front of the Great Northern depot in Great Falls. Above the cab of the engine, the new Union Station tower can be seen. The tower had been constructed 10 years earlier. (2007.17.309)

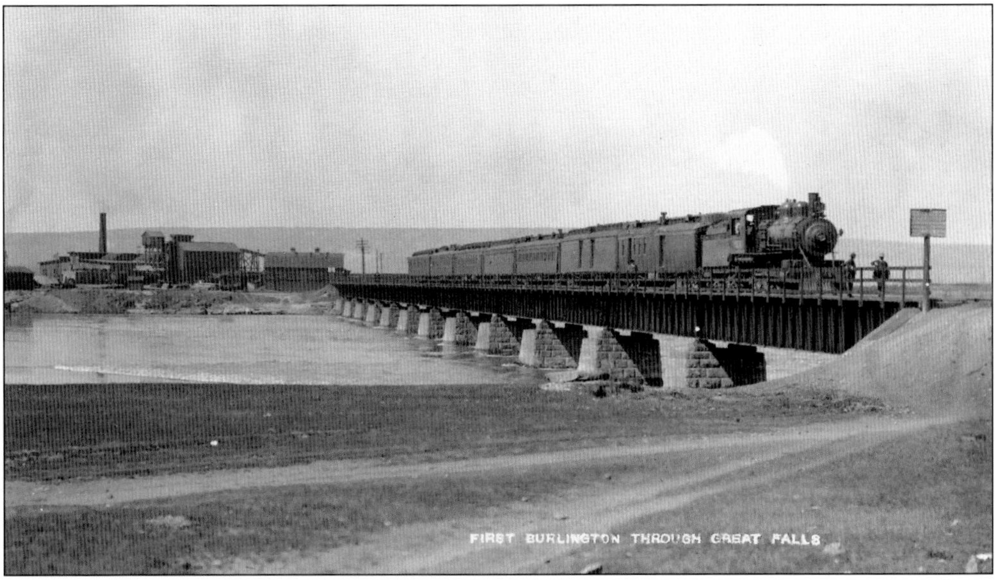

The first Burlington train through Great Falls crosses the Missouri River over the Great Northern Railroad Bridge at Broadwater Bay on the morning of May 25, 1909. The Great Northern rail yards and maintenance shops can be seen across the river. This was the first transcontinental train through Great Falls, and a huge celebration took place. The city was filled with celebrants who came for all the festivities, including numerous speeches, train rides, a parade, and other events. (PC92.1.4197)

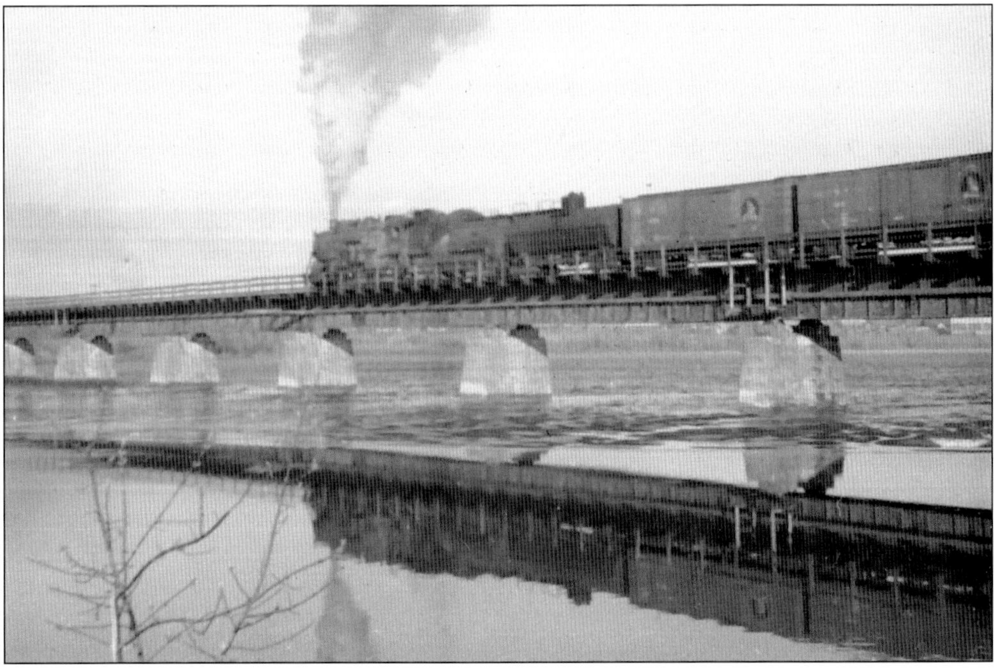

A steam-powered locomotive makes its way into the train yards in west Great Falls. It crosses over the Missouri River at the same point where the old wagon ford was located before the advent of bridges. This ford was used by Native Americans as well as buffalo, deer, and other wildlife for years before the arrival of settlers. Native Americans called it "Rock-Bottom Crossing." (MOE93.111.27H)

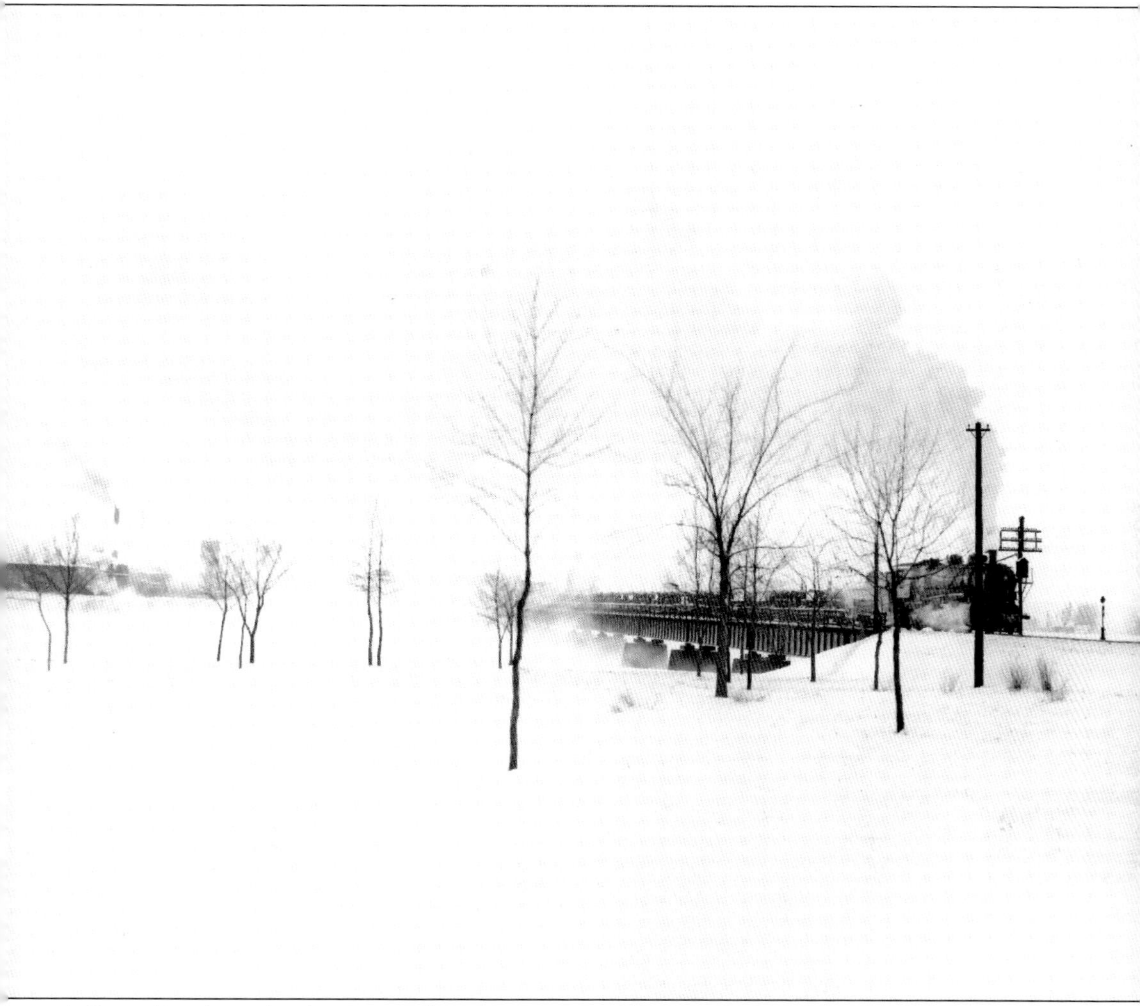

A Great Northern freight train makes its way across the Missouri River on a very cold winter day. This photograph captures the less-than-pleasant weather that many Montanans had to face each day in the course of their normal duties—railroaders were no exception. Judging from the amount of mist coming off the river, the temperature is most likely below zero. Even with the cold and hardships connected with working in north-central Montana in wintertime, the area retains a certain beauty on even the harshest day. (2007.17.821)

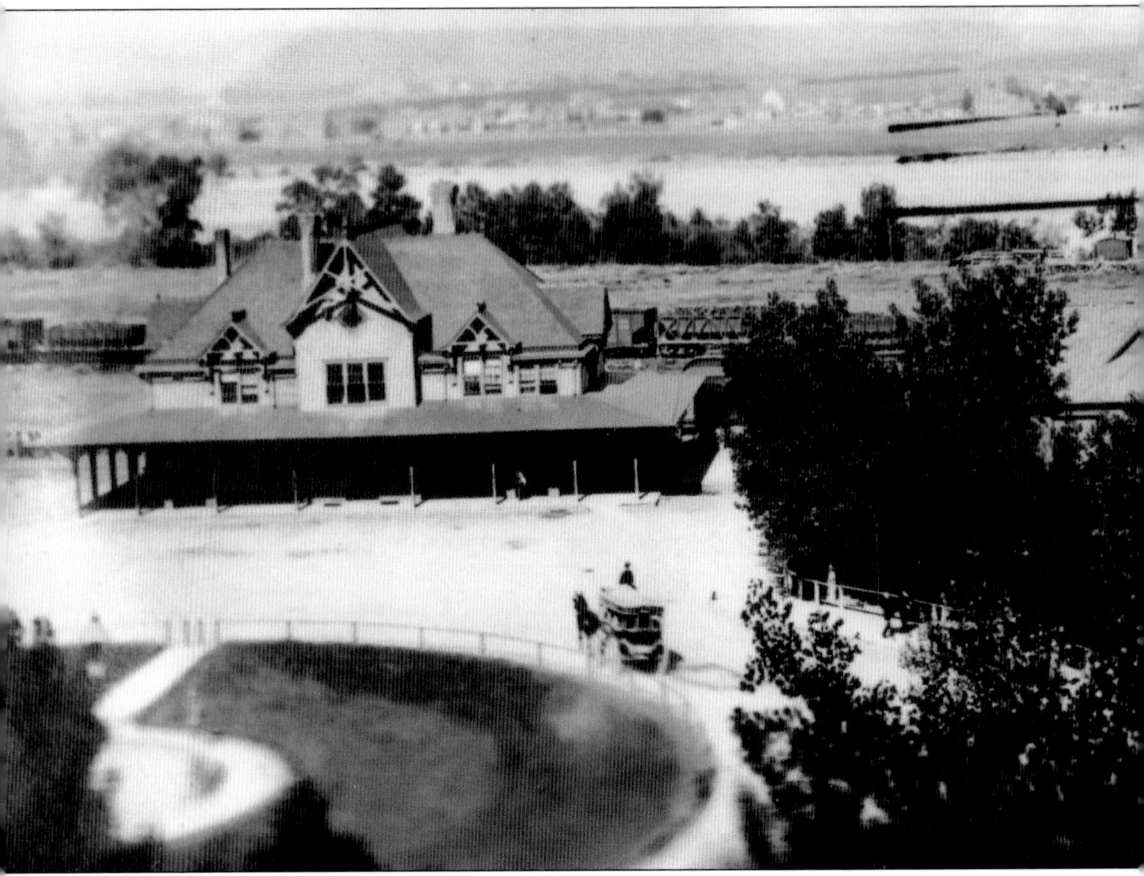

The Great Northern train station shown above was constructed in 1890 near the river on the west end of Central Avenue. It was the second train station to be located in Great Falls. The Great Northern would eventually close its original station (a converted boxcar) on the west side of the city in favor of this 1890 station. In 1910, a brick terminal was built just south of the original frame station. The frame structure, later used for storage, caught fire and burned down on November 4, 1915. (2007.17.305)

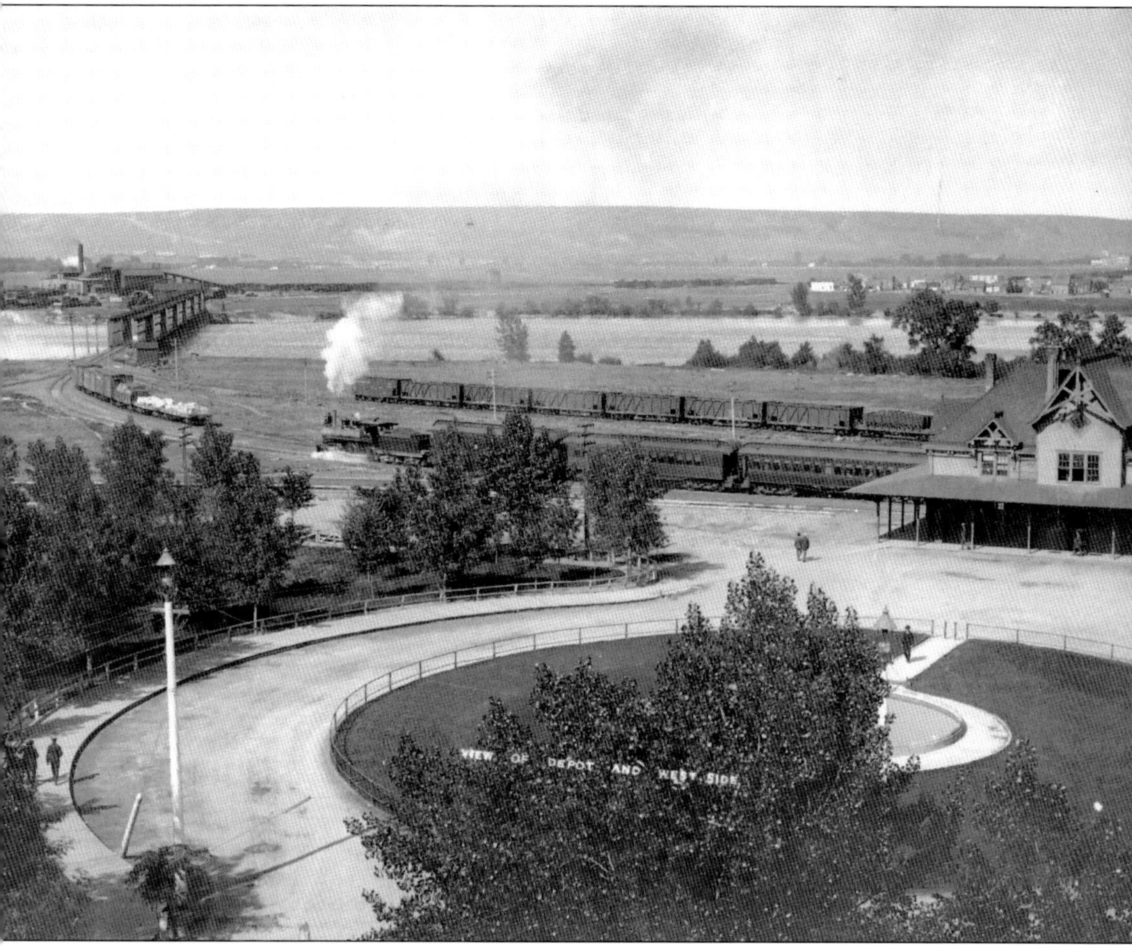

The original Great Northern depot is seen at the west end of Central Avenue with a portion of Johnstown visible across the river to the right. Johnstown had been in serious contention for the honor of maintaining the commercial center of the city. The construction of the Great Northern train station (locally known as "Union Station") in Great Falls and the closure of the train station in Johnstown by James J. Hill, president of the railroad and financier of the development of Great Falls, clinched it. (2007.17.845)

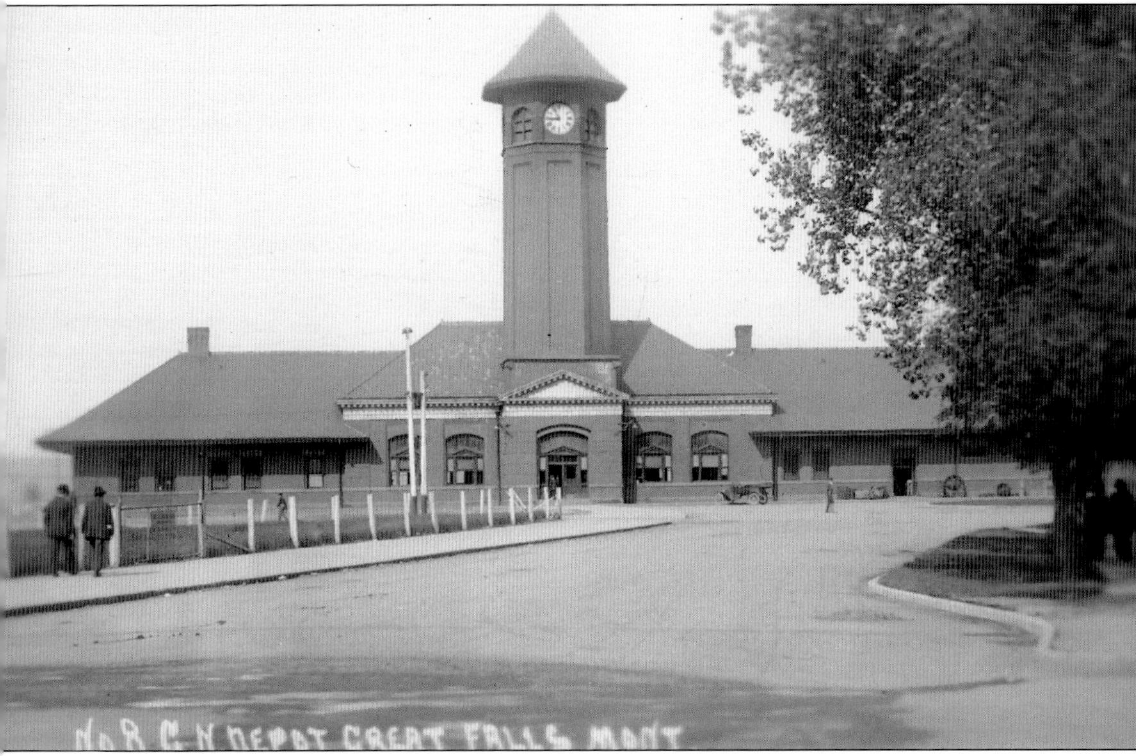

The new Union Station, opened on September 25, 1910, sported a 100-foot tower. The tower gave the station a commanding elegance that afforded residents as well as travelers a prominence easily identified from various areas of town. The new station was located a block south of the original frame station built in 1890. This new station was all brick and had nearly half a mile of brick pavement surrounding it. Over 300,000 bricks had been used in just the paving. At the time, the *Great Falls Tribune* said it formed "one of the most delightful promenades in the city." (PC92.1.77)

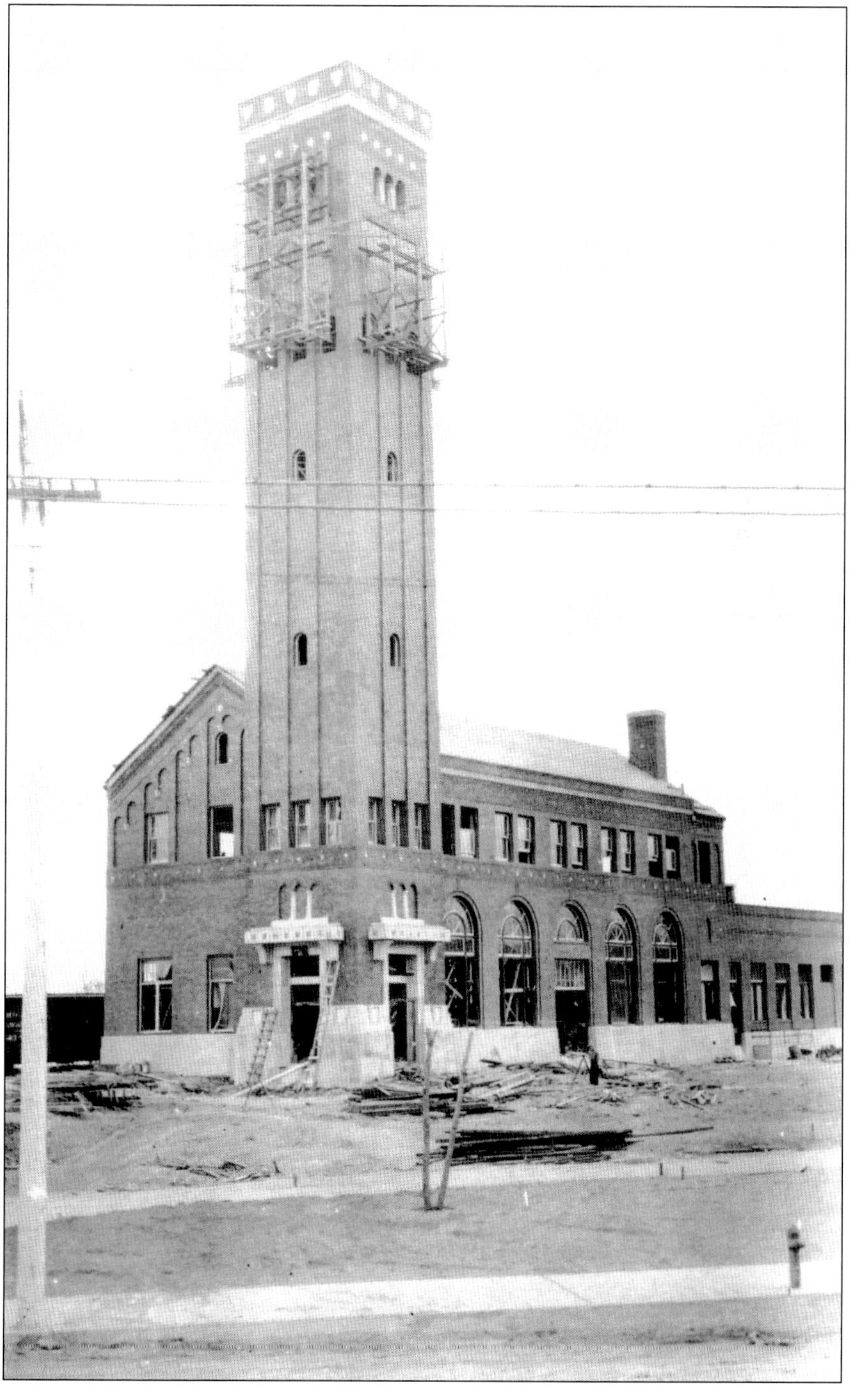

Construction of the Milwaukee Railroad station took place in 1914. This station sported a tower that was originally designed to extend 138 feet above the first floor of the structure. The tower was initially going to be a clock tower, but revised plans eliminated the clock faces and replaced them with the Milwaukee Railroad logo. The top of each of the tower's four sides thus featured the railroad's name written in a mosaic tile sign that was 13 feet square. (2005.11.21)

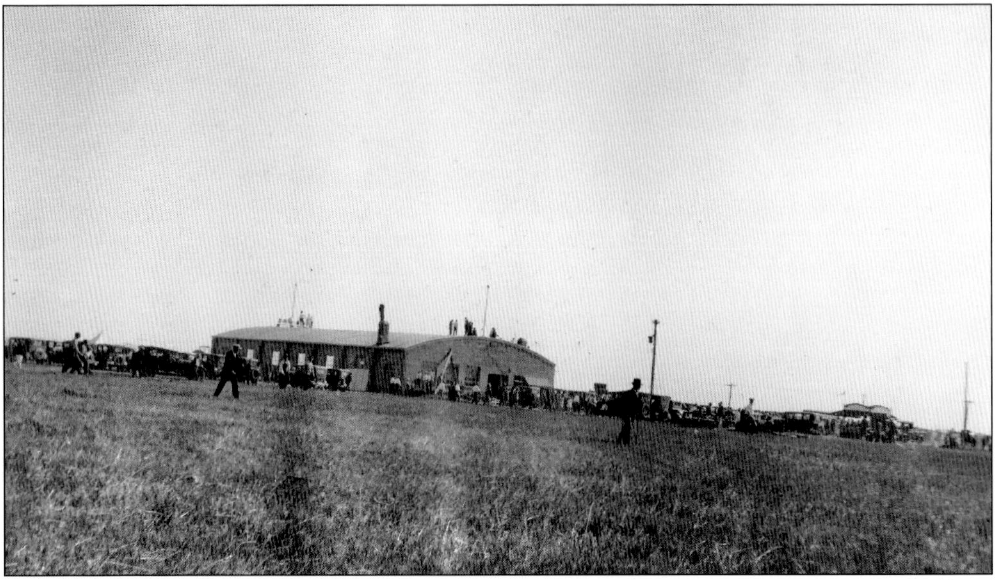

Earl Vance was an early pioneer in aviation and came to Great Falls about 1926. He purchased land north of town on a hilltop overlooking the city to build the original airport for Great Falls. The year 1928 saw Great Falls witness the first airmail flight into the city by National Park Airways, later to become Western Airlines. (MOE93.111.27I)

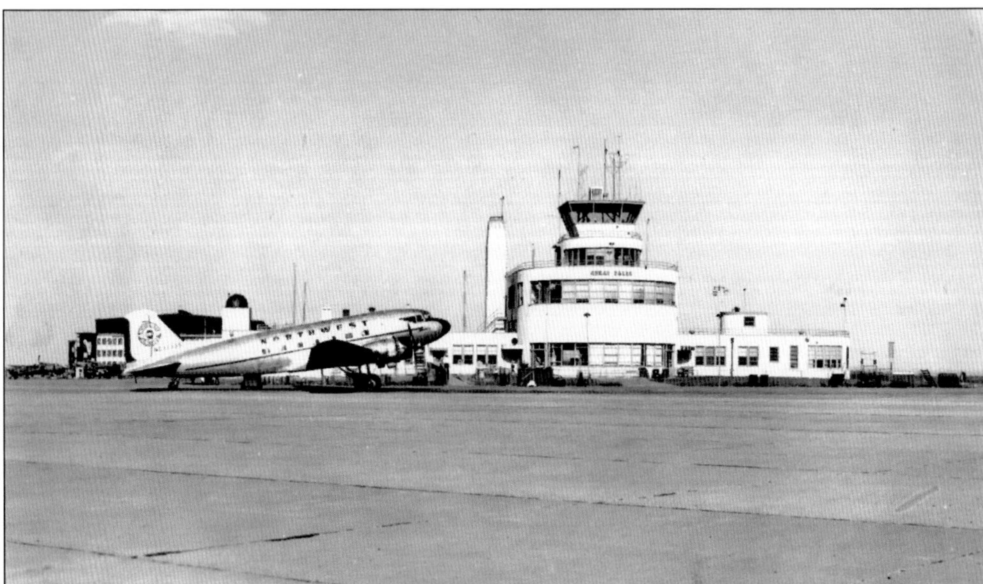

The newly built terminal for Great Falls Municipal Airport stood on Gore Hill west of Great Falls, 300 feet above the city. The city purchased land up on the hill in 1928, and the site was dedicated as an airport in 1931. Construction of the terminal, four runways, hangars, and other facilities was not completed until 1939. The hill was named Gore Hill and the airport was called Gore Field to honor the Gore family, who farmed there and originally owned the land. (2010.1.24)

Six

River City Views

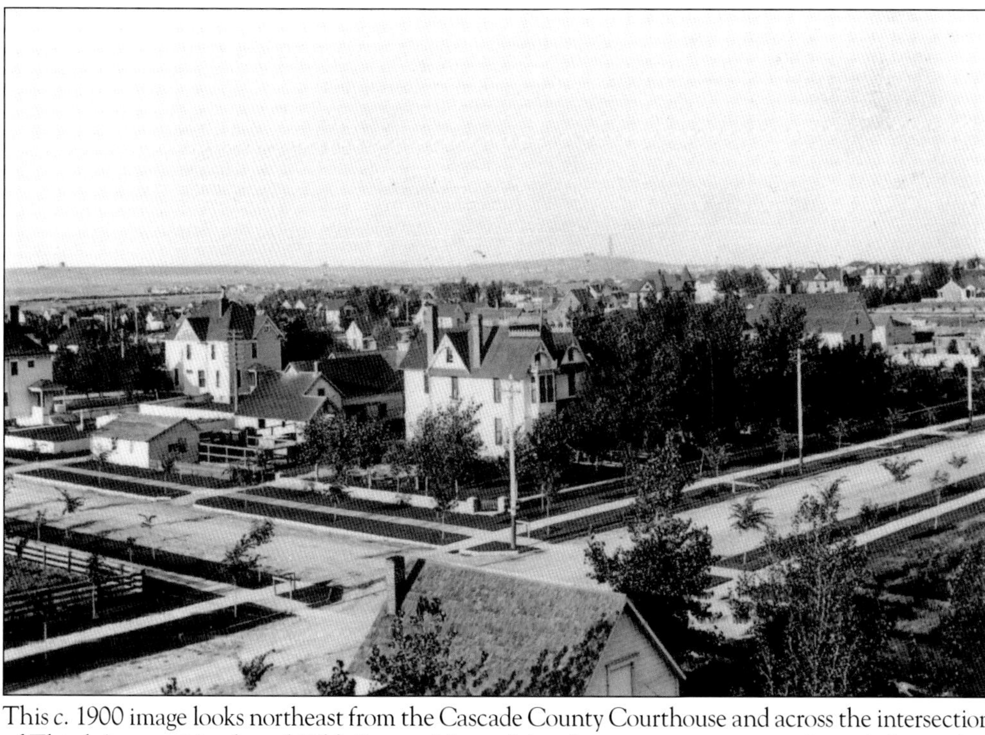

This c. 1900 image looks northeast from the Cascade County Courthouse and across the intersection of Third Avenue North and Fifth Street. Most of the elm trees are new growth, and the smelter smokestack on the horizon is the smaller, 150-foot stack. (2007.17.513)

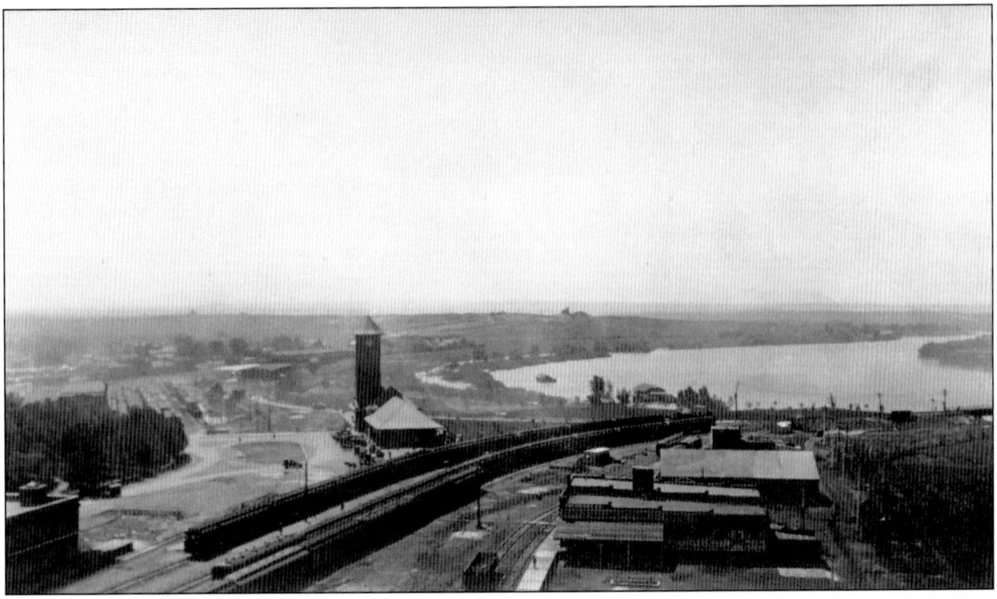

This c. 1920 bird's-eye view of the Great Northern train station was taken from the much higher tower of the Milwaukee Railroad station and looks upriver (south). Horses and wagons as well as a few early automobiles line up at the station, either picking up or dropping off passengers and their baggage. Two boathouses are visible on Broadwater Bay; the one nearest is on the shore, while the other one rests in the bay and is connected to shore with a walkway. (94.45.2)

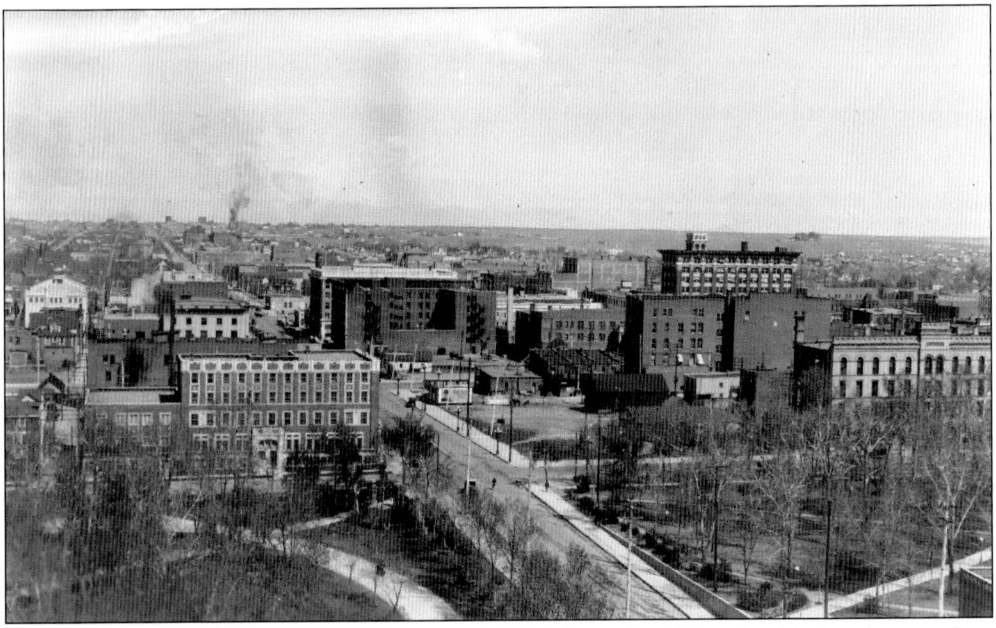

Downtown Great Falls is seen here in the early 1900s from the Milwaukee Railroad tower. First Avenue North is visible just as it exits from the railroad underpass near the river. The south end of Gibson Park with its driveway can be seen in the left foreground. On the right is Whittier Park. The intersection is First Avenue North and Park Drive. Park Drive starts at this intersection and goes to the left (or north). Sitting on the northeast corner of the intersection is the YMCA. (PC92.1.159)

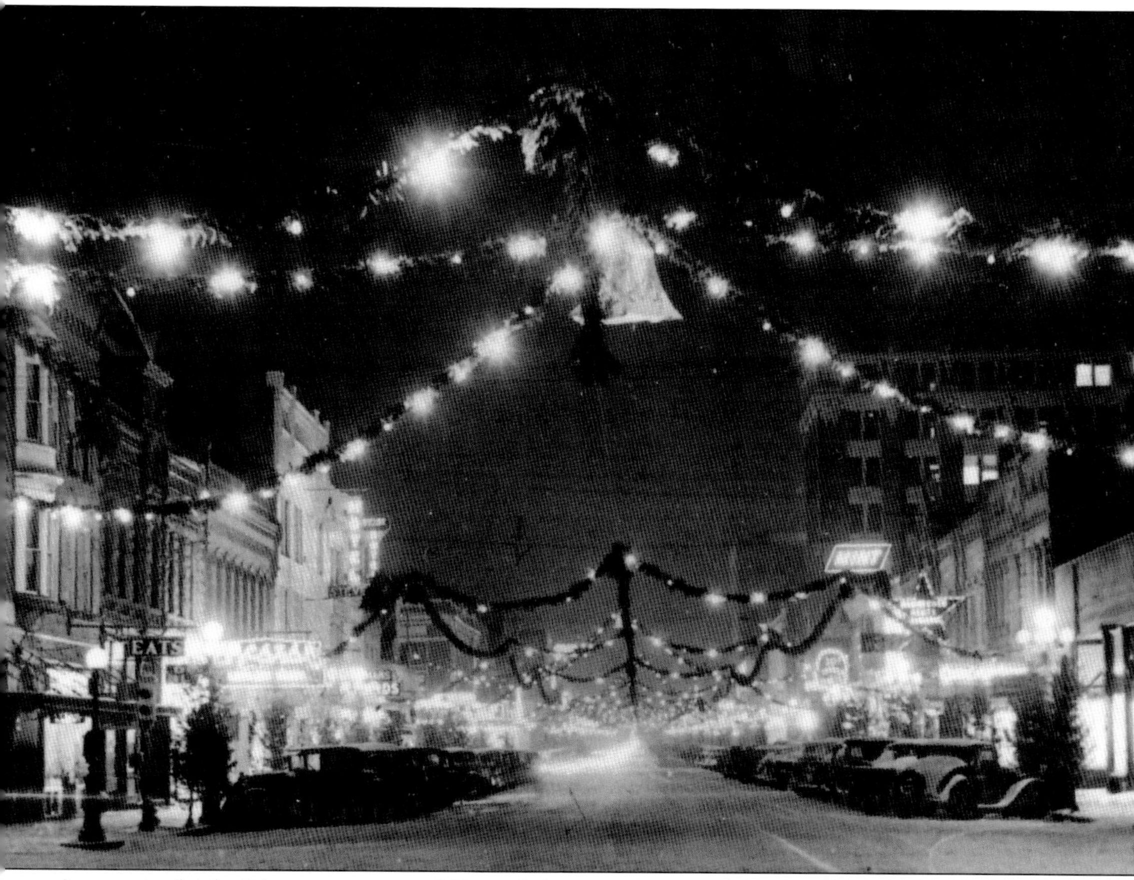

As seen in this holiday season view of Central Avenue, the city of Great Falls puts forth its finest to help celebrate the season. Looking east, the Alcazar Theatre is on the left. Murphy Maclay Hardware starts the businesses out on the right. The Mint Saloon, at 218–220 Central Avenue, was once Charles M. Russell's favored spot for passing the time with his friends. The vintage cars date this *c.* 1930 picture. (2007.17.514)

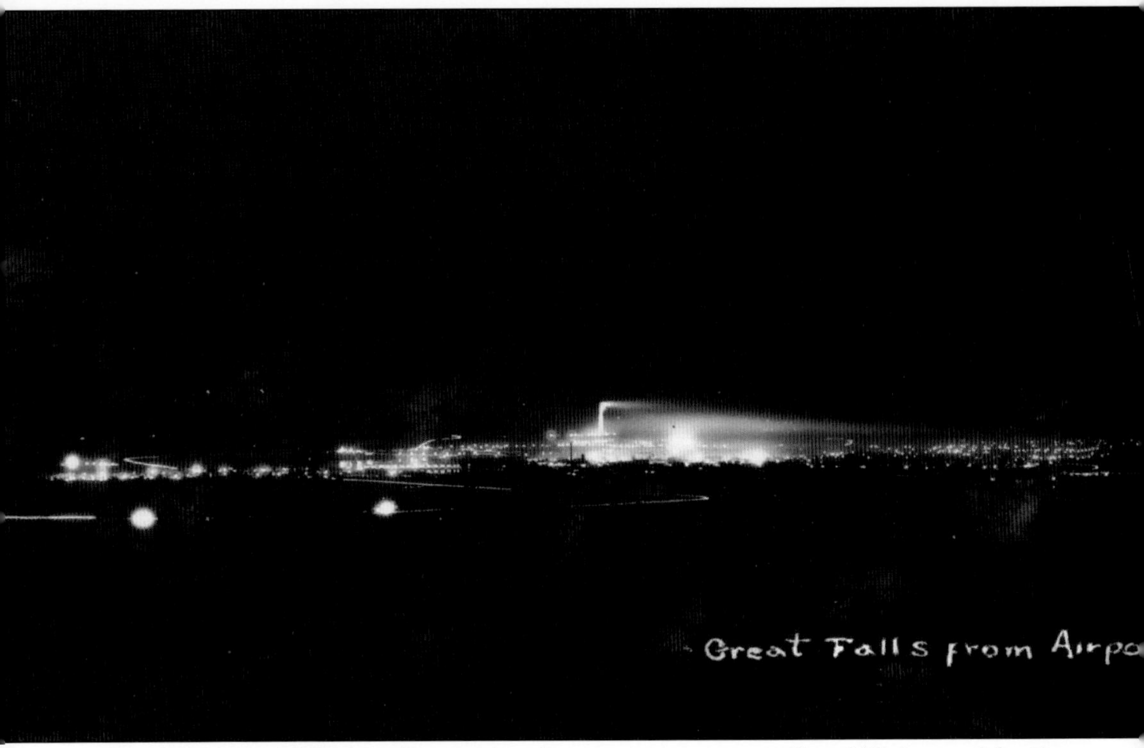

This shot of Great Falls at night was taken from a vantage point on Gore Hill, home of the Great Falls airport. Note the industrial smoke and haze being swept away by the prevailing westerly winds. The wind in Great Falls blows predominantly from the west and has earned the city the nickname "the Windy City." Even the area's first recorded visitors, Lewis and Clark, pondered why the wind blew so often and so hard at this particular juncture in their journey to the Pacific. (2006.84.24)

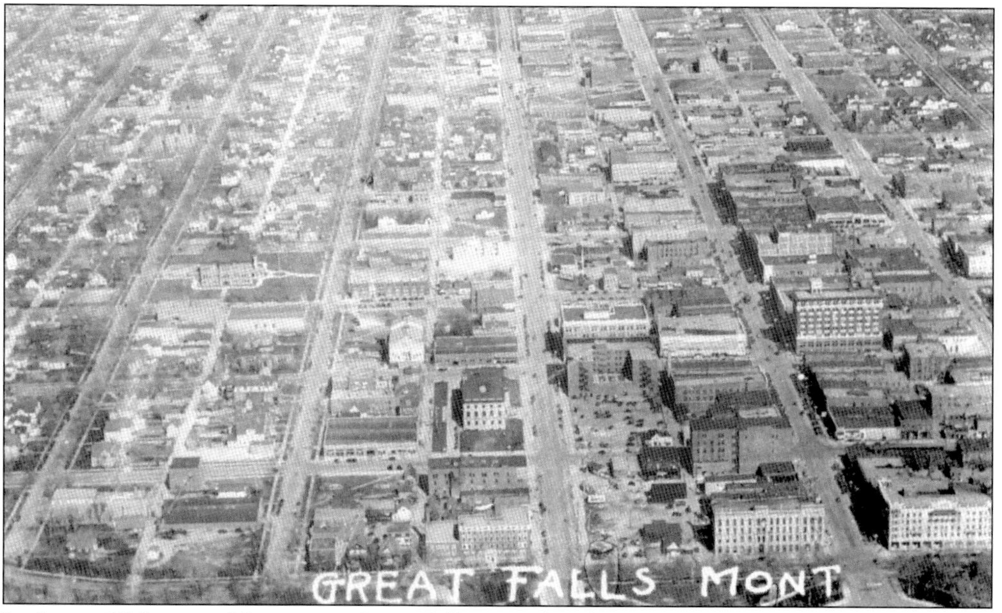

In this c. 1928 view of downtown Great Falls, note the absence of the Great Falls Civic Center. Development is clearly taking place in certain areas, but in other areas—such as the eastern end of Central Avenue—there is room for new growth. Great Falls at this time was still a heavy industrial center, with the Anaconda Copper Smelter, three (and soon to be four) hydroelectric plants, two major flour mills, and major growth in the agricultural arena. (2010.1.25)

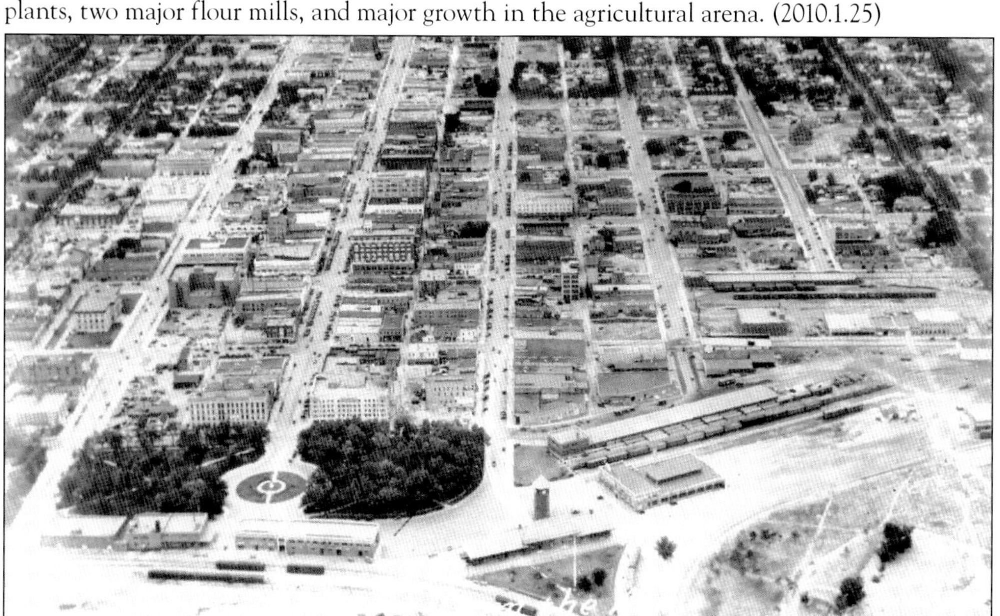

In this 1930s aerial view of downtown Great Falls, the park and circle at the west end of Central Avenue dominate the foreground along with the Great Northern Railroad station. The circle park at the end of Central Avenue would be replaced in 1939 by the construction of the Great Falls Civic Center, which would house all city government as well as provide for a grand theater. (2010.1.26)

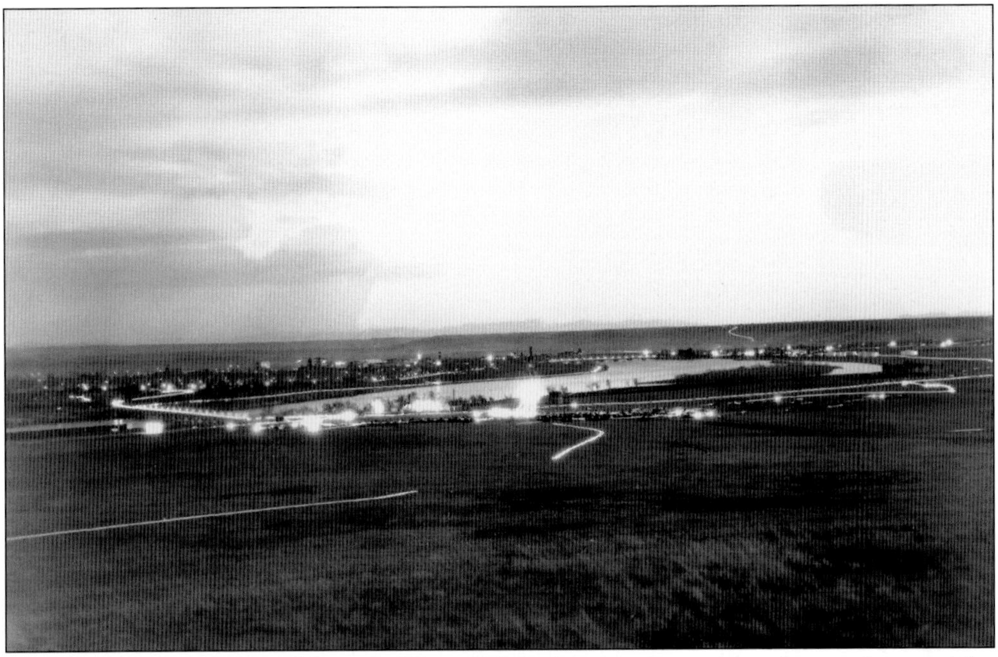

This panoramic 1928 view of the city of Great Falls looking southwest shows dozens of automobiles converging in the foreground as everyone gathers to celebrate the arrival of the town's first natural gas pipeline. The First National Bank building and the two railroad depots are visible, as are the Sunburst Oil Refinery tanks and the brick factory. (2007.17.867)

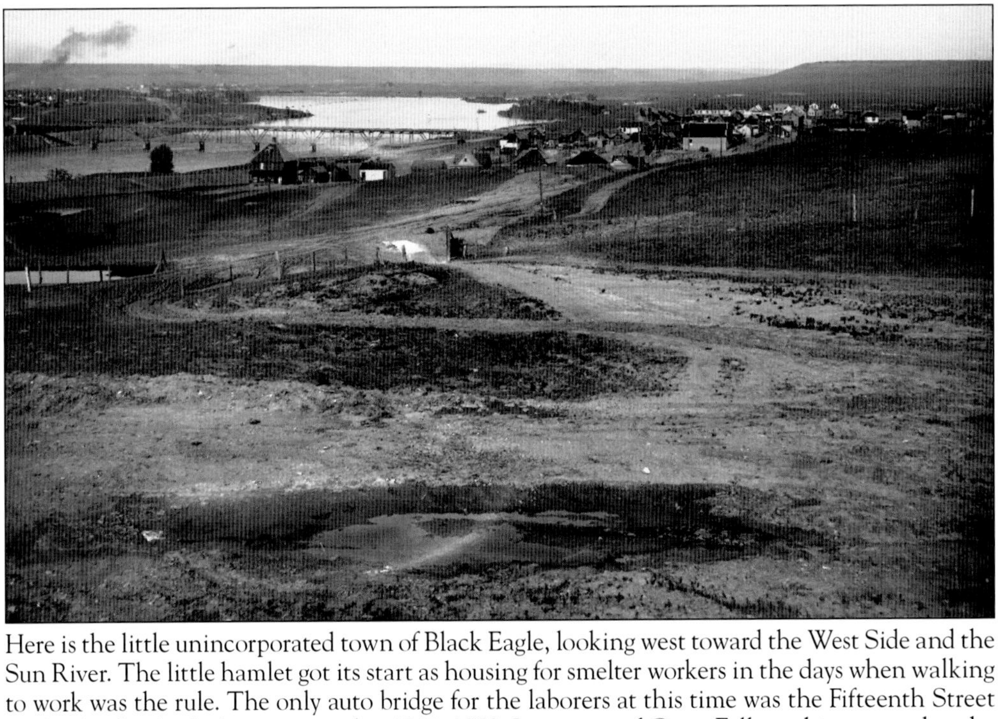

Here is the little unincorporated town of Black Eagle, looking west toward the West Side and the Sun River. The little hamlet got its start as housing for smelter workers in the days when walking to work was the rule. The only auto bridge for the laborers at this time was the Fifteenth Street Bridge (trolley bridge), constructed in 1891–1892. It connected Great Falls to this area and to the road to Fort Benton and Havre. The Tenth Street Bridge would be built later. (94.38.128)

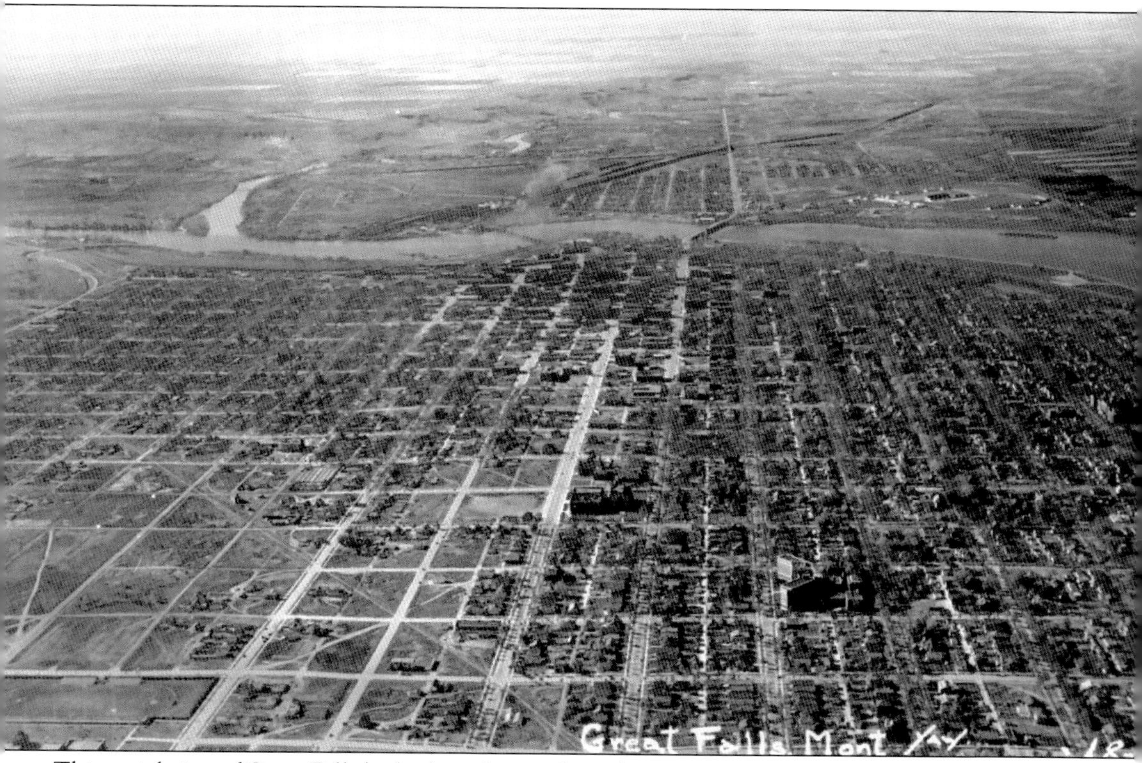

This aerial view of Great Falls looks directly west from the town's eastern edge. At the bridge over the Missouri just to the right of center, Central Avenue West continues on before it disappears in the farmland along the Sun River. West Great Falls was named Johnstown on maps made prior to 1900. It was named for John Largent, an early pioneer who attained prominence in the area. Some citizens aimed to develop Johnstown into the community's business hub. Paris Gibson wanted the city's business center closer to the hydroelectric sources and championed the idea that the city center needed to be on the east side of the Missouri. When the Great Northern Railroad established its main passenger terminal on the east bank and abandoned its west side passenger terminal, the issue was settled. Nonetheless, west Great Falls has always maintained a very prominent place in the city's business development. The Great Northern rail yards and freight trains, the Montana State Fairgrounds, and many successful and prominent businesses have kept the West Side at the forefront of economic development. (2006.84.59)

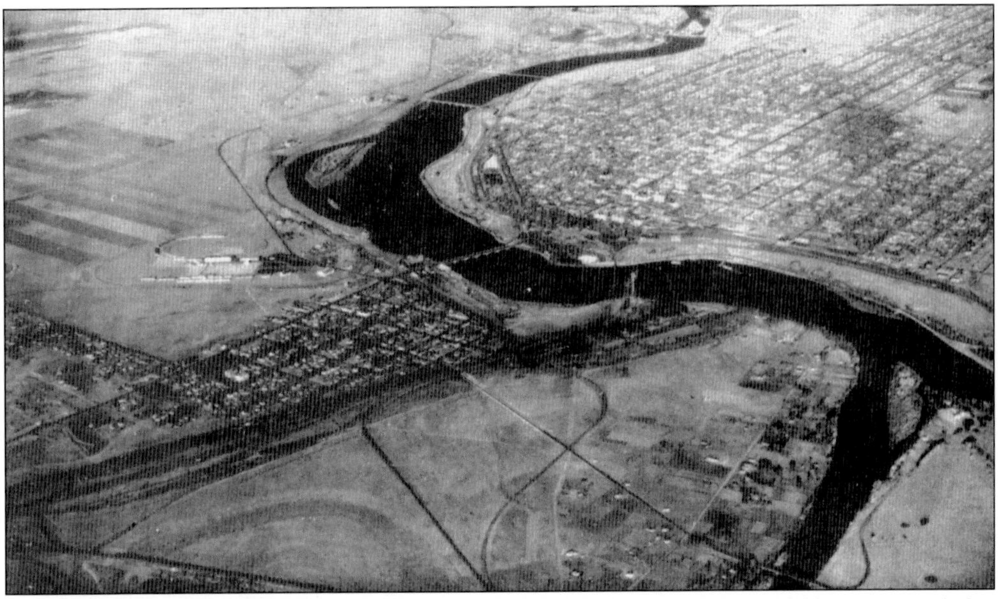

In the 1930s, at a point southwest of the city looking northeast, a photographer captured this image of Great Falls. Note the junction of the Sun River with the Missouri River. The impact of these two rivers joining at this point on the upper Great Plains made a perfect location for a large city. Ample water, arable land, mild topography, and a decidedly rapid drop in river elevations made this a perfect site for hydroelectric development. Along with the benefits of all that water, however, came the need for several bridges so that people could get across it. (2010.1.27)

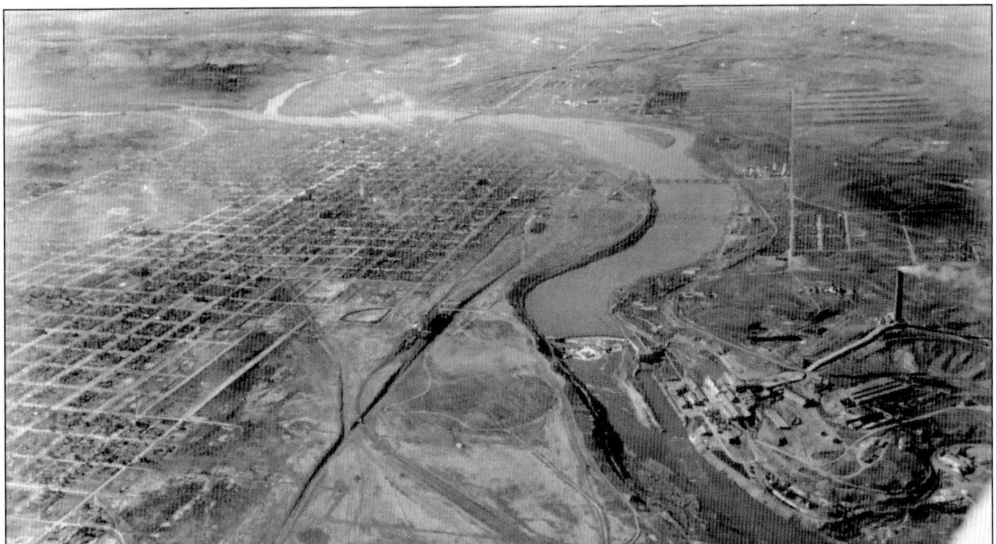

This c. 1940 view of Great Falls was taken from a point somewhere above Rainbow Dam/Giant Springs and looks south-by-southwest. Notice the prominence of Black Eagle Park in the foreground just to the right of Black Eagle Dam. Near Black Eagle Park can be seen the towering grain storage tanks of Royal Milling, later to become General Mills. Just to the left of the tanks is a baseball diamond. Also note the vast tracts of undeveloped land that lie in the city. The city grew up and built around these barren areas, only to go back and develop them in the years following World War II. (2006.84.60)

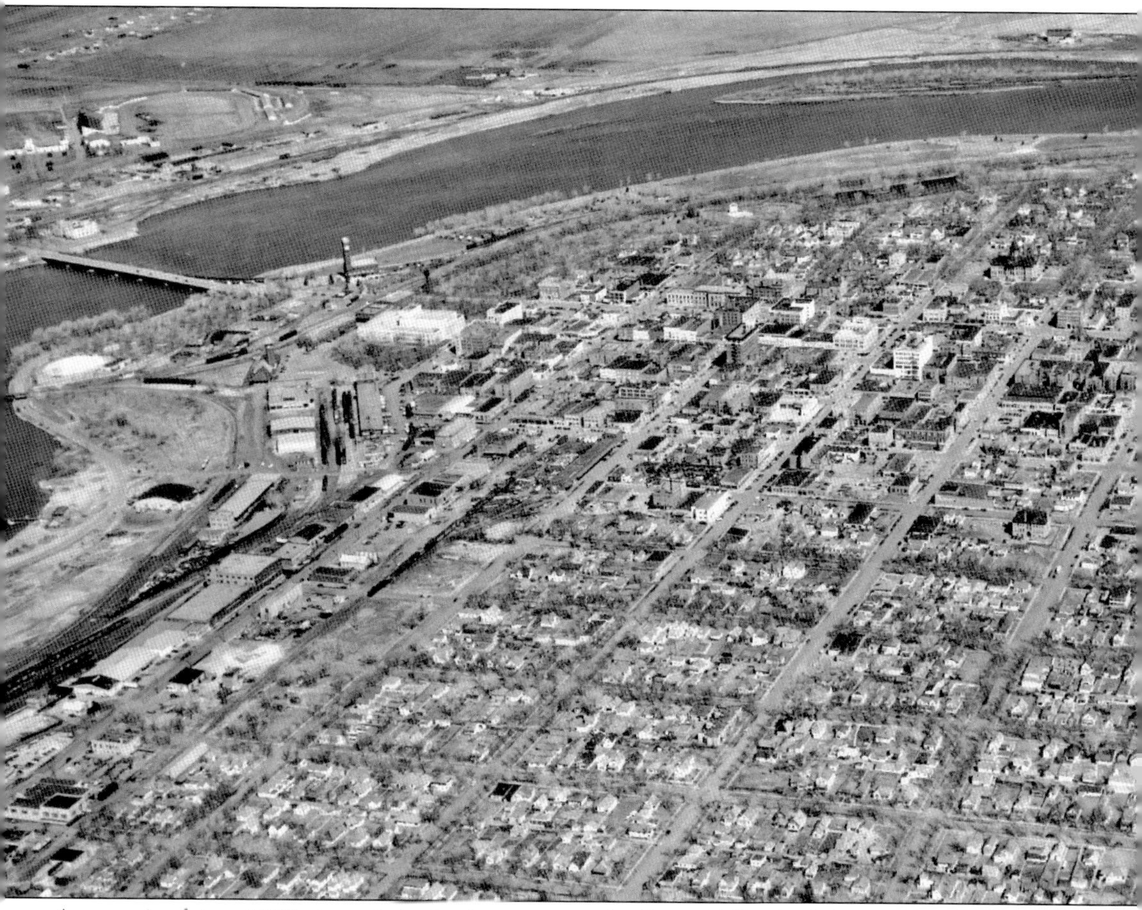

As seen in this c. 1950 view of the business center for Great Falls, the Missouri River clearly influenced the city's development. Due to its large size, it had played an important role in determining local transportation routes. Great Falls arose from its infancy around the spot where the First Avenue North Bridge connected the halves of the city. The river impacted automobile and train transportation as well as bicycle and foot traffic, electrical transmission, natural gas lines, and telephone communications. It provided many of the area's recreational opportunities, offering boating, fishing, and even swimming to residents and visitors. These activities have, in turn, played an important part in the development of Great Falls and in the character of the people who live there. From the beginning, the river has always been a primary consideration in the city's development—and rightfully so: Great Falls is fortunate to have such a natural wonder at its doorstep. (2007.17.877)

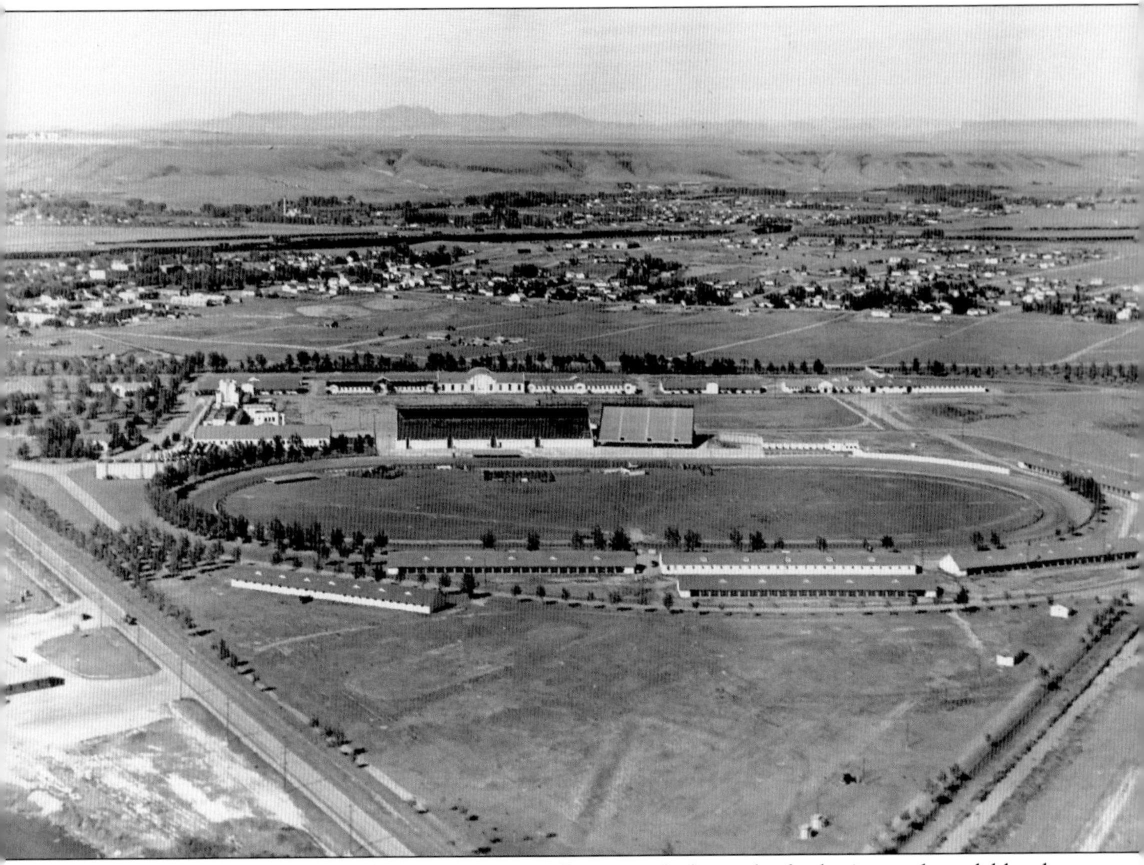

This *c.* 1940 photograph of the Montana State Fairgrounds shows the facility's grandstand, bleachers, horse barns, and art deco construction. The trees are still young. The west side has grown a little, but wide-open spaces remain undeveloped. In the background are the Adel Mountains and Square Butte. Hangars at the airport on Gore Hill are evident, as is the smokestack from the Great Falls Brewery on Fourteenth Street Southwest near the Sun River. (94.38.114)

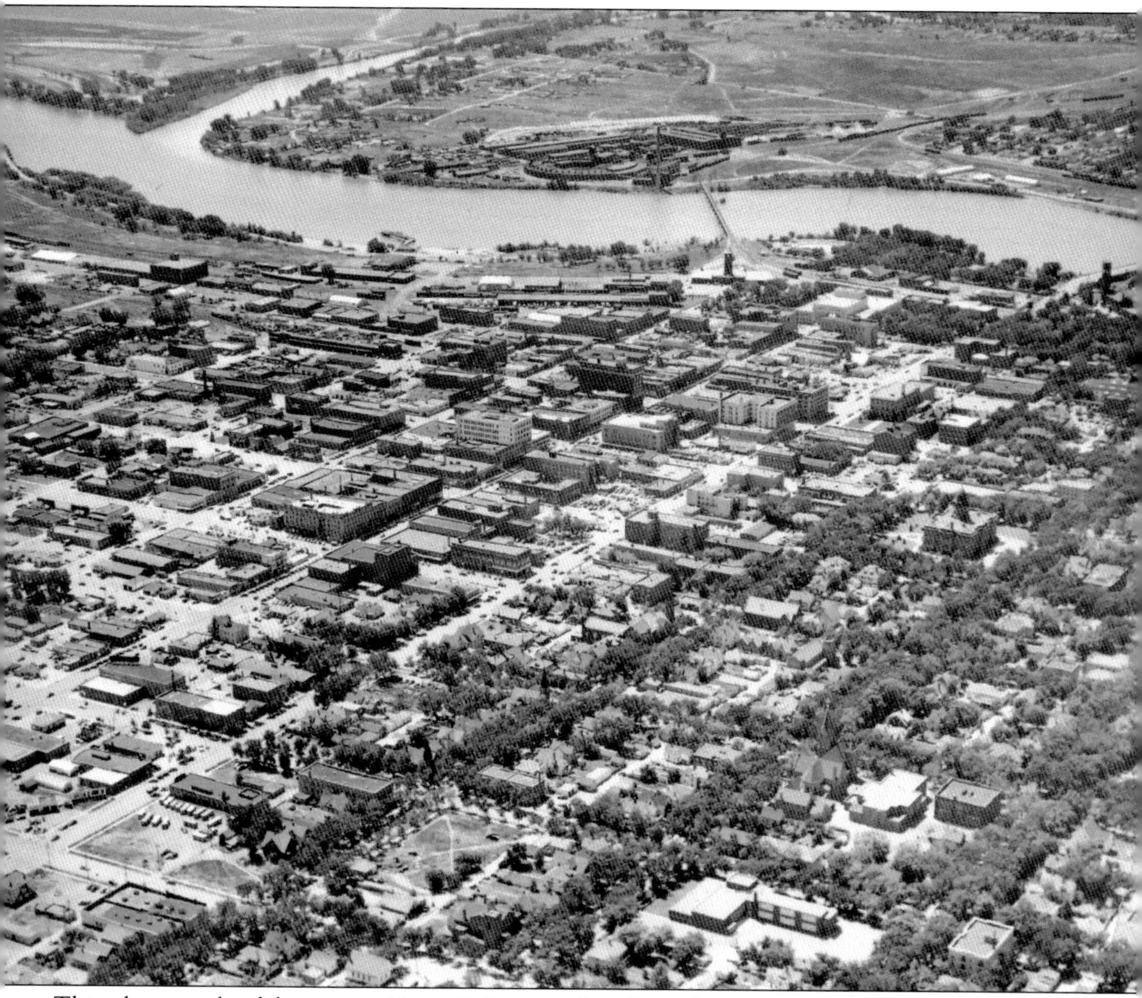

This photograph of downtown Great Falls was taken from the air on April 21, 1950, looking southwest. The treeless intersection in the lower left-hand corner of the image is Ninth Street and First Avenue North. The area to the south of the Sun River is farmland. The old boathouse rests on Broadwater Bay. A half-block piece of property sitting on Second Avenue North between Eighth and Ninth Streets is scarred with crisscrossing footpaths. Between the two bridges across Broadwater Bay is the Great Northern Railroad maintenance shop and roundhouse. (Harrington 1950APR)

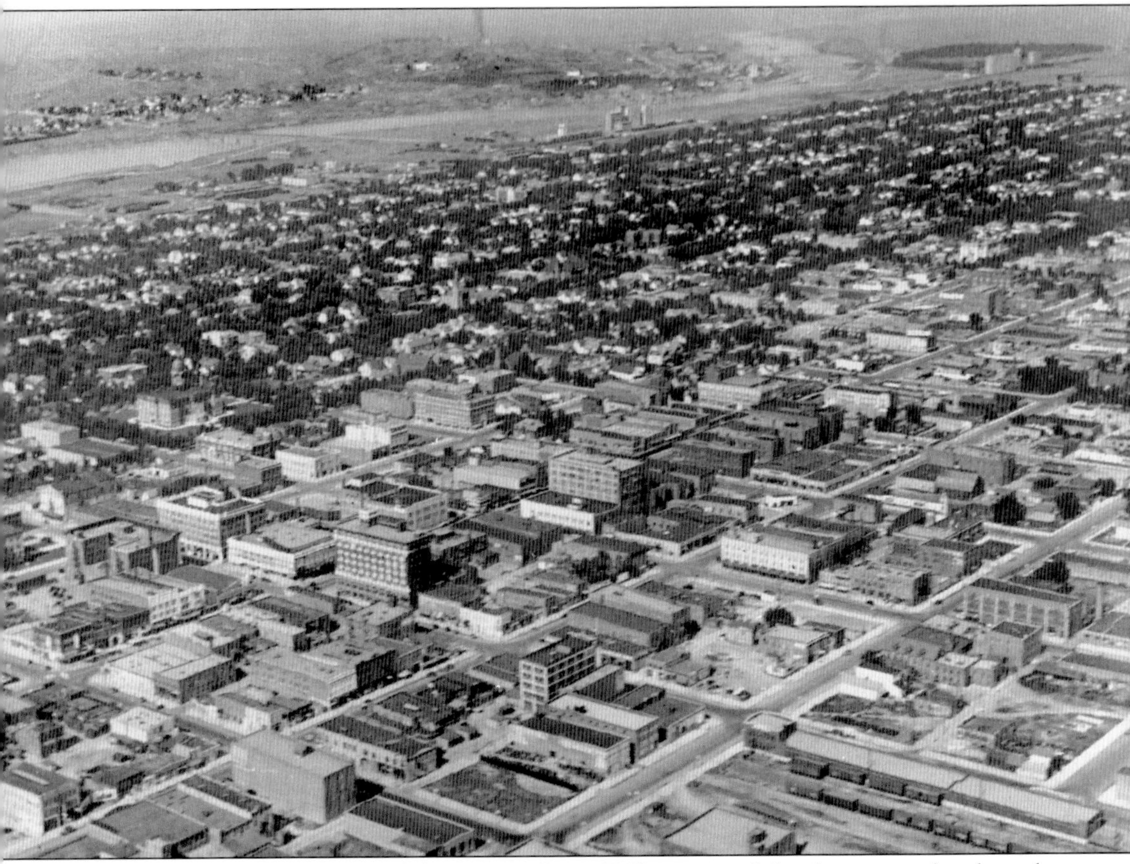

In this c. 1940 aerial view of downtown Great Falls, many of the downtown lots have been developed. In the center foreground is the intersection of Second Street and Second Avenue South. In the center background, just this side of the Missouri River, is the Montana Flour Mills Company. In the distance to the upper right are the General Mills elevators and flour mill. Just beyond the flour mill is Black Eagle Park. Across the river is the smelter, and just west of that is the small, unincorporated town of Black Eagle. (94.38.112)

Seven

Parks and Recreation

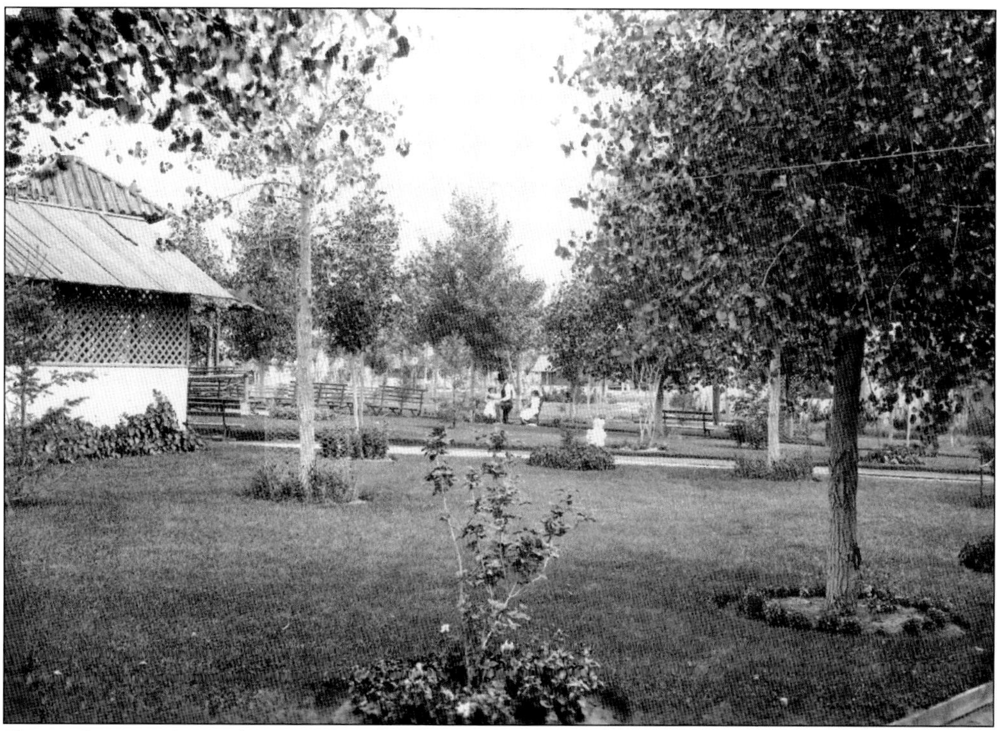

Shown here in the early 1900s, Black Eagle Park was a scenic and popular destination, as it sat above the Missouri River overlooking Black Eagle Dam, the falls, river, and smelter works. There were lots of shade trees, landscaping, tables, and benches, as well as shelters, making it very attractive to local residents. (94.41.62AA)

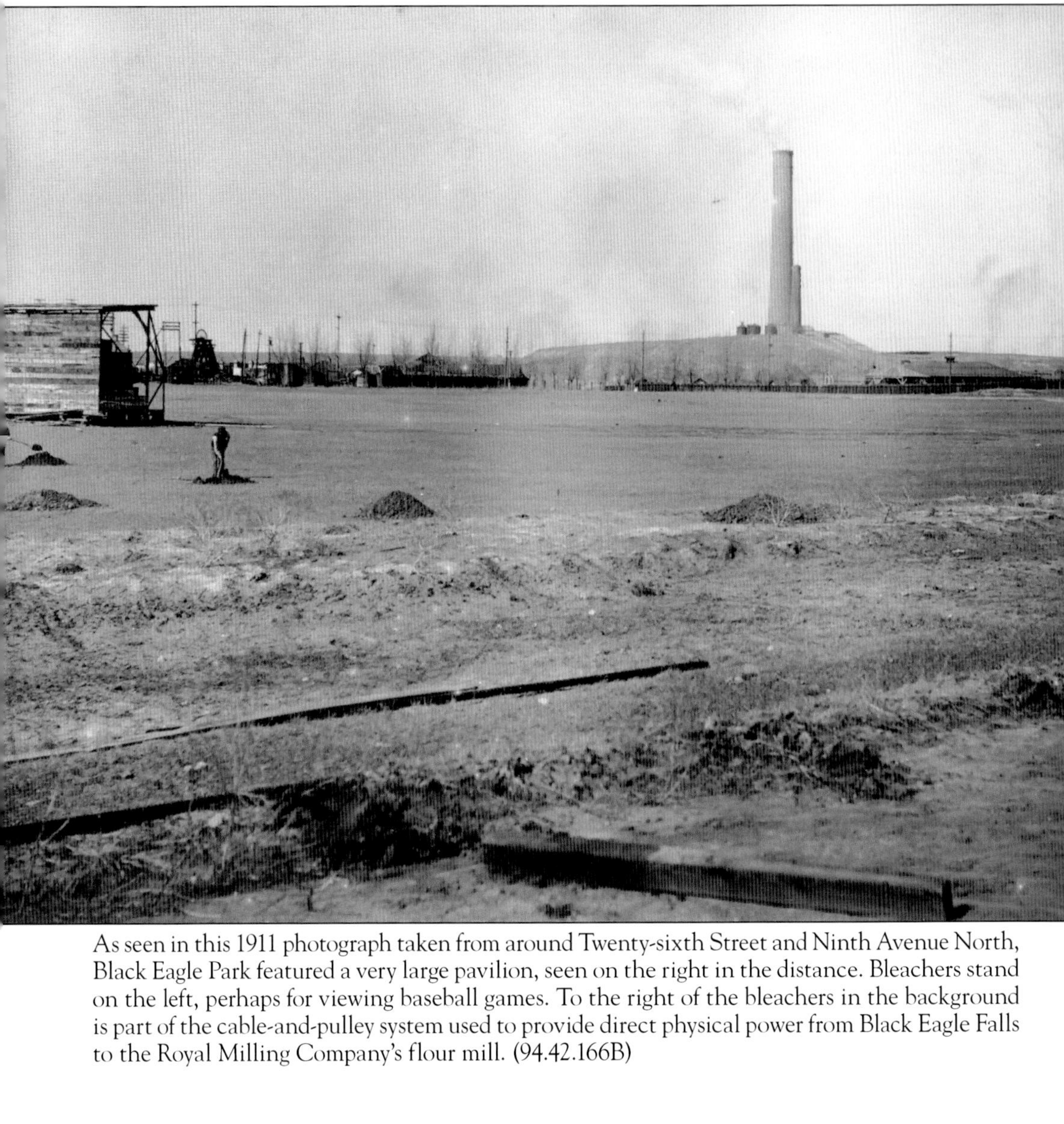

As seen in this 1911 photograph taken from around Twenty-sixth Street and Ninth Avenue North, Black Eagle Park featured a very large pavilion, seen on the right in the distance. Bleachers stand on the left, perhaps for viewing baseball games. To the right of the bleachers in the background is part of the cable-and-pulley system used to provide direct physical power from Black Eagle Falls to the Royal Milling Company's flour mill. (94.42.166B)

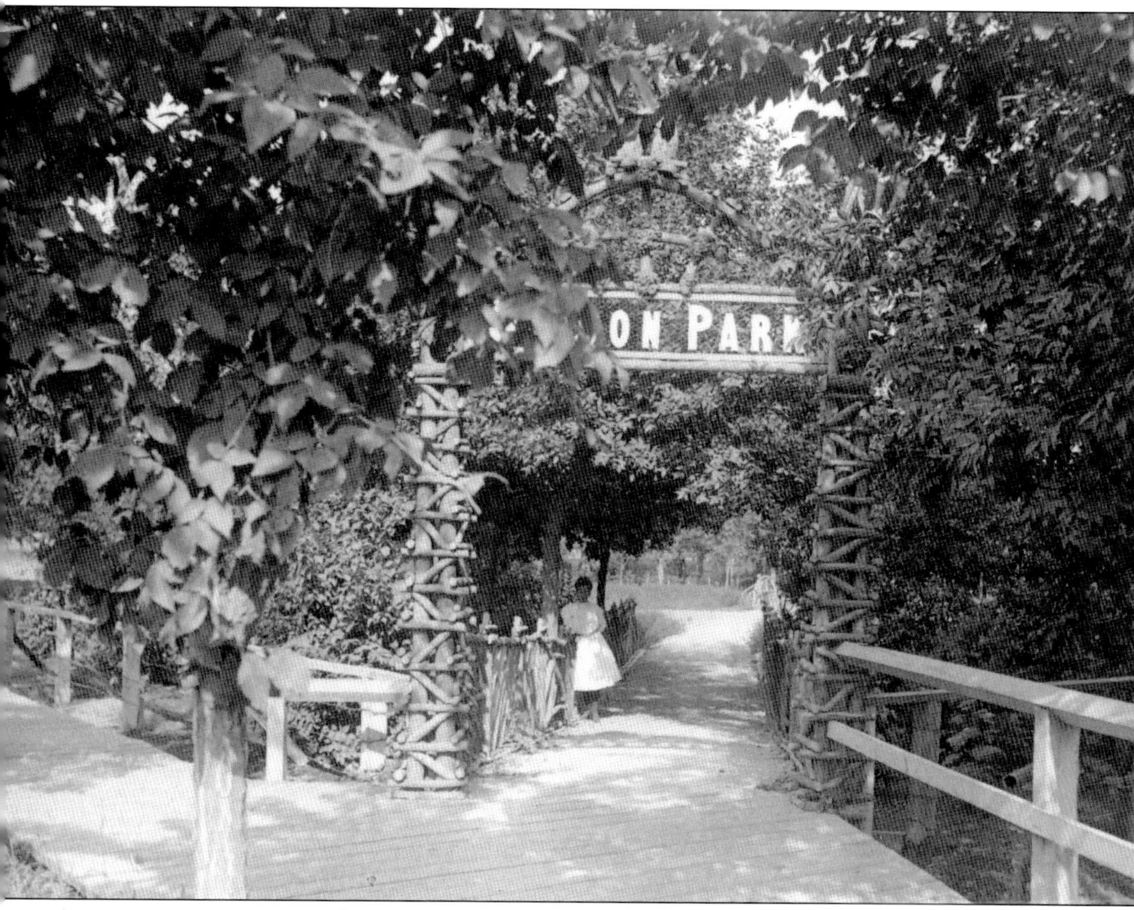

A gorgeous entrance to Gibson Park is enhanced here even more by a lovely young woman. The entrance is located near the intersection of First Avenue North and Park Drive. Curiously enough, Gibson Park started out as Cascade Park in 1887, and it wasn't until 1903 that the name was changed to honor 73-year-old Paris Gibson, founding father of Great Falls. (2007.17.644)

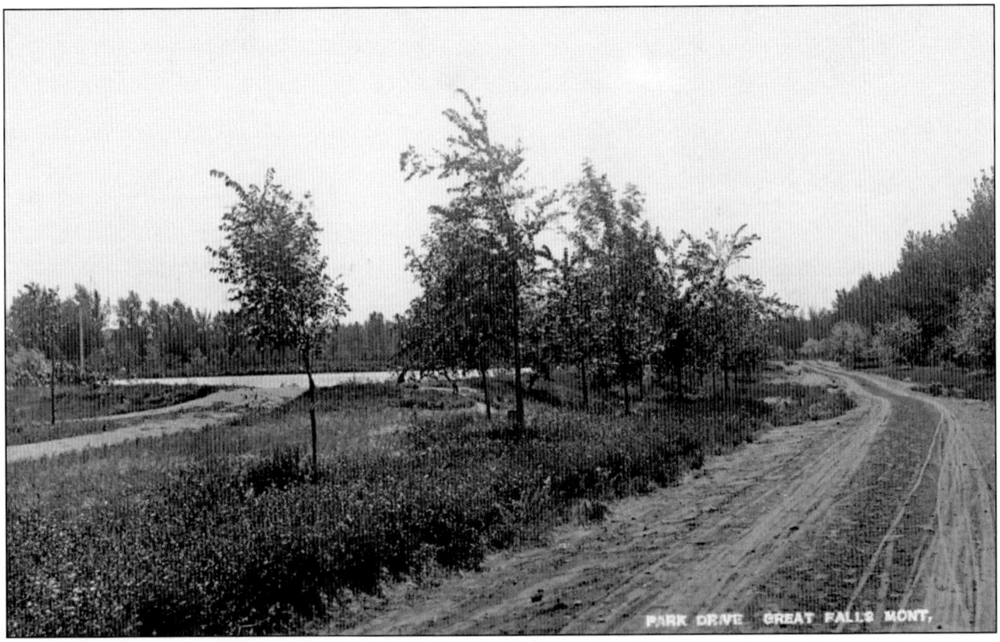

Gibson Park is shown here in a very early postcard scene. At this point, the roads are unimproved dirt, which works well for sightseers as long as the weather is dry. With rain, the roads could become a sticky gumbo quagmire that was next to impossible to negotiate. Gibson Pond is seen at left, as yet largely without improvements. (2010.1.28)

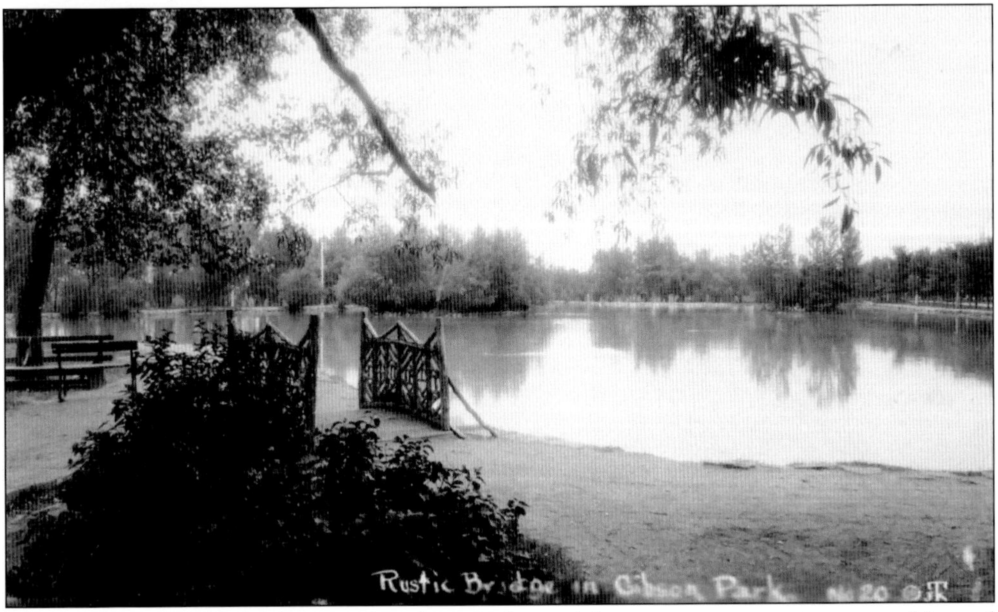

In this early postcard of Gibson Park and Pond, the city's largest, most attractive, accessible, and well-maintained park flourishes with flowers and shade trees. It had pens of wild animals and was a haven for birds, including a variety of waterfowl. This quaint bridge was one of many things that made the park so attractive to locals. The lake abounded with planted fish. The Missouri River flowed nearby. It was very close to downtown and also to the main thoroughfares of the city. (2010.1.29)

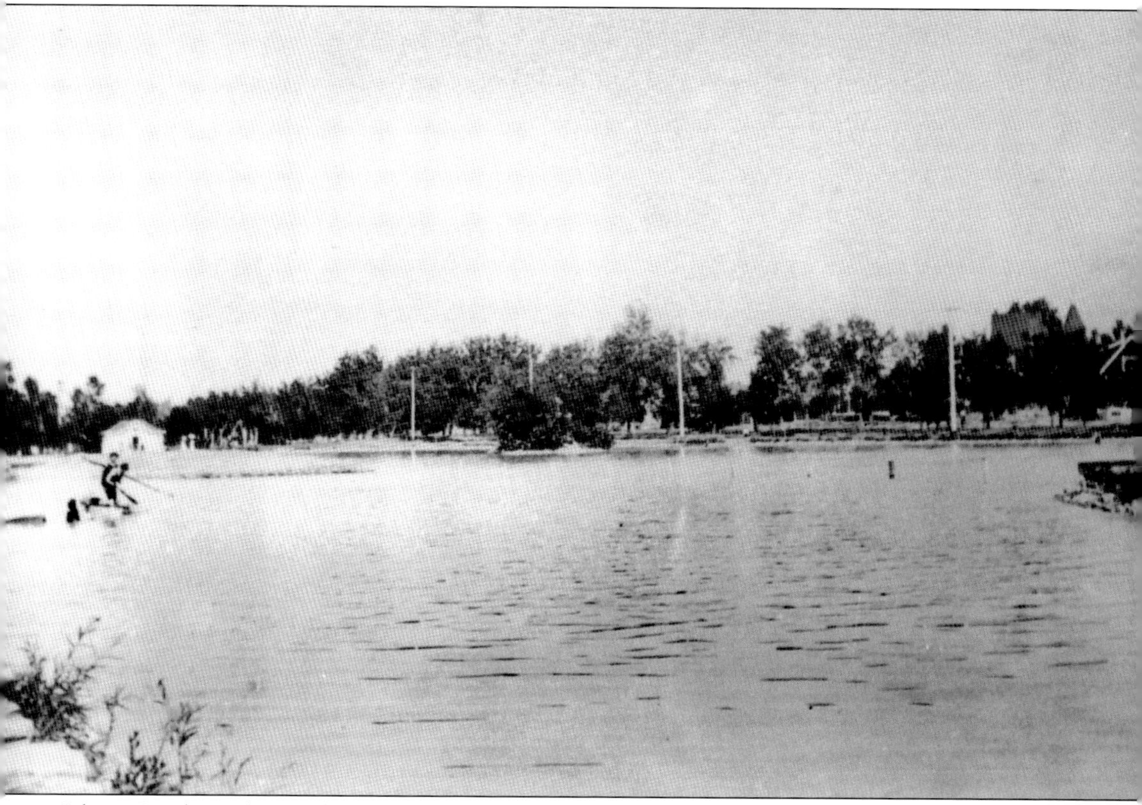

Gibson Pond was designed into the city plan early on. Paris Gibson, founder of the city, wanted to insure that his town had an adequate amount of what he considered essential for a beautiful town—parks and trees. This park pond, located just north of downtown, was originally used for all kinds of recreation, including boating and swimming. Two young fellows can be seen in this photograph as they try to maneuver their little watercraft across the treacherous waters of their imagination. (2007.17.311)

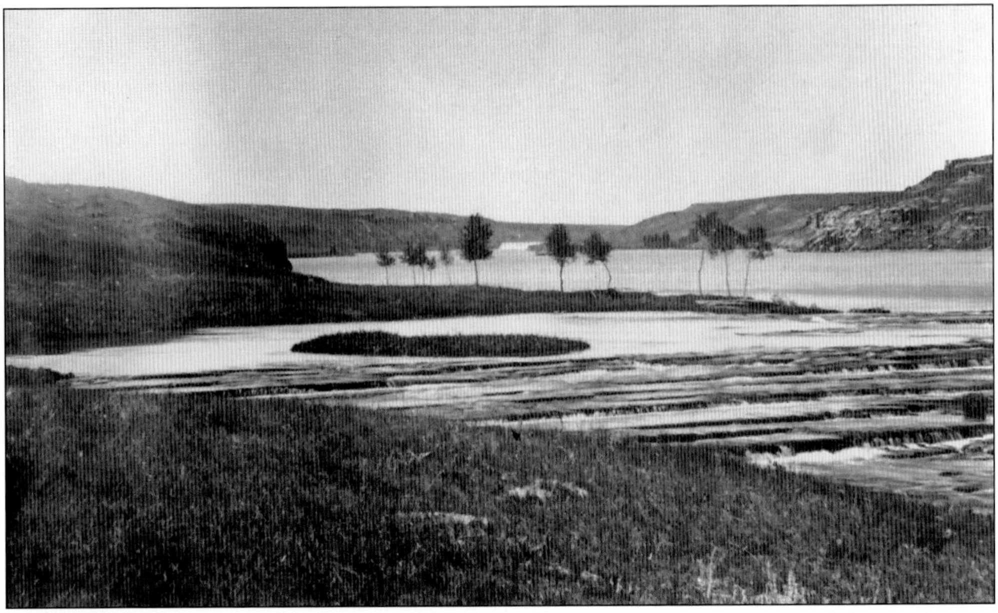

This 1884 image of Giant Springs is the earliest known photograph of one of the area's most famous landmarks. Beyond the odd-looking trees, the river can be seen turning to the right. Farther upstream, a small section of Black Eagle Falls is visible. Remarkably little vegetation can be seen between the springs and the falls. This may be due, in some small part, to the cooler climate that has ruled for the last several hundred years. This period, called "the little ice age," was much cooler than the present and may account for the limited vegetation. (94.38.179BB)

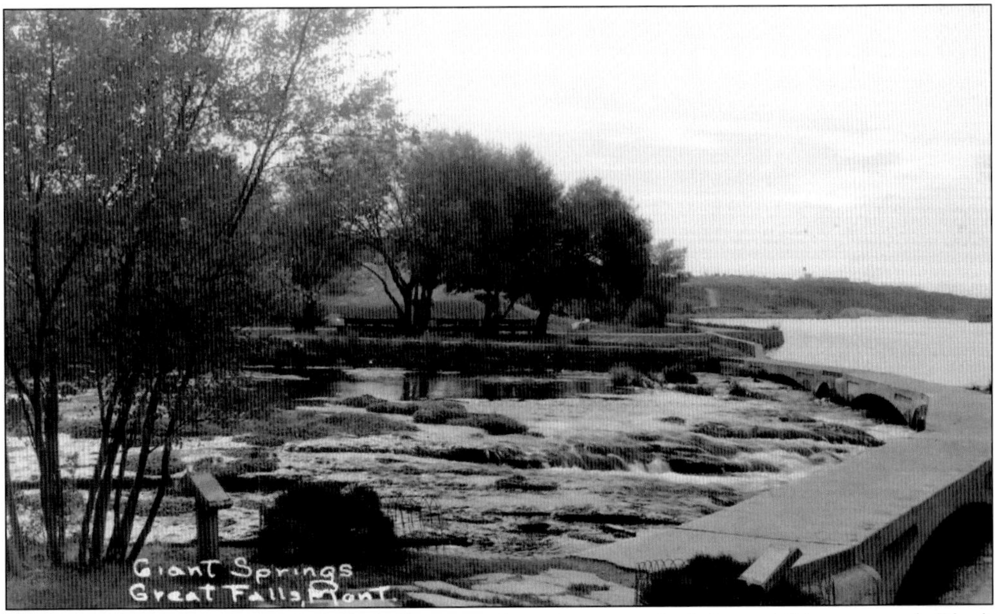

This is Giant Springs around 1940, looking south and west up the Missouri River towards Black Eagle Falls. Always a favorite spot for sightseers and picnickers, it was also a favorite fishing spot. The Montana State Trout Hatchery was also a point of interest for visitors. Development of this park began in the late 1920s, though it had been a major point of interest since the founding of the city. (2006.84.28)

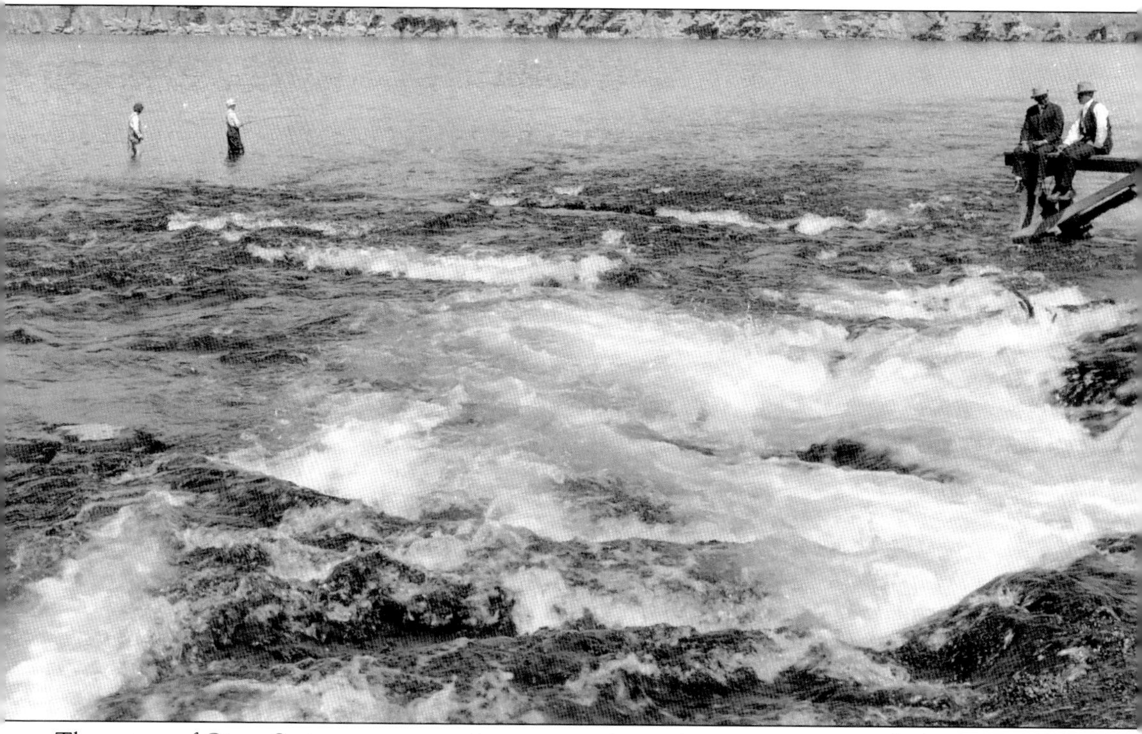

The waters of Giant Springs surge over the mossy rocks on their way to meet with the waters of the Missouri. Upon discovering the springs on June 18, 1805, William Clark wrote that he thought it was the largest spring or fountain he ever saw. This water was a favorite place for fishing or for cooling off during the summer. Both of those activities are taking place in this early photograph. The crystal clear water flows at a constant volume of 156 million gallons per day at a constant year-round temperature of 54 degrees Fahrenheit. (90.26.19)

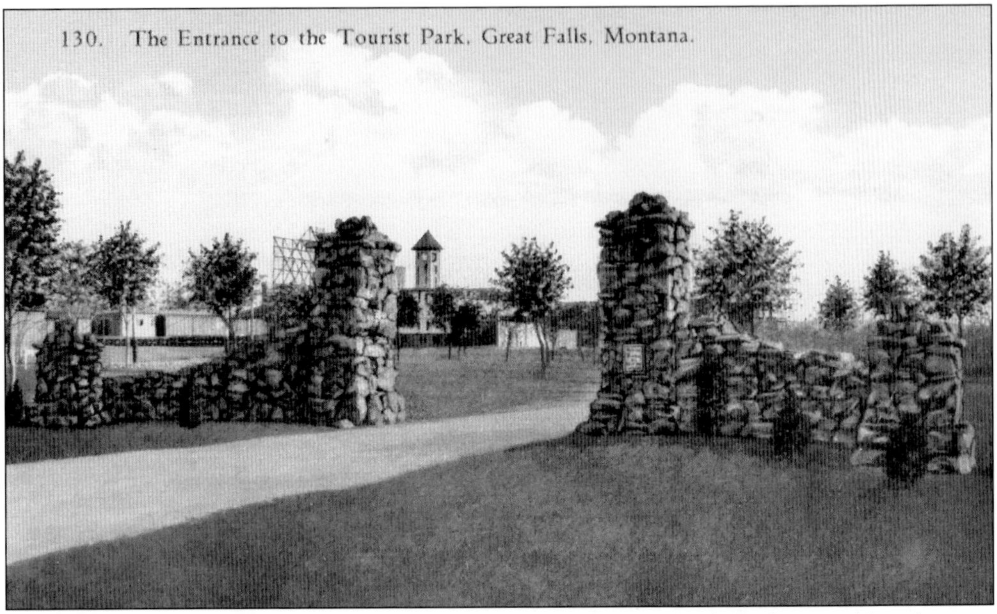

The Tourist Park, located on the south side of the First Avenue North Bridge, would evolve into a swimming pool and wading pond in the 1930s, but in the days when this postcard was printed, the park was still being used as a place to park the car and pitch a tent. In the background stands the Great Northern Railroad depot tower. (2010.1.30)

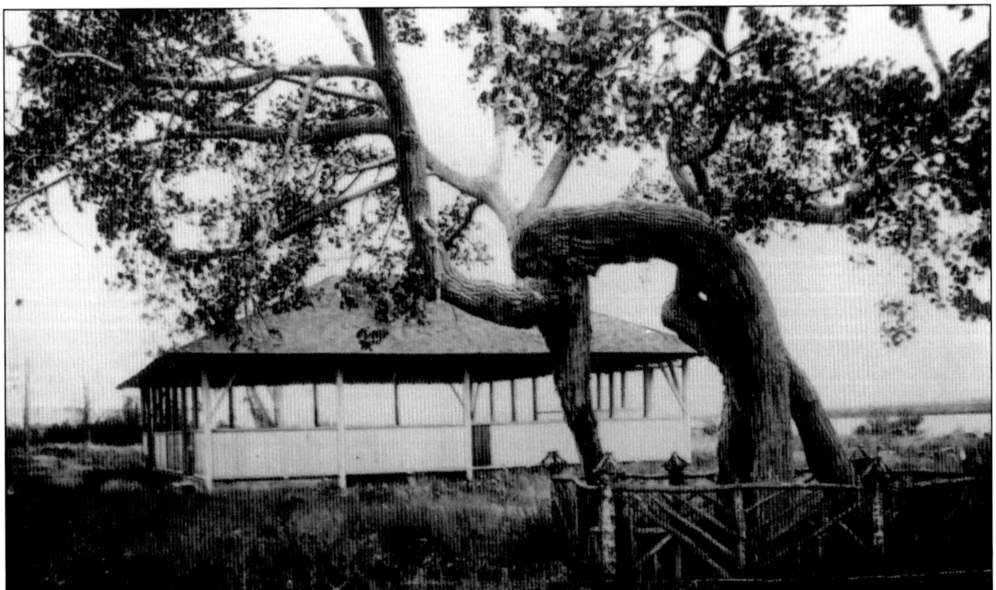

A large shady pavilion shelter near the Missouri River gave picnickers a chance to get out of the sun and relax. The curiously deformed tree near the shelter acquired the name "Lewis and Clark Tree," but nobody seems to know why. (Perhaps someone saw the letters "L C" in the tree's twisted trunk?) Note that the ornate fence around the tree was made with limbs to give it a very special rustic look. This dancing pavilion was part of the facilities at Riverfront Park, and when a band was available, dances were held there. This park later fell under the ownership of the Milwaukee Railroad, but it remained open to the public. (2007.17.6)

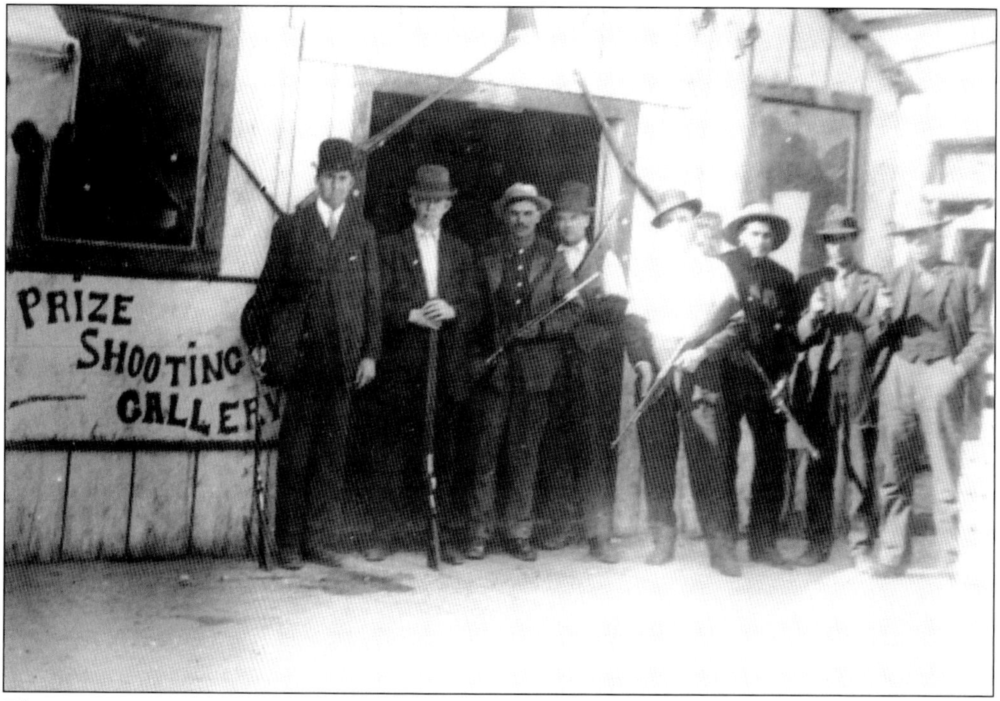

There were not many forms of recreation in early Great Falls, but one sport fit very well with the Western life: shooting. It seemed like everyone owned a gun, so what better way to capitalize on that than by opening a shooting gallery? Seen here in 1908, the Prize Shooting Gallery was located on Second Street South between Second and Third Avenues South. (2007.17.158)

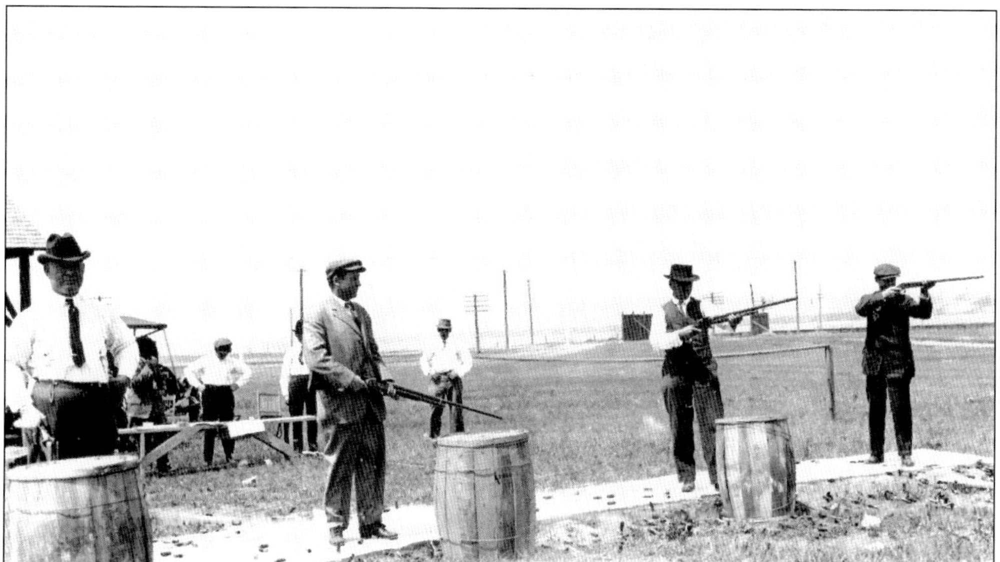
In this 1920s photograph, shooters at a range near the Sun River are after the clay pigeon, and from the look of the numbers of spent cartridges, they have been enjoying themselves immensely. Dressed in suits, these men are enjoying a "gentleman's sport." (2007.17.310)

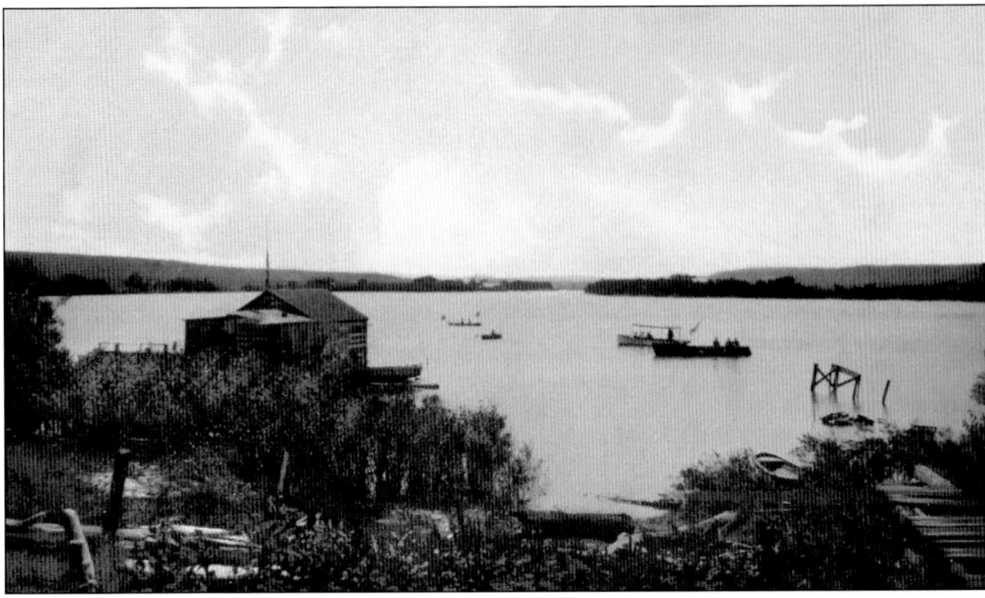

Broadwater Bay stretches out from the old boathouse just upstream from the Burlington Northern Railroad Bridge. On the *1893 Missouri River Survey*, this was the head of what was labeled "The Long Pool," which stretched upstream for 65 river miles. This was a favorite place for families to gather on warm summer days. Broadwater Bay took its name not from the broad expanse of water but from prominent Montanan Col. C. A. Broadwater—banker, businessman, rancher, railroad financier, and politician. However, the name seemed a good fit. (2010.1.31)

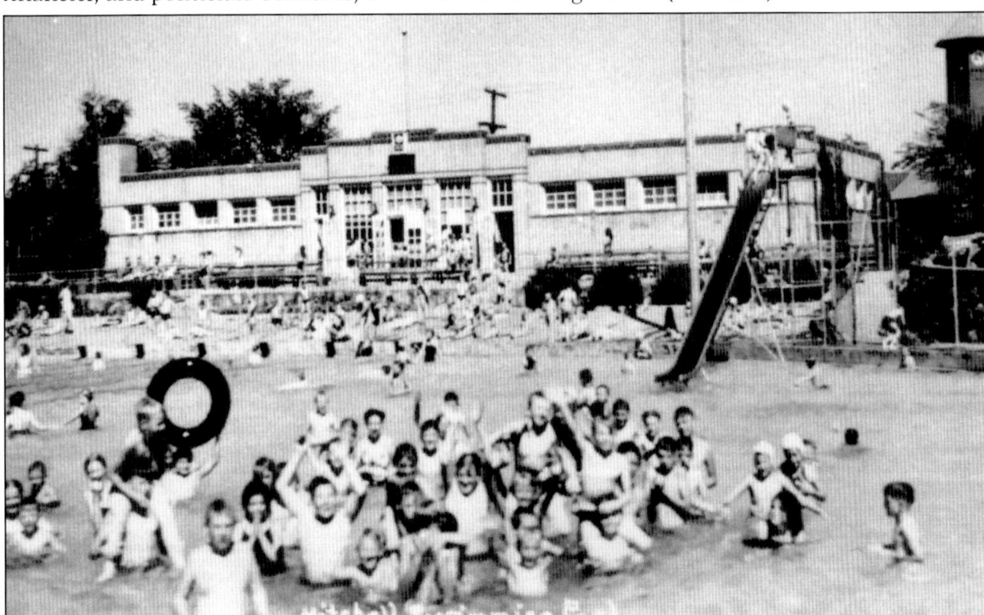

The first public outdoor swimming pool in Great Falls was the Mitchell Swimming Pool, completed and opened to the public in the 1930s. A city pool, it was operated by the Great Falls Parks and Recreation Department. As the only public outdoor pool in town, it was a haven for children all summer long. Here they could let their pent-up energy loose while staying cool and enjoying the camaraderie of their friends and schoolmates. (2007.17.1)

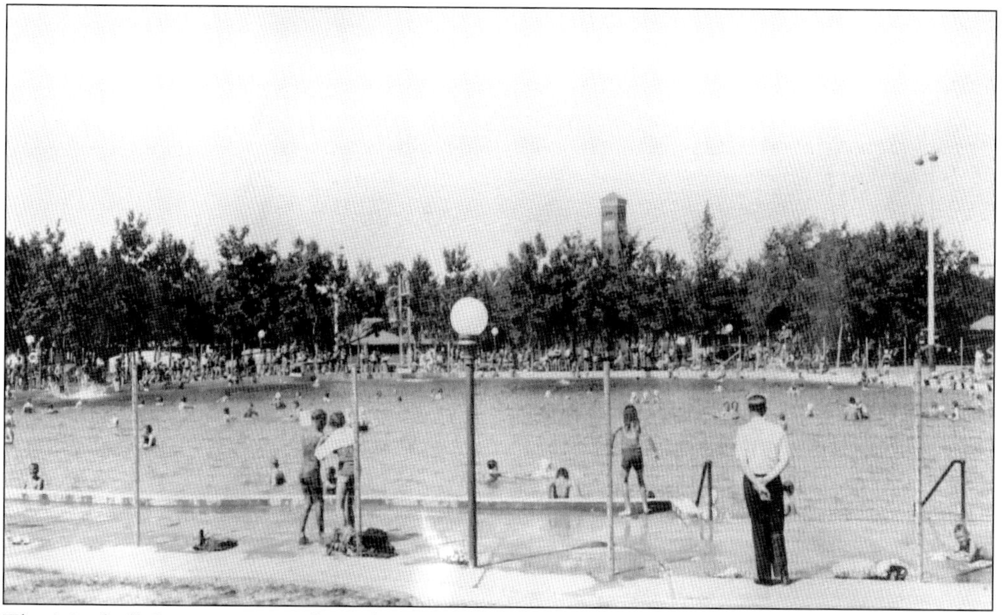

The Mitchell Swimming Pool was located very near the east bank of the Missouri River, just upstream from the First Avenue North Bridge. In this photograph, the Milwaukee Railroad station tower stands in the background. This large swimming pool was used not only as a spot to swim, exercise, sunbathe, or just cool off but also to meet and spend time with friends. Great Falls had very few other places that could be used as a common meeting place throughout the summer. (MOE93.11.27J)

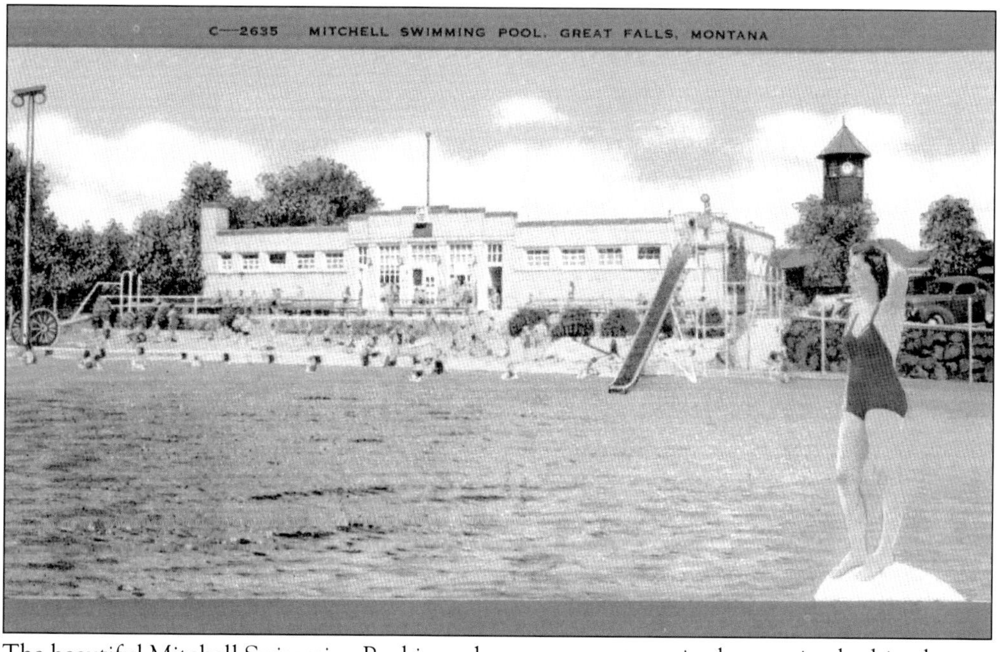

The beautiful Mitchell Swimming Pool is made even more attractive by a posing bathing beauty in this postcard from the late 1930s or early 1940s. (98.72.162)

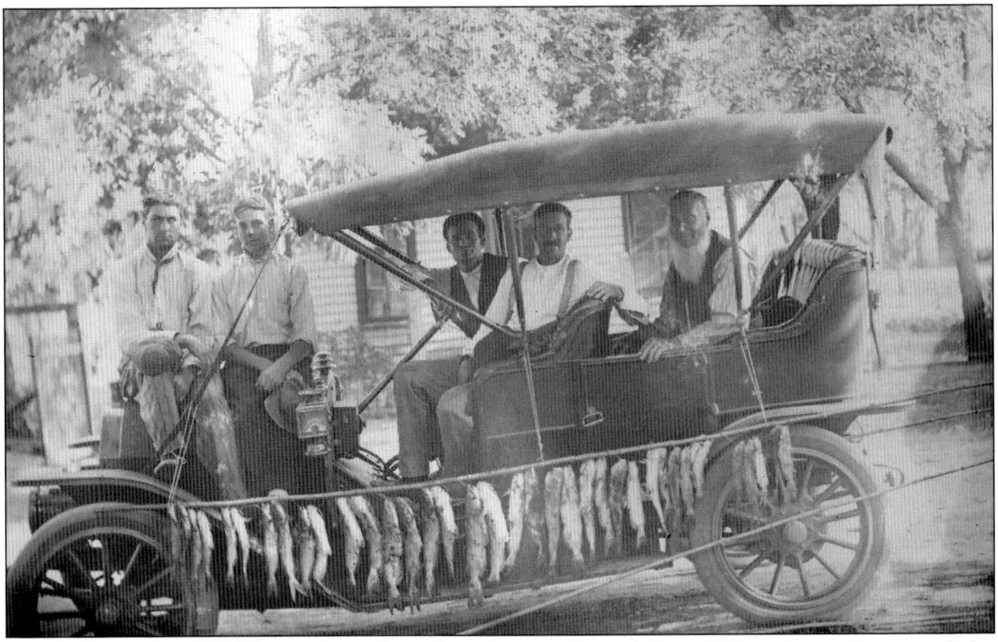

Recreation and sport fishing abound on the Missouri River. These fellows have discovered the bounty the river offers with a short drive downriver. Channel catfish are plentiful in the Missouri downstream from the last falls. From Morony Dam to St. Louis, catfish inhabit every stretch of the river. These fellows have had remarkable luck and took the time to share their bounty with the world through a photograph. (MOE93.111.27K)

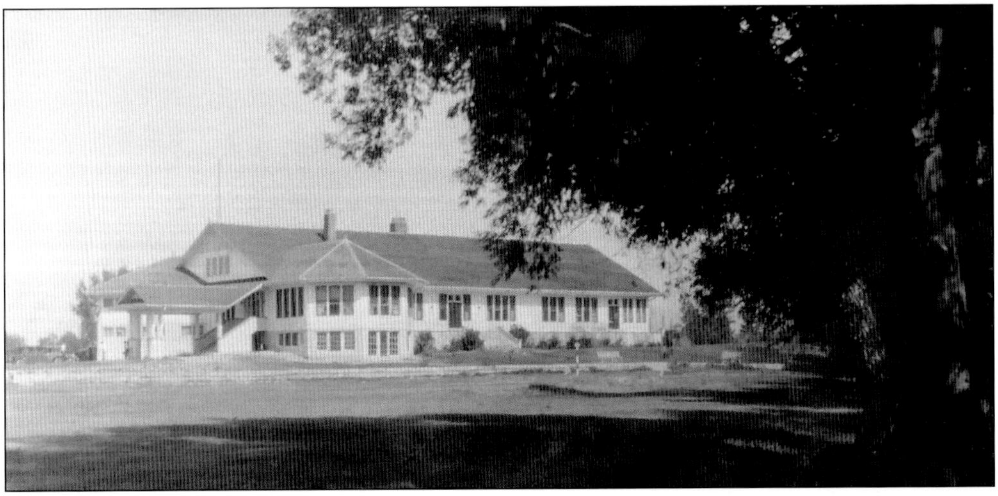

The Meadowlark Country Club Clubhouse was located on the west bank of the Missouri River very near the mouth of the Sun River. The Meadowlark Country Club boasted one of the finest golf courses in Montana and was very popular as a center of social functions as well as a place to play golf in one of the most attractive settings available—along the Missouri River. Organized in 1919, the Meadowlark Country Club bought land for a clubhouse from Paris Gibson for $47,500. The clubhouse was completed in 1921 and was formally opened on May 28 of that year. On the list of 139 original members was Charles M. Russell, the famous Western artist. The membership roster read like a "Who's Who" for Great Falls. Membership in the club at that time cost $50, an especially large sum of money in those days. (2006.84.18)

Eight

Great People

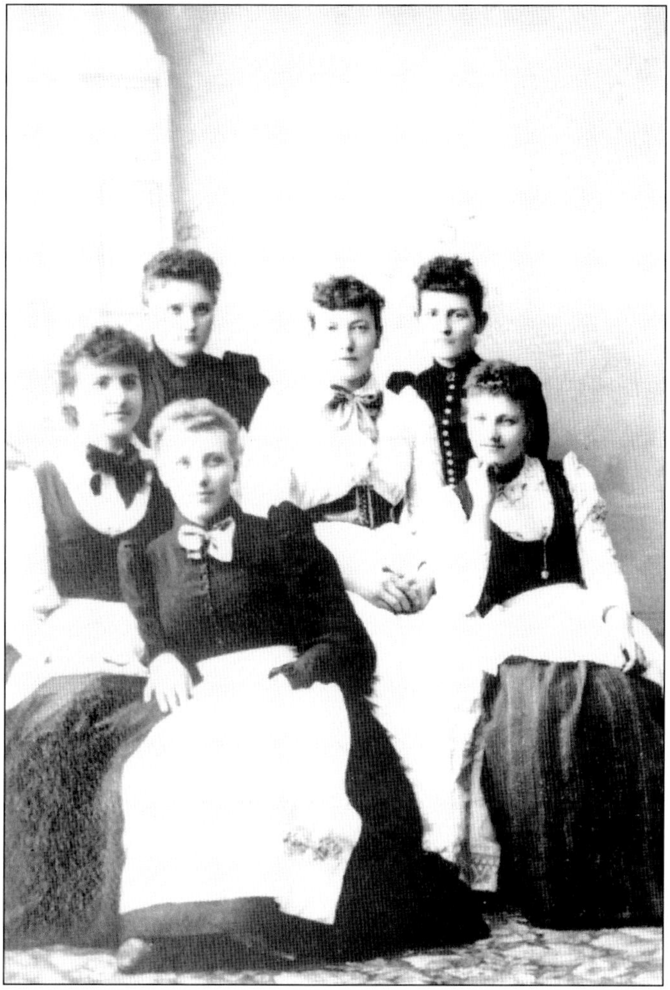

This group of charming young women worked at the Arcade Restaurant, 219 First Avenue South. The names of these girls, photographed in 1891 or 1892, are lost to the sands of time. The restaurant had several owners in those early years, including Thomas Howells, Walter Thompkins, and Clara Holt. The Arcade advertised, "Good meals for 15¢ and up. We serve good steaks, bread, butter, and first class coffee and tea with every meal." (2007.17.370)

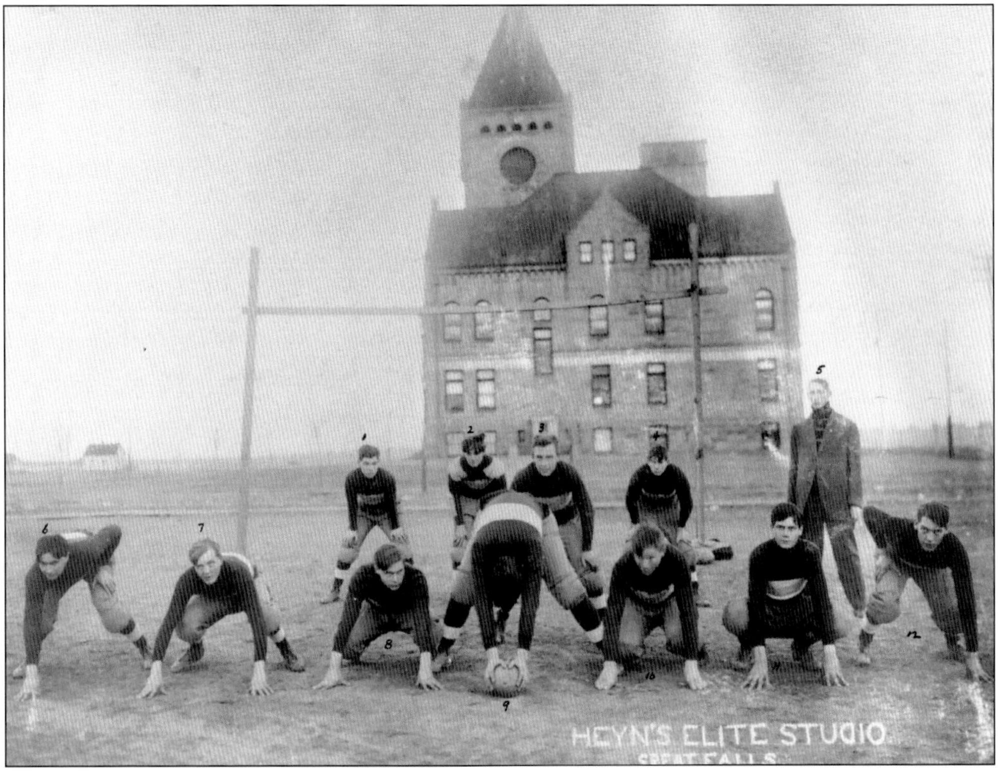

The Great Falls High School football team scrimmages in 1905 in the field on the west side of the school. The original Great Falls High School sat between Fourteenth and Fifteenth Streets and between Central Avenue and First Avenue North. In 1929, this became Paris Gibson Junior High School, and it would remain a junior high for the next 40 years. (2004.57.2)

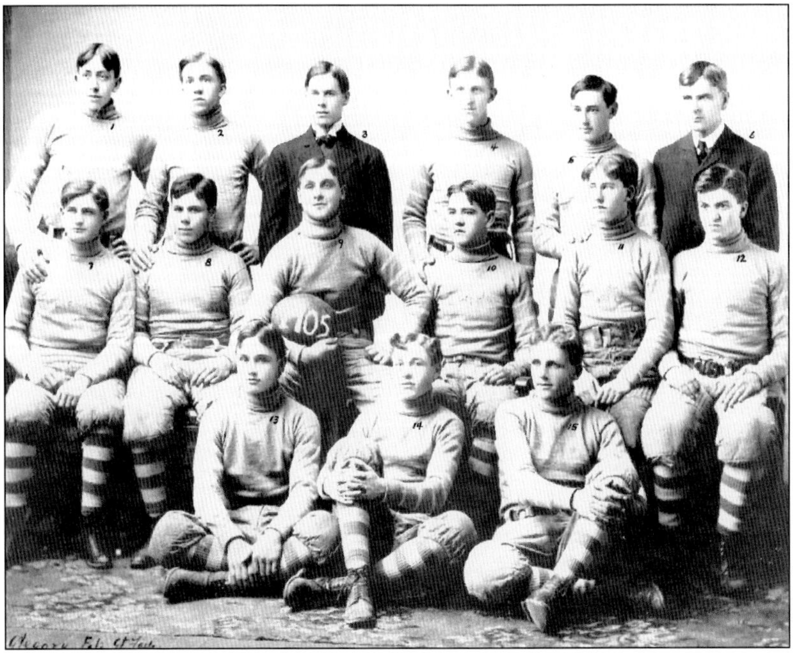

Players on the 1905 Great Falls High School football team included (1) George Campbell, (2) ? Sengbush, (3) ? Birkenbule, (7) Oscar Vogel, (8) ? Williams, (10) ? Copeland, (11) Roy Dailey, (14) Steve Doyle, and (15) ? Fisher. The other players pictured here are unidentified. (2004.57.3)

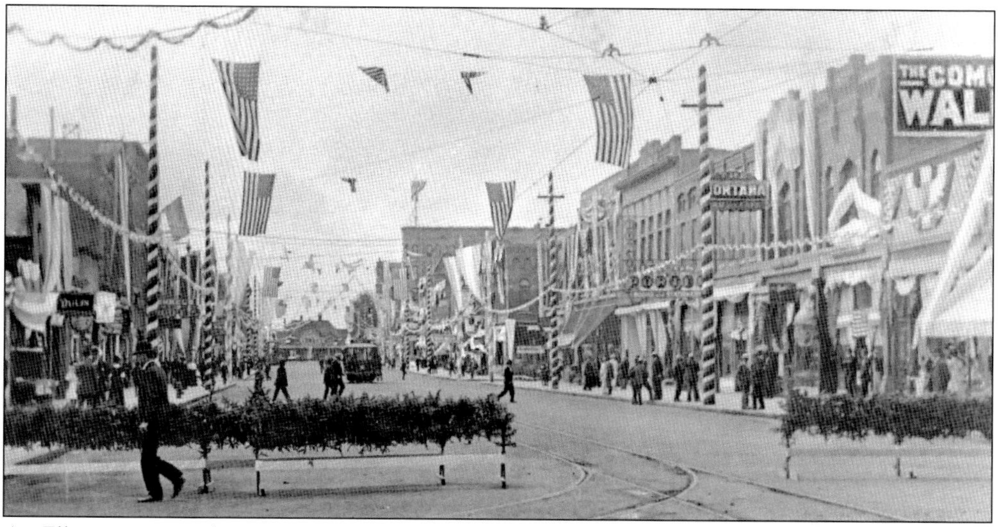

An Elks convention began in Great Falls on Wednesday, August 12, 1908. These early conventions were a very important economic boost for the community. Businesses started touting the convention a week beforehand to promote sales of items in connection with the event. On August 5, an advertisement for Verge's Store asked, "Are you 'Fit' for the Elks' Convention? Are you fit to receive the Elks? The Elks' convention will be a GALA OCCASION for Great Falls. It will be a jolly occasion. At least a thousand of Montana's gayest, jolliest, bravest men will be here for THREE DAYS. They should be entertained in an elegant way by Great Falls' prettiest, dressiest, smartest women." The advertisement goes on at length about what a young woman should buy to prepare herself for the Elks. This photograph was taken at Central Avenue and Fourth Street. (2007.7.515)

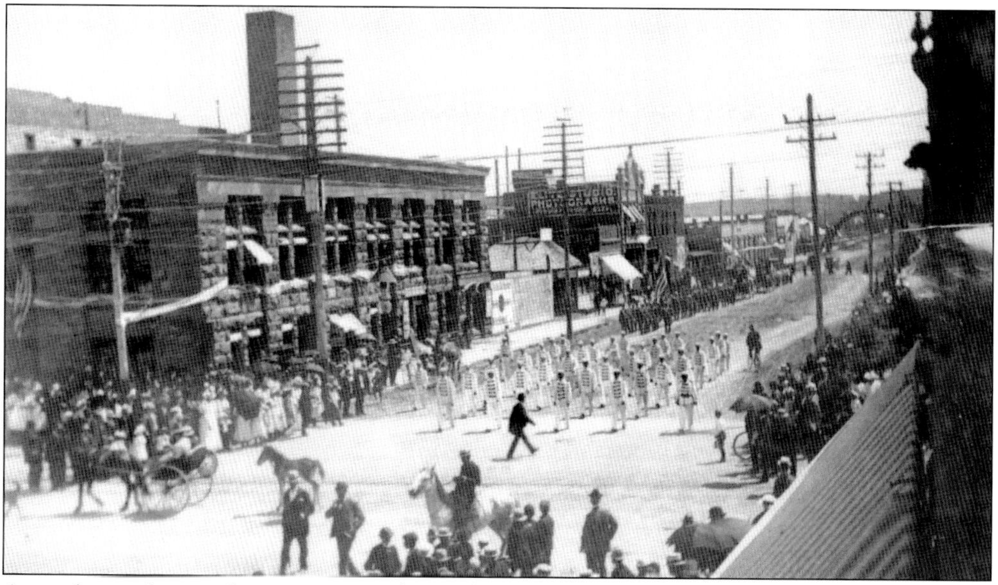

An early parade is working its way north on Third Street South as it approaches Central Avenue. The Flambeau Marching Band can be seen approaching in its smart white uniforms. The sandstone blocks from the original First National Bank's lower levels can be seen on the corner. In 1913, the bank would expand to add a steel superstructure in support of what would become the tallest building in Great Falls. Elite Photographic Studio can be seen across the street and down a block. (2007.17.517)

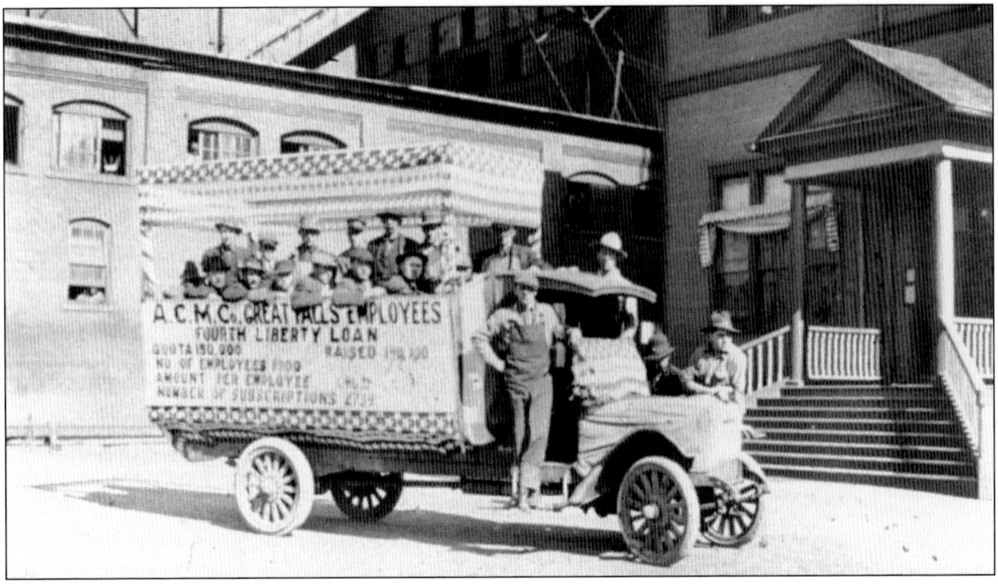

World War I inspired a tremendous amount of national pride, as shown in this photograph. Employees of the Anaconda Copper Mining Company all proudly join the Liberty Loan Truck as it makes its rounds of the grounds at the smelter on the north side of the Missouri River near Black Eagle Falls. Their quota was $150,000, and thus far they had raised $140,100 from their 1,900 employees. (96.98.23)

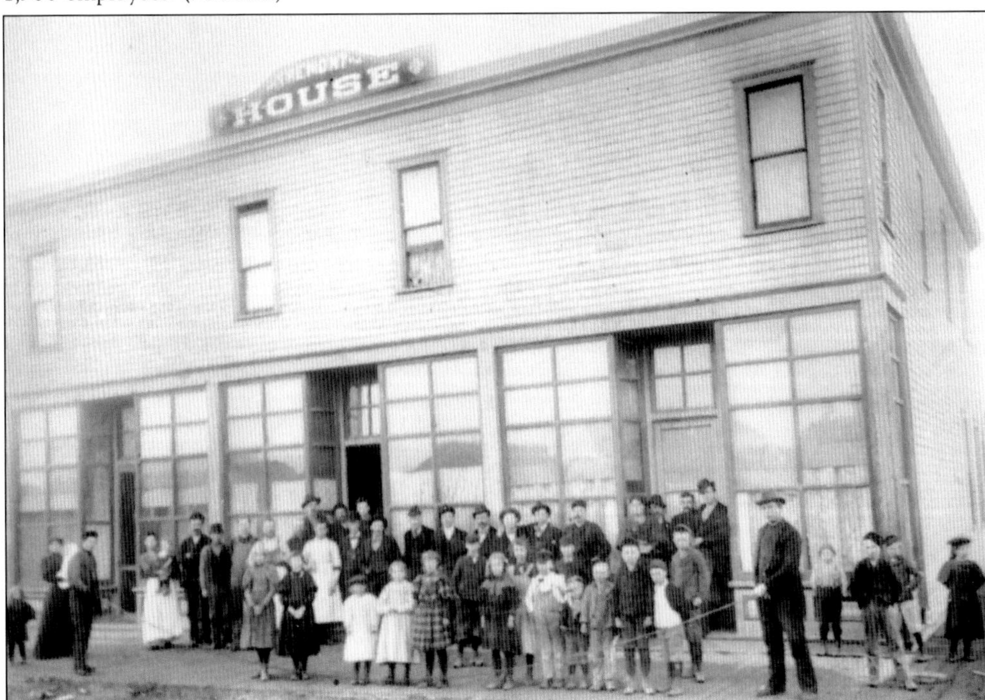

In this late-1890s photograph, a large group stands in front of the Tremont House, a hotel at 505 Fifth Street Southwest in Johnstown. The two gentlemen holding opposite ends of a long rope in front of the children appear to be ready to help with a game of jump rope. (2007.17.484)

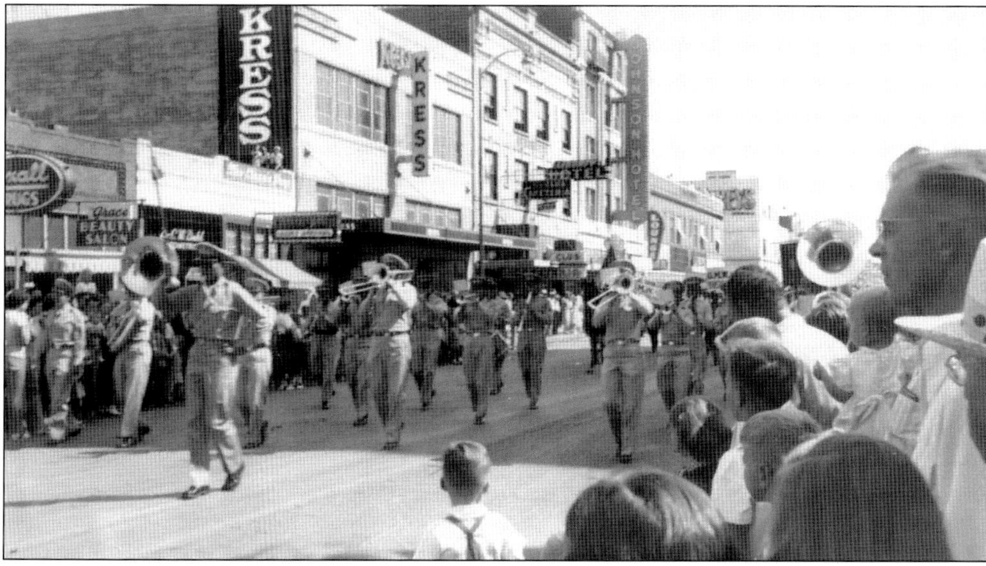

A U.S. Air Force band is seen here marching between Fourth and Fifth Streets on Central Avenue headed west. Rexall Drugs, the Kress Five-and-Dime, and the Johnson Hotel are visible. This looks to be about 1952 or 1953. (2010.1.32)

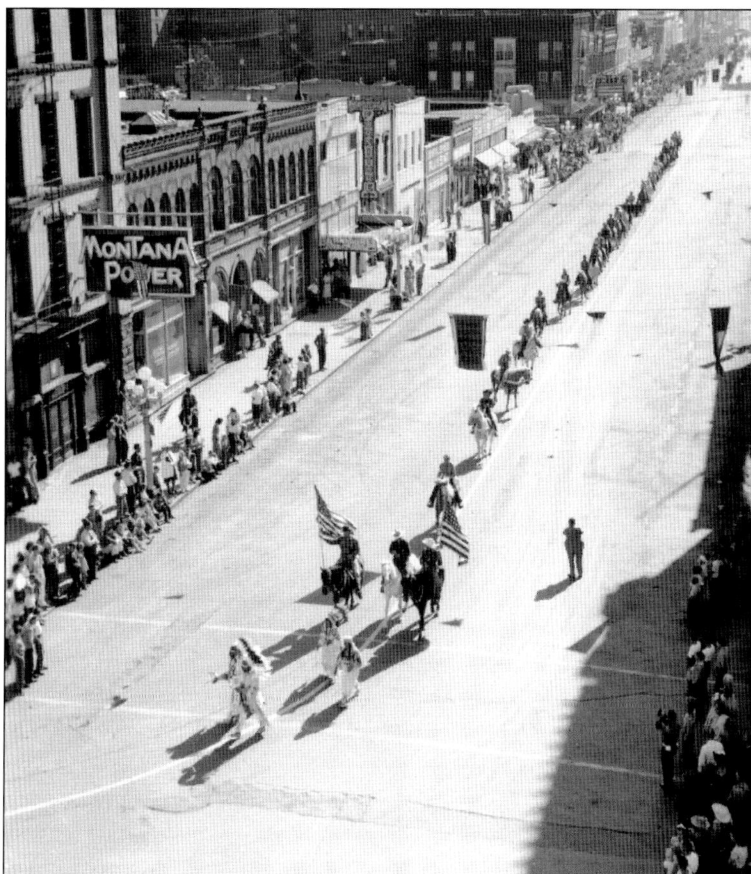

A North Montana State Fair contingent passes in front of the Great Falls Civic Center, Park Hotel, and Montana Power Building in this August 7, 1944, photograph. They march west on Central Avenue and turn north down First Street at the civic center. The parade is complete with Native Americans sporting their finest regalia and cowboys proudly carrying the American flag. Onlookers are lined up as far as the eye can see. (2003.80.69)

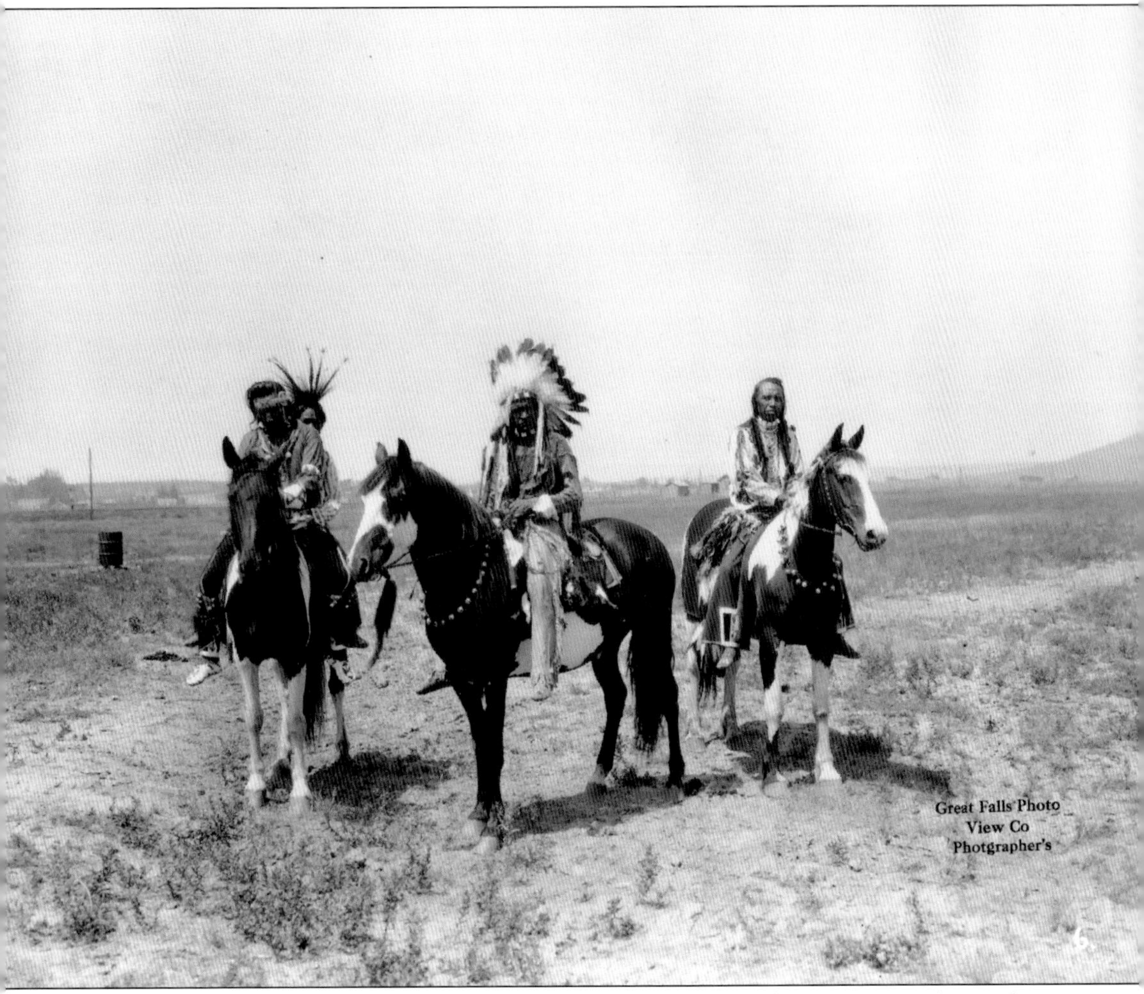

Native Americans, believed at the time to be Blackfeet, display their native regalia on the west side of Great Falls around 1910. (2007.17.416)

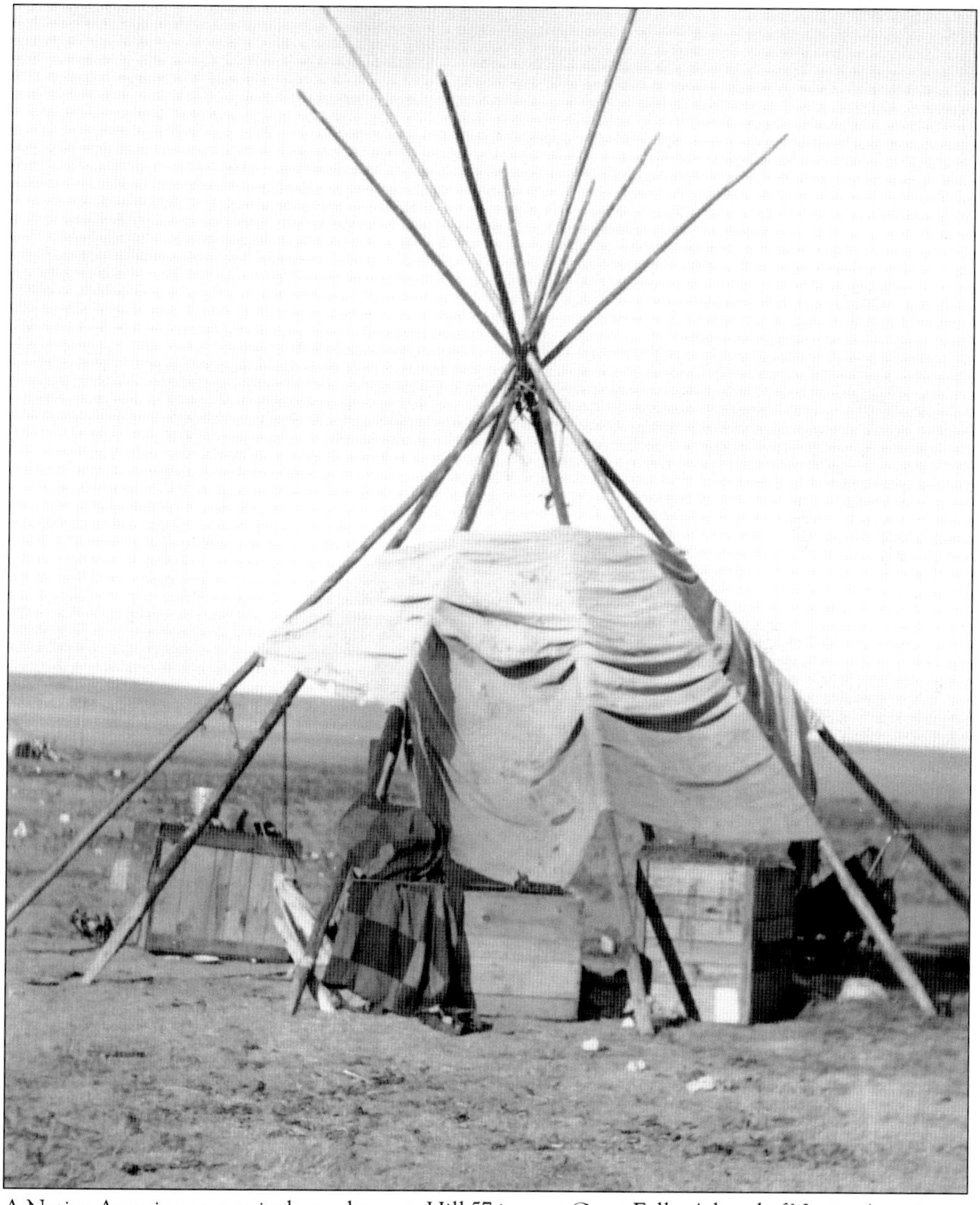

A Native American tepee is shown here on Hill 57 in west Great Falls. A band of Native Americans had settled here around 1900 and lived in primitive conditions. Very few amenities of any kind are visible in this 1914 photograph—a few shipping crates for crude furniture, a blanket, a piece or two of canvas covering, and very little else. Winter would bring unbelievable hardship to the people living here. Hill 57 got its name as a result of a Heinz Food salesman arranging rocks in a huge "57" on the hillside and painting them with whitewash some time in the first couple of decades of the 1900s. This unusual advertising symbol could be seen for miles. (MOE93.111.27A)

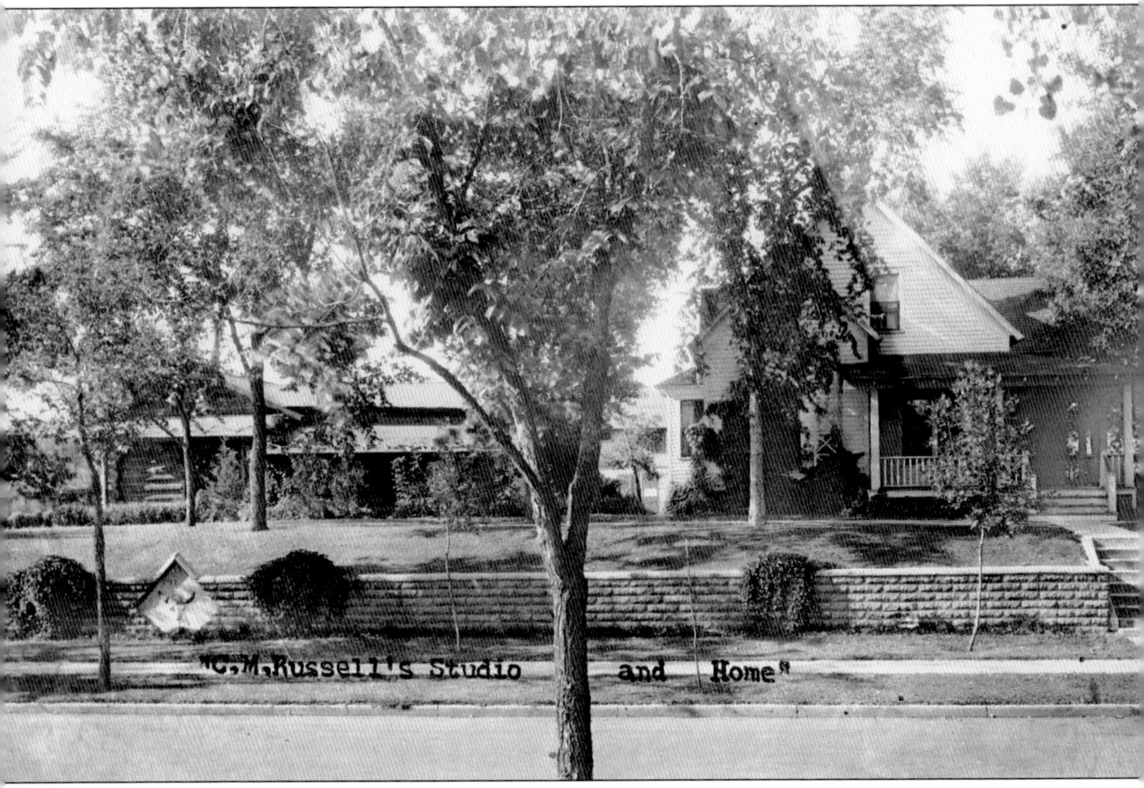

Charles M. Russell's log cabin studio is on the left, and his home is on the right. He and his wife, Nancy, moved to Great Falls about a year after their 1896 wedding in Cascade. Not long after moving here, they had a home built on Fourth Avenue North between Twelfth and Thirteenth Streets. In 1903, Charles had a log cabin studio built next door. He wanted it designed to remind him of his friend Jake Hoover's cabin in the Judith River country, where Russell had spent a lot of time shortly after coming to Montana. The Russells and their adopted son, Jack, lived here until Charles Russell's death in October 1926. (92.1.80)

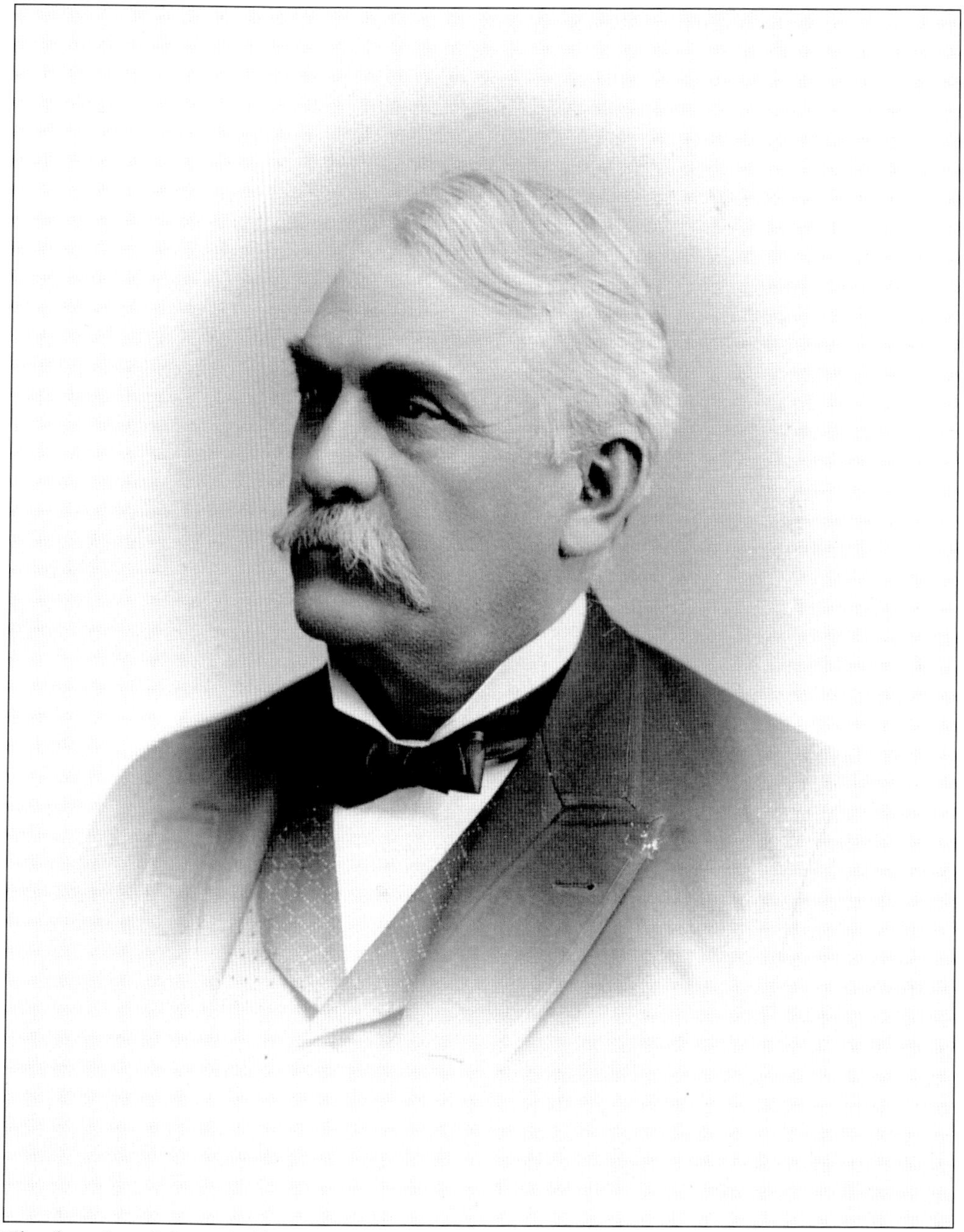

The founder of Great Falls, Paris Gibson, was a St. Paul and Minneapolis entrepreneur in the flour milling and later the woolen textile industries. When the economy slumped in the 1870s, he left Minnesota to try his hand at sheep ranching in Montana. He had a ranch about 20 miles east of Great Falls and learned of the falls from reading a copy of the Lewis and Clark journals. Investigating the falls and visiting them several times with his two sons and H. P. Rolfe, Gibson envisioned the potential for hydroelectric development, which had just made its debut. Having no capital, he contacted his longtime railroader friend James J. Hill, who had sufficient capital. Gibson invited him to Montana surreptitiously on a fishing trip. Hill was sold on the idea when he saw coal mined at Sand Coulee Creek—and the rest is history. (94.38.161)